One Day We Will Live without Fear

One Day We Will Live without Fear

Everyday Lives under the Soviet Police State

Mark Harrison

HOOVER INSTITUTION PRESS
STANFORD UNIVERSITY | STANFORD, CALIFORNIA

With its eminent scholars and world-renowned library and archives, the Hoover Institution seeks to improve the human condition by advancing ideas that promote economic opportunity and prosperity, while securing and safeguarding peace for America and all mankind. The views expressed in its publications are entirely those of the authors and do not necessarily reflect the views of the staff, officers, or Board of Overseers of the Hoover Institution.

www.hoover.org

Hoover Institution Press Publication No. 665
Hoover Institution at Leland Stanford Junior University,
Stanford, California 94305-6003

First printing 2016
22 21 20 19 18 17 16   9 8 7 6 5 4 3 2 1

Manufactured in the United States of America

The paper used in this publication meets the minimum requirements of the American National Standard for Information Sciences—Permanence of Paper for Printed Library Materials, ANSI/NISO Z39.48-1992. ♾

Cataloging-in-Publication Data is available from the Library of Congress.
ISBN-13: 978-0-8179-1914-6 (cloth : alk. paper)
ISBN-13: 978-0-8179-1916-0 (epub)
ISBN-13: 978-0-8179-1917-7 (mobi)
ISBN-13: 978-0-8179-1918-4 (PDF)

Contents

To my sisters and brother:
Elizabeth, Dinah and Joyce, and John and Anne

Preface

Remembering how in so strange a time
Common integrity could look like courage.

"Talk" by Yevgeny Yevtushenko (1960)[1]

"People in Russia say that those who do not regret the collapse of the Soviet Union have no heart, and those that do regret it have no brain," Russian President Vladimir Putin told German television viewers in 2005.[2] His words suggested that to bring back the Soviet Union is desirable but unrealistic.

What kind of a country was the Soviet Union? What was it really like? No book could capture the everyday lives of hundreds of millions of people over several generations. But for some of those hundreds of millions on some days, life was like this. They lived the stories in this book.

My stories tell of everyday lives in a police state. By accident or design, ordinary people become entangled in the workings of Soviet rule. Famous people step in and out of my stories, but the central characters are people whose names will have been remembered only within their families: a budding artist, an engineer, a pensioner, a government office worker, a teacher, a group of tourists. The events are drawn from the 1930s to the 1970s. The first story takes place in the Far East on the Chinese border and the last in the western borderlands of the Baltic region.

My stories are based on historical records. I found them while investigating other matters in the Library & Archives of the Hoover Institution, which holds many documents of the Soviet Communist Party and state. I did not choose the stories by following a research design. Rather, they chose me; they grabbed me and would not let me go. They chose themselves for their humanity and their inhumanity, shining a clear light on many tragic, funny, and bizarre aspects of Soviet life.

In every story, something happens that triggers an investigation. A mistake is made, or is it something worse? Then, an investigation follows. Who is to blame, and is the hand of the enemy at work in the events under investigation? The evidence is often one-sided because the characters speak only through the investigator. Some find a voice through witness statements or interrogation summaries. Others find a voice when private conversations are reported or intercepted. Some voices are not heard, but can be read between the lines.

Chapter 1 ("The Mill") takes place in wartime. An ambitious security officer in a remote outpost plays a deadly game with local residents. His superiors know and approve. Years later the story is uncovered. What sort of vindication awaits the victims? The story provides background for later chapters, including Stalin's violent rule and the turn away from mass terror after he died.

In chapter 2 ("Truth Hurts"), a woman comes back to work after sick leave and is rushed into a decision that she gets catastrophically wrong. She is a censor; the decision concerns a dubious political cartoon. Lots of people suffer from her mistake—more than we know, probably, because this is 1937, the year of Stalin's Great Terror.

Chapter 3 ("Heretics") is set in Soviet universities and colleges in the late 1940s. Each story begins with a denunciation. We see the many strange ways in which teachers and scientists could get on the wrong side of each other, their students, and the authorities. Every accusation is examined minutely, no matter how ridiculous. The Paris Commune, potatoes, genetics, relativity, and anti-Semitism all have their turn.

Chapter 4 ("The Mafia") begins soon after Stalin's death. Soviet life is thawing. An old man with time on his hands writes to the local papers about mismanagement and fraud on the local collective farm. At first he is annoying; then he becomes a threat. The locals join forces against him: the farmers, the party, the police, even the KGB. The old man ends up losing everything. Then, Moscow steps in. But wait—whose side are you on?

By the time of chapter 5 ("You Have Been Warned"), the secret police had learned to deal bloodlessly with dissent and deviance. It was cheaper and kinder to frighten people than to kill them. A first line of defense was the "preventive" interview. Some case histories are told from the 1960s and 1970s—straight, comic, and mysterious. This chapter dwells on the Kaunas riots of 1972, a moment when secret policing failed.

Chapter 6 ("A Grand Tour") recounts a visit by a group of Soviet tourists to North America in 1970, seen through KGB eyes. It explains how Soviet citizens got to travel outside their own country and the restrictions they traveled under. Above all, it shows the trouble they could get into on their travels. At any time they could bump into real or imagined spies or say or do the wrong thing.

In chapter 7 ("One Day We Will Live without Fear"), an Israeli citizen returns to Soviet Lithuania for a family reunion. The local KGB is mobilized for her visit. The authorities call up past records, intercept letters, tap phones, follow her in the street, interrogate neighbors, and call up informants. What's going on? The KGB asked the same question. We learn something about the purposes of surveillance.

The book is laid out to meet the needs of more than one kind of reader. The stories in each chapter can be appreciated by anyone, including those with little previous knowledge of Russia or communism. For those who come equipped with specialist knowledge or who wish to acquire it, every chapter provides primary and secondary sources, including a list of archival documents and what I have drawn from them in the context of the existing scholarly literature. An afterword considers the reliability of Soviet archival records and their relationship to historical truth.

★ ★ ★

From the 1930s to the 1970s, the Soviet police state underwent considerable change. From something bloody and brutal it became sophisticated, refined, and sparing. But the problem that the police state had to manage did not change, and its underlying principles remained the same. These principles are spelled out in chapter 1. In other chapters I refer briefly to these principles from time to time, but I have tried to write in such a way that no reader will feel obliged to flick back and forth between chapters in order to follow the narrative.

In addition to this common message, the chapters of my book have a common target, which is the human tendency to see the past as more comfortable than the present. For memory has been kind to the Soviet state and other states like it. Introducing his "inside story" of the secret police of the German Democratic Republic (the GDR, or East Germany), Gary Bruce wrote:

> Surveys of East Germans conducted after the revolution of 1989 suggest that there is indeed an increasingly positive view of the

> GDR. In evaluating the statement, "One felt spied upon. You couldn't trust anyone," 43 percent of East Germans answered "True, that's exactly how it was" in 1992, but only 25 percent gave the same response in 2004. Similarly, 72.6 percent of East Germans claimed in 1990 that there was "complete surveillance" in the GDR, whereas only 42 percent would agree with that claim in 1995.[3]

East Germans are not alone in this. Russians too feel nostalgia for the past. VTsIOM, the All-Russian Center for the Study of Public Opinion, has regularly asked respondents to evaluate positively or negatively the historical periods under different rulers. In 1994, Stalin's period (the mid-1920s to 1953) was rated positively by 18 percent of respondents.[4] After that his positive rating rose year by year, reaching 37 percent in 2007 before falling back to 28 percent in 2011.[5] Another source of data on Russian opinion is the independent Levada Center, which broke away from VTsIOM in 2003 following a dispute over increased government supervision. The Levada Center has asked Russian respondents for their views of Stalin repeatedly since 2006. The proportion replying that Stalin played a definitely or probably positive role in Russia's history has never fallen below 40 percent and rose to 52 percent in December 2014.[6]

An aspect of Russian nostalgia is regret for the passing of the Soviet Union. In 1991 the Soviet Union broke up into fifteen independent republics. The largest of these were Russia and Ukraine; the smallest were Estonia and Latvia. In Russia itself, 73 percent of the electorate voted in favor of preserving the Soviet Union in the referendum of March 1991, and between two-thirds and three-quarters continued to regret the collapse of the Soviet Union in polls conducted by VTsIOM up to 2001. After that the proportion began to decline. But, as recently as December 2012, an absolute majority continued to lament the Soviet Union's abrupt end.[7]

This regret is shared by President Putin, who also described the collapse of the USSR as "the greatest geopolitical disaster of the [twentieth] century."[8]

When Russians express a desire to return to the past, they support this by recalling that the communist state cared for popular welfare and that the ethnic groups of Soviet society lived together in harmony. In July 2000, for example, a VTsIOM poll asked Russians to characterize how life was lived in Soviet times. The single most popular answer, chosen by 42 percent of respondents, was that there was an absence of conflicts based on nationality (for example, Russians versus Ukrainians). Another popular answer, with 37 percent, was the state's "concern for ordinary people."[9] This perspective on the past can be seen in more recent data, for example, in December 2012 when the Levada Center polled respondents on reasons to regret the Soviet collapse. On this occasion, 39 percent pointed to increased mistrust and bitterness in society; that is, they recalled the Soviet period as a time of trust and friendship among people.[10]

It is far from unusual to look back on the past with nostalgia. Bryan Caplan has documented a universal "pessimistic bias" in matters of the economy; most people tend to see the present and future as fraught with economic problems, while threats in the past are perceived as less acute. Caplan points out that there is no reason to think that this bias is limited to economics.[11] Perhaps all cultures have a consciousness of decline, which sees our world going from bad to worse. We are richer and live longer, healthier lives in more freedom than our forebears; yet somehow we think we have frittered away their legacy. We endow the past with the virtues of simplicity, morality, and community that we believe we have lost.

In this respect, Russians are no different from the rest of us. The consequences of Russians' nostalgia may be more severe, however, if they end up mistaking the actual qualities of dictatorship and totalitarianism.

In Russia, it appears, many people now look back on Stalin as an effective national leader and the Soviet Union as a caring community that somehow, accidentally, acquired a secret police, thermonuclear weapons, and other countries. The records of the time tell a different story.

Acknowledgments

The Hoover Institution on War, Revolution and Peace at Stanford University has held a Workshop on Totalitarian Regimes each summer since 2003. Led by Paul Gregory, the workshop focused in its initial years on the Hoover Archives' wonderful collection of records relating to the Soviet state and Communist Party. (Since then, the annual invasion of scholars from around the world has broadened to include specialists in other countries formerly in the Soviet bloc, China, and the Middle East.) At dinner the participants would compete to narrate the most unusual document of the day. I am an economist; I soon realized that the evidence that economists gather rarely makes good stories. Overriding the biases of my training, I began to gather the stories that I liked best, thinking sadly that I would never be able to use them in my own research.

The idea of collecting my stories into a book was born from a conversation with Paul Gregory at one of the early workshops. My greatest debt is to Paul for his inspiring intellectual leadership and guidance. Paul established the Hoover Institution Workshop on Totalitarian Regimes on the basis of a farsighted vision: to understand the sources and persistence of the dictatorships that exist today, we must grasp in detail their historical origins and working arrangements. I am privileged to have been a part of this enterprise.

I am profoundly grateful to the Hoover Institution and its Library & Archives. Since 2003, the Hoover Institution has honored me with various affiliations: I have been a visiting fellow, a W. Glenn Campbell and Rita Ricardo-Campbell National Fellow, and a research fellow. The Hoover Institution has supported my work through grants that have enabled me to visit the Archives and to take leave from my teaching duties. Hoover Archives Director Eric Wakin and his predecessor, Richard Sousa, have directly championed this book. The Hoover Archives staff made it miraculously easy for me to do my work. In naming Linda Bernard, Carol Leadenham, and Leonora Soroka, I do not forget what I owe to the many Archives staff members whom I cannot name because their efforts were made behind the scenes and out of my sight. At the Hoover Press, as my writing advanced, senior publications manager Barbara Arellano and book editor Barbara Egbert freely offered valuable insights, advice, and assistance.

In the world of Russian studies, I am a research fellow at the University of Birmingham's Centre for Russian, European, and Eurasian Studies. I am grateful to its director of the time, Derek Averre, for giving me a desk in 2008 where, after three years as a department chair, I could sit, breathe, and reflect on my roots in Russian studies. I also thank the Library of the University of Birmingham for access to its unique Baykov collection.

In my other life I am an economist. The University of Warwick and its Department of Economics have supported my work generously through grants of research leave. When I have had the opportunity to explain my project, my colleagues have listened patiently and responded with enthusiasm. Warwick's ESRC Centre on Competitive Advantage in the Global Economy, where I am a research associate, has shared the costs of my research travel. Its unique research agenda has embraced a rethinking of how social organizations, norms, and beliefs affect not only the way we behave from day to day but also the way that economies have developed over the long run. I have promised that the insights I have found will eventually contribute, somehow, to this research.

I have gained immeasurably from many discussions with all those who have joined the annual meetings of the Hoover Institution's workshop. Among them have been Golfo Alexopoulos, Anne Applebaum, Eugenia Belova, Leonid Borodkin, Ed Cohn, Katya Drozdova, Saulius Grybkauskas, Alex Hazanov, David Holloway, Emily Johnson, Deborah Kaple, Stephen Kotkin, Andrei Markevich, Donal O'Sullivan, David Satter, Robert Service, Lynne Viola, Amir Weiner, and Inga Zaksauskienė. Inga gave her time freely to help me with Lithuanian sources, and I thank her for her kind assistance.

Many other friends and colleagues have responded generously to my requests for advice. These include Arvydas Anušauskas, Melissa Feinberg, Eric Jones, Peter Law, Elena Osokina, Christopher Read, and Amanda Swain. I thank Melissa and Amanda particularly for giving me access to their writings.

Paul Gregory, Anne Harrison, Samuel Harrison, Peter Law, Roy Owen, Judith Pallot, Amir Weiner, and Inga Zaksauskienė kindly read parts of the typescript and told me what they thought. I assure them all that my love remains strong; I will get over it. After forty years of publishing in social science and history I have learned that I am a novice in telling stories. I owe special thanks to two people who read the entire book—parts of it more than once—with a view to the art and craft of writing. Barbara Egbert and Jamie Harrison took on my vision and helped me try to tell my stories like a storyteller.

Some of the "principles" of police states, described in chapter 1, made their first appearance in a lecture entitled "What do Secret Policemen Really Do? Lessons from history and social science," that I gave at Haverford College on October 30, 2013; at the University of Warwick (within the ESRC Festival of Social Science) on November 7, 2013; and at Stanford University (within the Hoover Institution Workshop on Totalitarian Regimes) on July 24, 2014. I thank the organizers and the audience for their responses. Previous versions of chapters 4 and 5 were circulated as working papers. Chapter 4 appeared under the title "Whistleblower or Troublemaker? How One Man Took On the Soviet Mafia" as PERSA (Political Economy Research in Soviet Archives) Working Paper no. 54 (University of Warwick, Department of Economics, 2008) and as TWERPS (The Warwick Economic Research Papers) no. 890 (University of Warwick, Department of Economics, 2009). An early version of chapter 5 appeared as "You Have Been Warned: The KGB and Profilaktika in Soviet Lithuania," PERSA Working Paper no. 62 (2010), and was published under the title "You Have Been Warned" in the *Hoover Digest* (2011, no. 1). It also formed the substance of a presentation, entitled "The KGB: Success and Failure on the Western Border," to the Fiftieth Anniversary Conference of the Centre for Russian, European, and Eurasian Studies of the University of Birmingham, June 7, 2014. Again, I thank the organizers and the audience for their comments.

About the Author

Mark Harrison is a professor of economics at the University of Warwick. He is a research fellow of Warwick's ESRC Centre on Competitive Advantage in the Global Economy, the Centre for Russian and East European Studies at the University of Birmingham, and the Hoover Institution on War, Revolution and Peace at Stanford University. He visited Russia first as a schoolboy in 1964, again as a graduate student in 1972, and on many occasions since then. He has published many books and articles on Russian economic history, the international economics of the two world wars, and the historical political economy of dictatorship, including most recently *The Economics of Coercion and Conflict* (World Scientific Publishing, 2015). He received the Alec Nove Prize for Russian, Soviet, and Post-Soviet Studies in 1997 and the Russian National Prize for Applied Economics in 2012.

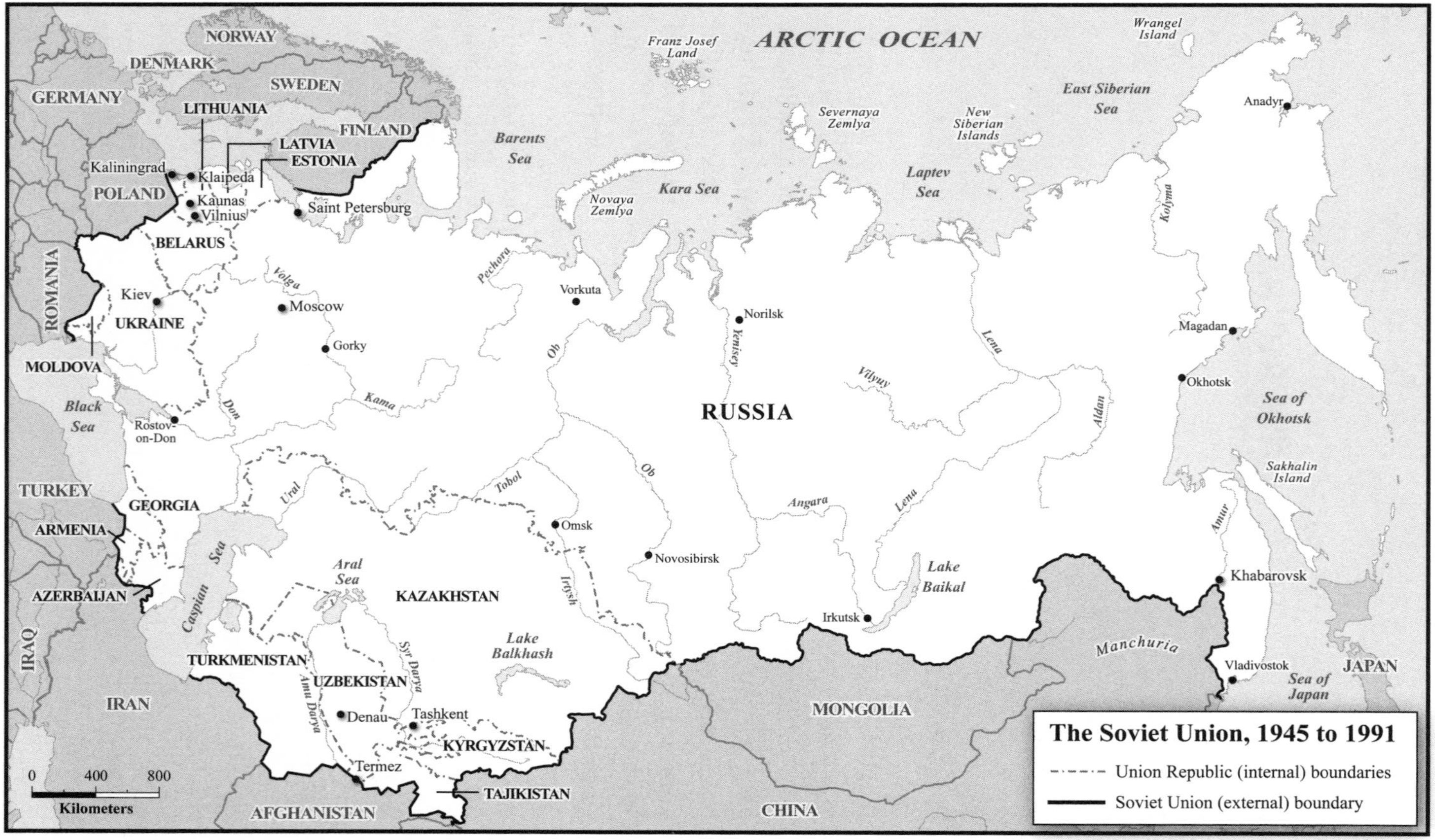
The Soviet Union, 1945 to 1991
Union Republic (internal) boundaries
Soviet Union (external) boundary
ARCTIC OCEAN
Franz Josef Land
Wrangel Island
East Siberian Sea
Severnaya Zemlya
New Siberian Islands
Barents Sea
Kara Sea
Laptev Sea
Novaya Zemlya
Anadyr
NORWAY
DENMARK
SWEDEN
GERMANY
LITHUANIA
FINLAND
LATVIA
ESTONIA
Kaliningrad
Klaipeda
POLAND
Kaunas
Vilnius
Saint Petersburg
BELARUS
ROMANIA
Kiev
UKRAINE
MOLDOVA
Volga
Moscow
Gorky
Pechora
Vorkuta
Norilsk
Yenisey
Kolyma
Magadan
Okhotsk
Lena
Vilyuy
Ob
Kama
Don
Black Sea
Rostov-on-Don
RUSSIA
Aldan
Sea of Okhotsk
Sakhalin Island
TURKEY
GEORGIA
ARMENIA
AZERBAIJAN
Ural
Tobol
Omsk
Angara
Amur
Caspian Sea
Aral Sea
KAZAKHSTAN
Irtysh
Novosibirsk
Lake Baikal
Khabarovsk
Irkutsk
IRAQ
TURKMENISTAN
UZBEKISTAN
Amu Darya
Syr Darya
Lake Balkhash
Manchuria
Vladivostok
JAPAN
Sea of Japan
IRAN
Denau
Tashkent
KYRGYZSTAN
MONGOLIA
Termez
TAJIKISTAN
AFGHANISTAN
CHINA
0
400
800
Kilometers

CHAPTER ONE

The Mill

The cell is packed and airless. Night falls, but no one sleeps. Whose turn will it be? You wait. In the small hours the guards come to the door. They call your name; it's your turn. You say goodbye as you step over the others. The guards march you down into the basement. They push you through a doorway. The executioner steps behind you and fires a bullet through the back of your head.[1]

Stanislav Bronikovsky escaped a death like that in 1937.[2] Accused as an "enemy of the people," he was arrested and imprisoned. Suspicion alone was enough to condemn most of those detained in that year. Stanislav was lucky to be still alive when the executions were halted for a time. He was released for lack of evidence.

A few years went by, and then Stanislav was detained again. He had not intended any harm, but this time there was compelling evidence against him: it seemed that he had betrayed his country to Japan. Nothing could prove his innocence. He might have thought he was a victim of the worst luck in the world.

On April 24, 1943, Stanislav was tried and sentenced to death. Two days later the guards took him down to the execution cellar.

Stanislav was just fifty when he was killed. The name Stanislav, which means a person destined for fame or glory, is not uncommon in Russia, but it is originally from Poland. This particular Stanislav was originally Polish, born in Warsaw at a time when Poland was a province of the Russian Empire. Now he was a Soviet citizen living in Khabarovsk, which is six thousand miles from Poland and about as far as you can go from Warsaw in any direction without crossing an ocean. More exactly, Khabarovsk is in Russia's Far East, close to the Pacific and sitting on top of the Chinese border. How and why Stanislav made this long journey is not recorded, but at the time he lived in Khabarovsk he was working as a building engineer.

Stanislav never knew the truth of the events that led to his death. He was not a victim of bad luck; he was the object of a game. The game was devised and played by the Soviet Union's top secret policemen. Its officers were certainly ambitious and most likely bored. They played the game to show they were doing something and perhaps to have something to do. The Japanese were irrelevant; they played no part in the matter at all.

Peace and quiet in a world at war

By the end of 1941, almost the entire northern hemisphere was at war. Deadly fighting was in progress across Europe, around the Mediterranean Sea, and over and under the Atlantic. Warfare in China had exploded into the Pacific.

In a world at war there were not many major frontiers where neighbors were still at peace. One of the few peaceful frontiers ran between the Soviet Union and the Japanese colony of Manchuria (modern Heilongjiang Province in northern China). The fact that this frontier was peaceful might be thought surprising. Japan's military leaders, who were steeped in violent nationalism, had spent much of the interwar period gazing across the sea to the natural wealth and empty spaces of Siberia, calculating their chances of detaching that territory from the young Soviet state. In 1931 the Japanese Army occupied Manchuria, bordering Siberia to the north. In 1939 the Japanese fought a border war with the Red Army. Although undeclared, this was a major conflict involving pitched battles with tanks, planes, and thousands of casualties on each side.[3]

Losing that war, the Japanese gave up on Siberia. They switched their efforts to consolidating control of the Chinese mainland. They also went to the south, looking for the softer targets represented by British, French, and Dutch colonial possessions in Southeast Asia. There the US Navy stood in their way. This is how Japan's turn away from Siberia led directly to the surprise attack on America's Pacific Fleet in Pearl Harbor on December 7, 1941.

A few months before Pearl Harbor, in April 1941, the USSR and Japan concluded a treaty of neutrality and nonaggression. This treaty held, miraculously, until August 1945. It lasted so long for a simple reason: while Japan was fighting America and the Soviet Union was fighting Germany, neither country wanted another war.

On the Soviet side of the peaceful Manchurian border, the town of Khabarovsk was the last major eastbound stop on the Trans-Siberian railroad before Vladivostok and the Pacific coast. Founded as a garrison town in the previous century, Khabarovsk was now the headquarters of the Far Eastern military district. Its central quarter had imposing municipal buildings, with broad streets and squares for marching and parades. On the outskirts an industrial region was growing up, with workers packed together in dormitories and barracks.

In Khabarovsk all was quiet and the war was a long way away. To find the war from Khabarovsk you would have to travel five thousand miles to the European front in the west, or more than a thousand miles south to central China where China's Nationalists were locked in a struggle with the Japanese Army.

Like every Soviet city, Khabarovsk had a local office of the NKVD. "NKVD" stands for the Soviet ministry of the interior; the senior branch of this ministry was the secret police, responsible to Moscow for the loyalty of the local population. Put yourself in the shoes of the local NKVD commanders. With the world in flames you sat on the frontier, but this was the quietest frontier city in the country. In fact, here was the only border where *nothing was happening*. How could you prove to Moscow that you were doing your job? How could you distinguish yourself, when all the excitement was somewhere else? Perhaps, also, how could you overcome the maddening tedium of provincial life, with only work and vodka to fill the evenings?

Chief Goglidze of the Khabarovsk NKVD found the answer: he would put on a play.

A killer rises

Thickset and saturnine, Sergei Goglidze was in his early forties. Georgian by birth, he joined the Bolsheviks young and fought for them in Russia's Civil War. After that, he rose quickly through the ranks of the Soviet border troops and security police to become interior minister of the Transcaucasian Soviet Republic. The Transcaucasus, so called because the region is separated from Russia by the Caucasus Mountains, was one of the Union Republics of the USSR from its foundation in 1922. In 1936 the Transcaucasian Republic was split into three: Georgia, Armenia, and Azerbaijan. Goglidze became the first interior minister of Soviet Georgia.[4]

Goglidze's career brought him from the outer edge of the Soviet empire to its center. He advanced through his relationship with Lavrenty Beria, who was Stalin's man in the Soviet Transcaucasus and acted as leader of the Transcaucasian and Georgian Communist parties. Later, Beria commanded millions of forced laborers and ran the Soviet Union's atomic bomb project. He had a receding hairline and rimless spectacles. These gave him a passing resemblance to another famous mass murderer, a similarity that Stalin recognized by calling him "my Himmler."

Along the way, Beria became Goglidze's patron. According to one story, the relationship was based on a guilty secret: when Goglidze joined the Bolsheviks he lied about his family background. He claimed to be from the rural poor when in reality his parents were classified as kulaks. "Kulak," meaning a clenched fist, was a traditional term of abuse for the richer (and supposedly tight-fisted) farmers. The Bolsheviks adopted this term, inciting the rural poor to wage class war against their more prosperous neighbors. In 1930 Stalin ordered the kulaks to be expelled from the villages and resettled in Siberia while the remaining peasants were forced into collective farms. As there was no clear definition of who was a kulak, any farmer who resisted could fall under suspicion. If Goglidze was suspected of a kulak family background, he hid the fact. Exposure could have ended his career. Beria knew Goglidze's secret, and kept quiet in return for Goglidze's absolute personal loyalty.[5]

Goglidze's path to Moscow was opened by the Great Terror of 1937. The year before, in 1936, Stalin put Nikolai Yezhov in charge of the NKVD, giving him the assignment with which his name would be forever associated: to carry out the Great Terror. Even today Russians sometimes call the Great Terror *Yezhovshchina*—the "Yezhov business." Through Yezhov, Stalin managed two waves of mass imprisonment and killing, one public and the other secret.[6] In public, tens of thousands of citizens were put on trial as "enemies of the people," many of them former members of the Soviet political, cultural, and scientific elites. The "enemies" were accused of espionage, sabotage, and murder, usually in coordination with foreign enemies. Crushed by psychological pressure and torture, most confessed; all were found guilty and sentenced to long terms of imprisonment or execution. The show trials demonstrated to the public how its enemies were encircling the Soviet Union's borders and infiltrating its councils and how everyone should be on guard against the smallest signs of treachery.

The Great Terror also had a secret aspect, the "mass operations" and "national operations" of the NKVD that Stalin launched in the summer of 1937. The secret victims outnumbered the public victims by an order of magnitude. The public trials condemned tens of thousands, but the secret operations detained 1,600,000 people in a few months; nearly half of them were executed and the remainder were sentenced to long terms of imprisonment for "counterrevolutionary crimes." The purpose of the secret operations could not have been to intimidate or deter anyone, for that purpose would have been defeated by secrecy. Their purpose was to eliminate forever the people whom Stalin and his security advisers considered to be the misfits of Soviet society: the proven enemies, the security risks, those with whom there could be no reconciliation because of their origins, their past actions, or the sense that they could never be relied on.

Nowhere was safe. In Georgia, where Lavrenty Beria ran the party and Goglidze ran the NKVD, around 12,000 were arrested; most were executed.[7]

In early 1938, Stalin brought the Great Terror to an end. Now he faced the problem of what to do with the executioners. Soaked in blood, Yezhov had become a liability—and not only Yezhov but all "his" men. In April, Stalin brought Beria from Georgia to Moscow and made him Yezhov's deputy, responsible for state security. Beria brought his own men with him, including Goglidze. This saved Goglidze, who might otherwise have gone down soon afterward with many of Yezhov's other executioners. It also brought him to the center of Soviet politics.

In the following months, Yezhov's men were gradually moved out of the NKVD while Beria's men moved in. Yezhov found himself isolated. In November, he was demoted from minister of the NKVD to something much less important: minister for water transport. Beria took his place in the NKVD. Yezhov was arrested in April 1939, charged with organizing a counterrevolution. He was shot in February 1940. Meanwhile, nearly one thousand NKVD officers were arrested, including most of the regional bosses at Goglidze's level.[8]

Protected by Beria, Goglidze prospered. At age thirty-seven, he found himself head of the NKVD in Leningrad, Russia's second city. For many upwardly mobile young men of his generation, this was a moment of opportunity because the terror, having created so many vacancies for them, now subsided, leaving them in place to consolidate their new authority.

In Leningrad, Goglidze got to work, which meant first of all cleaning out Yezhov's men. Then, in April 1941 Goglidze was sent to the borderland republic of Moldavia, which the Soviet Union had seized from Romania the previous year. On this new territory he organized mass arrests and deportations of the people thought likely to be hostile or unreliable. He might have expected some reward for this, but further advancement was mysteriously denied. His rise might have seemed unstoppable, but suddenly it stopped. When war broke out in June, he was sent as far from Leningrad as it was possible for anyone to go without leaving Soviet territory: five thousand miles to the Far East. There, he became head of the NKVD for Khabarovsk.

Goglidze's career had brought him from the periphery of the empire to the center—and back to the periphery. Why? It's not clear. On the plus side, no one knew at that stage whether the Far East would remain quiet. If it blew up, Goglidze would become the central figure on the Far Eastern home front. But there was a clear minus, which everyone surely understood: in this most centralized of states, the place to be was at the center. And Goglidze would be stuck in Khabarovsk, far from the center, through the war and long after the war was over—in fact, for ten long years.

Potential enemies

Who were the targets of the Great Terror? Stalin aimed the terror first of all at the hundreds of thousands of people who were embittered because the revolution had taken away their property, status, or liberty. These were the people already listed in NKVD files. If anything was going to go wrong, they would be the "usual suspects."[9] But this was not all. Stalin took aim also at the wider circles of people who were not disloyal, but whose loyalty was skin-deep: they supported Soviet rule perhaps only when it benefited them directly, or when it went unchallenged. A compelling interpretation of the Great Terror is that Stalin correctly foresaw what was coming—a huge war that would break out with Germany if not with Japan. Such a war would face millions of Soviet citizens with a choice. Would they fight for Soviet rule? Or would they oppose it, either actively or passively by adopting an attitude of wait-and-see?[10] In Stalin's calculus, it was best to find the waverers and kill them now: not only the actual, conscious enemies, but the unconscious ones. How could you be an enemy unconsciously, without knowing it? The unconscious enemies were those who would break faith with the revolution and go over to the enemy in a future war, *even if they thought of themselves as loyal now*.[11] Better find them and kill them first, while they were only potential traitors, before they had done any harm, rather than wait for them to turn into real traitors when they could do critical damage.

How could you know who was a potential enemy? You couldn't be certain, so you had to guess. What Stalin did was to guess, based on broad classes of people who might be thought to have a tendency to disloyalty on average. The guesses he made provide a key to the fate of Stanislav Bronikovsky. For Stanislav was a member of two such broad classes. One, he was born in Poland, now a foreign country and a hostile power. Two, the revolution had already imprisoned him once. On that first occasion he had been released after a time. His case did not come up for trial until the Great Terror was dying down, so he was still alive to be released "for lack of proof of guilt." Perhaps he had been a loyal citizen before his first arrest. But was he loyal afterward?

In effect, the NKVD had already formulated one of the answers to a question that the sociologists Alex Inkeles and Raymond Bauer asked in a classic survey of Soviet war refugees in Europe and America in the early 1950s. The question was: what made people hostile to Soviet rule? Inkeles and Bauer created a measure of underlying anti-Soviet feeling, and looked for influences in their respondents' life histories. Their research showed that the single most important factor associated with this hostility was "experience of arrest by the secret police of oneself or a family member."[12]

By imprisoning him once, Soviet rule had handed Stanislav a grudge against the Soviet state. Was he now a potential enemy? How would he behave under pressure? Given the opportunity, would he betray the motherland?

The theater

Two great rivers join at Khabarovsk: the Amur from the west and the Ussuri from the south. Over hundreds of miles their channels mark the border between Russia and China. At Khabarovsk the

Amur is already a mile wide. It will roll on to the northeast for four hundred miles more, flowing into the Pacific at a settlement so remote that even today you cannot reach it by road.

These great waters separate Russia from China. But at Khabarovsk, where they come together, a finger of land protrudes between them from China into Russia. This little promontory, rolling and lightly wooded, provides the only land border between the two countries for hundreds of miles. Here, a few miles from the town, entirely on Soviet territory, members of the NKVD built a kind of open-air stage. On the side of the stage that lay toward the town they marked the land "Soviet Union." On the other side, in the direction of China but well inside the border, they marked the land "Manchuria." They drew a line down the middle, and this line became a make-believe border. On the "Soviet" side they erected a "Manchurian Border Police Post." Opposite to it, they placed a "District Japanese Military Mission." They staffed both border posts with their own men of the NKVD, divided by European and Asiatic appearance and dressed in Soviet and Japanese uniforms as appropriate.

The make-believe border was not a sideshow. In the nine years of the installation, the NKVD laid out more than a million rubles on maintenance. It's hard to represent that sum in real terms, but it was a lot of money. Based on average wages in December 1946, a million rubles would have employed around fifteen factory workers full time over the nine-year life of the operation.[13]

Who dreamed up the make-believe border? That's not clear. It was April 1941 when Goglidze's predecessor in the Khabarovsk NKVD asked Moscow to approve the commissioning of the theater. Goglidze was still in Leningrad. The project was to be ready by June 1, just before the war started. Goglidze was not sent to Khabarovsk until sometime in July, after war had broken out. So it was not Goglidze's idea, but he would run with it when the time came.

The theater was ready. Moscow would produce the play. Goglidze stepped in as director. The professional members of the cast had their costumes and props and knew their lines. Only the lead character would be an amateur. A new star would be recruited for each performance. The company called this play "The Mill."

A secret mission

Stanislav was chosen, most likely, because he was a usual suspect. He already had a record arising from his arrest in 1937, the year of the Great Terror. Might he be a spy? There was no particular reason to think so; but this is not how the NKVD worked. The Mill operatives decided to check him out. They brought Stanislav in and gave him a mission: to go into enemy territory and carry out surveillance for the motherland. His instructions were precise and detailed: he should give the Japanese authorities a true account of his life story, including his earlier arrest and imprisonment, and explain that he wished to defect. On September 1, 1942, as Khabarovsk's brief summer came to an end, Stanislav crossed the border into "Manchuria."

At the "District Japanese Military Mission," Stanislav was immediately detained. Held for a month, he was interrogated as an illegal border crosser. He stuck to his story. He did not reveal either his NKVD "recruitment" or his "mission," but he did come to an agreement. A "Japanese intelligence officer" recruited him to work for Japan and he was pushed back over the "border" to the Soviet Union.

Back in his homeland, not realizing that he had never left it, Stanislav reported truthfully that his spying mission had failed. He told the NKVD officers that the "Japanese" had detained him and tried to recruit him. In fact, his Soviet interrogators already knew every detail of what had happened "on the other side."

They knew Stanislav's every word was sincere. Stanislav had never had any contact with foreign intelligence; he had never even left the country. It didn't matter. They arrested him for passing information about Khabarovsk to the Japanese.

Based on the evidence, they sent Stanislav for trial by the Special Assembly of the NKVD. He was charged with counterrevolutionary crimes: "betrayal of the motherland" (Article 58-1a of the criminal code) and "anti-Soviet propaganda" (Article 58-10). These were capital charges.

In the Special Assembly

The Special Assembly provided a form of trial for counterrevolutionary crimes. The arbiters were a handful of highly ranked officials, all from the NKVD: the deputy ministers, the commissioner for the Russian Republic, the chief of police, and the minister of the Union Republic where the offense was committed. The Special Assembly was established in November 1934 as part of a "reform" of the Soviet system of repression.

To Stalin, repressive laws and courts were necessary, but not sufficient. The law did not always predictably punish the categories of people he wanted to exile, imprison, or destroy. Even if the law covered the case, the courts were sometimes unreliable. For example, judges often demanded adherence to rules of investigation and evidence. Sometimes they responded to procedural violations by diluting charges and reducing penalties.

The early 1930s were the most radical, formative years of Stalin's dictatorship. The country's resources were forcibly channelled into industrialization and rearmament. The urban economy was fully nationalized; tens of millions of peasants were dragooned into "collective" farms, a chaotic process that led to millions of famine deaths. Stalin gave the security police of the time, the OGPU, sweeping powers to sentence more than half a million people to imprisonment and exile without going through the courts.

Then, in 1934, came consolidation. The OGPU was transformed into the interior ministry, the NKVD. Most of its extra-judicial powers were removed; only a Special Assembly was left, supposedly to deal with the most sensitive cases and the most dangerous criminals outside the court system.[14] Judging by appearances, therefore, this reform was designed to restore the rule of law in most cases. But the outcome was quite different from restraint and reform. For Stalin now plunged Soviet society into wave after wave of new repressions, culminating in the Great Terror. The result was a huge increase in the number of especially serious cases.

The economic historian Paul Gregory has argued that Stalin wanted a compact and stable security establishment under his direct oversight. He also wanted to be able to turn the dial of repression up and down at will. It would have been impossible for him to do both while maintaining and adhering to legal propriety. Stalin resolved the dilemma at the expense of due process. By permitting periodic resort to "simplified methods" of investigation and interrogation, Stalin could push the NKVD to achieve much higher caseloads when each wave of repression reached its crest. At such moments the typical NKVD officer could meet the targets of several men in more normal times.[15]

Simplified methods meant relying completely on evidence supplied by the NKVD, with or without a confession, to prove guilt; using torture to extract confessions; excluding the defendant from the trial and proceeding without witnesses or legal representation; and ruling out any appeal. A death sentence would be carried out within days, sometimes within hours.

The Special Assembly was in existence for 969 weeks (between 1934 and 1953). In that time, it issued 442,531 sentences, a number that averages out at around 450 per week.[16] In wartime the Special Assembly could order the death penalty, and in the 216 weeks of the war it ordered the deaths of 10,101 people, or nearly 50 a week. But every member of the Special Assembly also had a full-time job to do, so in a typical week the Special Assembly was in session for only a few hours. On May 31, 1939, for example, deputy prime minister and former chief prosecutor Vyshinsky complained:

> Recently at each session the Special Assembly has considered 200–300 cases. Thus, less than one minute is devoted to the consideration of each case on average.[17]

And that was before the war broke out. The workload of the Special Assembly was higher in wartime, peaking at nearly 1,500 cases a week in 1942. By 1943, when Stanislav came up for consideration, the flood of cases had levelled off to around 500 a week. Thus Stanislav's case was submerged in the flood. He would have been lucky if the members of the Special Assembly had time to read out the charges.

It would be wrong to suppose that Stanislav was condemned without evidence, however. Years later, investigators found his file with an envelope attached. Inside, it appears, was the transcript of his interrogation by the "Japanese." The transcript revealed Stanislav's disclosure of his personal biography, his declared intention to defect to Japan, and his willingness to work for the "foreign" intelligence service. A covering note stated:

> The photograph copies of [Stanislav] Bronikovsky's plans and confessions attached to the investigation file under separate cover were obtained by the Khabarovsk NKVD counterintelligence

> department through a notably important and reliable agent network. Under no circumstances and in no way may these documents be utilized in Bronikovsky's interrogation, because this would involve the exposure of a valuable agent network.

More victims

Stanislav was not the only victim. The Mill was in operation for eight years, from 1941 to 1949, and over that time 150 people fell into it. Not all were executed as a result. One, a local government trade official, went through the Mill in December 1944. According to his own testimony, the "Japanese" tortured him for six days, at the end of which he gave away his NKVD assignment, denounced the Soviet Union, and was recruited to work for "enemy" intelligence. In due course the Special Assembly sentenced him to ten years in a labor camp, which he apparently survived. (But why only ten years? He was lucky no one was checking Special Assembly sentencing standards for consistency.)

Another victim was less fortunate. He saw through the deception and told his interrogators that he understood the game. One of Goglidze's officers became anxious. Might the accused man be interrogated in an open court? Might he be sent to a labor camp where he could confide in other prisoners? In January 1944 the Khabarovsk NKVD wrote to one of Beria's men in Moscow, Bogdan Kobulov:

> If [the prisoner] is sentenced to some term of detention then it stands to reason that in the camps he will increase his provocative activities and cause a lot of problems for the investigation about keeping secret the setup that has been arranged.

Kobulov, an experienced killer, had the case transferred from the courts to the Special Assembly. This ensured the prisoner's speedy execution.

The end of the Mill—and of the Miller

The last year of the Mill's operation was 1949. This was four years after the Japanese surrender, so it might be surprising that the run of the Mill went on for so long. The Soviet Union declared war on Japan on August 8, 1945, fulfilling Stalin's promise to the Allies at the Yalta conference, and the Japanese signed an unconditional surrender on September 2, so the Soviet campaign lasted three weeks. In those few weeks there was plenty of action. In one of the largest operations of World War II, Soviet forces stormed over the border into Manchuria. There they attacked and speedily overwhelmed the Japanese occupation forces.

The defeat of the Japanese in Manchuria should have stripped away the pretense of the "District Japanese Military Mission" on the far side of the fabricated border in the scrublands on the little promontory between the rivers outside Khabarovsk. But somehow, the Mill continued its run for four more years. Perhaps this was because China's civil war between the Communists and Nationalists spread to Manchuria.[18] While it continued, the NKVD officers on the far side of the false border could dress up as Chinese Nationalists instead of Japanese occupiers. We don't know. But the Mill closed down only in 1949, the same year that China's Communists declared victory and the Nationalists retreated offshore to their last stronghold, the island of Taiwan.

The play was over. Deprived of entertainment, Goglidze cooled his heels in Khabarovsk for two more years. Then a breakthrough came: in 1951 he was recalled to Moscow. After a weary decade as a provincial security boss, Goglidze was suddenly a first deputy minister! The occasion was the so-called MGB (ministry of state security) affair. On Stalin's orders, the previous minister, Viktor Abakumov, was arrested and charged with covering up Jewish conspiracies against the state—including a plot by the Kremlin's own doctors to kill Stalin. Stalin's job for Goglidze was to press the investigation forward.[19] And Goglidze would undoubtedly have succeeded, given what we know of his talents and his awareness that his life depended on getting the results that Stalin wanted.

Instead, however, Goglidze's career took another sharp turn. On March 5, 1953, Stalin died. His successors moved rapidly to dismantle the system of mass terror. Nikita Khrushchev and other leaders conspired to eliminate the influence of Beria, whom they viewed as a common threat to their own lives. Beria and his men were arrested and condemned on charges of treason and espionage. It was their turn to be taken down to the cellar in the basement, where Beria got special treatment: he was shot in the forehead by an army general.[20] Among the men who died that night was Sergei Goglidze.

Uncovering a crime

The fate of Stanislav (and others, for he was not the Mill's only victim) came to light in 1956. Or perhaps it is inexact to say that the case "came to light." It would be truer to say that it came out of darkness and into shadow, for Stanislav was exonerated without publicity and the circumstances remained secret for the lifetime of the Soviet state.

How did Stanislav's case come to be reviewed? By 1956 it had become convenient to look again at such matters, although not in public and only within a very limited circle.

With Stalin's death, the surviving leaders of the ruling party united temporarily to rid themselves of their common enemy, Lavrenty Beria. After that, they began to struggle against each other for power. A short, thickset man full of restless energy and blunt language, Nikita Khrushchev came to lead those who wanted a more radical turn away from Stalinism. In February 1956 he made a long, near-impromptu address to a secret session of the twentieth Soviet party congress, in which he denounced Stalin and some of his many crimes. (But not all of his crimes, and Khrushchev did not go into his own personal guilt, for he too had taken a most active part in the Great Terror.)

The men whom Khrushchev now charged with complicity in Stalin's crimes were largely those who were already condemned and shot—Yezhov and Beria, and their closest subordinates. Now that they were dead, it was helpful to search out the evidence against them, so that they could be charged with true crimes as well as the fabricated ones for which they had been condemned. (At first Beria was said to have been a foreign agent and spy.) To come up with hard evidence against Beria and his assistants, the investigators had to identify some real victims and exonerate them. Thus, on April 11, 1956, a military tribunal reviewed Stanislav's case and set aside the guilty verdict of the Special Assembly "in the absence of evidence of a crime."

That autumn the party launched an internal review of the Mill. The investigators were officials from the party's Commission of Party Control (responsible for looking into wrongdoing by party members) and its department of administrative organs.

That review has left three documents. A 2,000-word report, dated September 26, 1956, yields the bones of our story. Two shorter documents lie in the same file. One we'll save for later. The other, dated October 12, addresses the report to three authorities for their consideration and action. The chief of the Party Control Commission is asked to consider the "party accountability" of those responsible for the Mill. (Translation: should the party discipline or expel those of its members who share responsibility and are still alive?) The USSR chief prosecutor is asked to accelerate judicial review of remaining cases involving the victims. The Mill had 150 victims, but at the time of writing, the report notes, only twenty-seven cases had been reviewed, with the original charges dismissed in every case. And the chief of the KGB, the newly reformed security police, is asked to consider "the expediency of employment in the KGB of persons implicated in the aforementioned violations."

In October 1956 the chief of the KGB, to whom this last request was addressed, was Ivan Serov. A career soldier and security officer, Serov rose under Stalin to the upper echelons of the state security system. Tireless, competent, loyal, without fear or scruple, he seems to have been a model Soviet apparatchik. Never a contender for supreme authority, he had just the right amount of ambition to survive. In the struggles that followed Stalin's death, Serov allied himself tightly to Khrushchev. In 1954 the security service was renamed the KGB and the new leader of the country appointed Serov to take charge of security.

It fell to Serov, therefore, to review the surviving members of his staff who had previously worked together in the Mill. But who were they?

Weighing guilt

The party investigation found many officials and operatives who had known about the Mill. This included people in Moscow as well as in the Far East.

In Khabarovsk, approximately twenty local security officials were involved in the fabrication of testimony. By 1956 some were retired, while others still worked for state security. Here were some of the people whose further careers Ivan Serov would have to review.

Some of the Mill operatives seem to have taken on their assignments under duress. In 1941 three officers had been sentenced to long terms of imprisonment for "violations of socialist legality." This might mean nothing, or it might mean that they were among the torturers and executioners whom the NKVD found it expedient to sacrifice after the excesses of the Great Terror. In any case, in 1943 the Khabarovsk NKVD obtained the early release of these officers from the Gulag so that they could work at the Mill. In short, they were already compromised. Their superiors could send them back to the Gulag, or downstairs to the executioner, at the stroke of a pen. Their lives depended on unquestioning cooperation.

Another operative facing the same predicament was the chief of the "District Japanese Military Mission." A Japanese citizen, he entered the Soviet Union in 1937 as an agent for the Japanese Army in Manchuria. Arrested by the NKVD, in May 1940 he was sentenced to death for espionage. Afterward, his sentence was commuted to ten years in a labor camp. He too was recruited to work at the Mill.

No one involved in this work could afford a conscience. One who failed in this was a Chinese cook in the "Japanese" border post. On November 21, 1947, he could no longer contain the things he had seen. He smashed the dishes and destroyed the made-in-Japan kitchen equipment. Anxious that he might escape across the border, his colleagues shot him down. These people were used to violence. One member of the posse, a Chinese undercover worker, was separately implicated in the deaths of two other employees.

If you had to judge the collaborators in the Mill in a court of law, you wouldn't want to paint them all with the same brush. In Khabarovsk there were enthusiastic scoundrels working alongside others who were recruited under pressure or became reluctant. You'd also want to know about the orders they got from Moscow, where the burden of responsibility was surely heavier for those higher up the chain of command.

Among the Moscow officials allegedly responsible for the Mill were four who were already dead: Lavrenty Beria himself, his deputies Vsevolod Merkulov and Bogdan Kobulov—and Sergei Goglidze. All had been tried, condemned, and executed on the same December day in 1953, just months after Stalin's death.

The ultimate authority for the operation of the Mill is said to have been traced to Beria and Merkulov, but our report is oddly silent about the specific evidence for this. Was it merely expedient to blame them? It's entirely plausible; these people were all steeped in blood. Beria and Kobulov, for example, were Stalin's instruments in the secret massacre of twenty-two thousand Poles—officers and others—in the Katyn forest in 1940, but another half century would pass before this crime could be admitted. In 1956 it might have been convenient to find lesser crimes of which Beria and others could be convicted after their deaths.

The specific responsibility of others is clear. Kobulov was the Moscow official who arranged a quick death for the prisoner who guessed the secret of the Mill. Goglidze ran the operation in Khabarovsk from beginning to end.

By 1956 these people were condemned, dead, and buried. The party investigators would have seen them as safe targets, perhaps even necessary targets. A more difficult problem was presented by some of those who were still around and in positions of responsibility.

One who was still around was Peter Fedotov, Moscow's chief of counterintelligence. The Mill was a counterintelligence operation because the mission of counterintelligence was to frustrate the designs of Japanese intelligence to recruit Soviet agents—even though the only Japanese involved were NKVD imposters and double agents. In Moscow, Fedotov signed off on every step that Goglidze took in Khabarovsk, including the execution of people who were known to be innocent.

Conveniently, in April 1956 Fedotov was demoted from chief of counterintelligence to deputy director of the KGB's higher school publishing house. In that role he was no longer involved in operation decisions, although he would be involved in choosing the training manuals available to the next generation of young KGB officers. Now Fedotov was one of those implicated in the Mill, whose future in the KGB needed to be reviewed. The person charged with reviewing his future was Ivan Serov, Khrushchev's new KGB chief. Evidently, Serov decided that demotion was enough—for now.

There was one other person whose future Serov needed to review. This was himself, because he too was implicated in the Mill. The memorandum of September 12, 1956, that initiated the investigation quotes from a letter dated May 6, 1941:

> Deputy minister Serov has been informed. He has approved the organization of the mill and has asked [that you] present a budget estimate. Provide the estimate today.

Now Serov was one of the highest officials in the Soviet state, so the memorandum that found him personally responsible for approving the Mill was an unexploded bomb. Wisely, the party investigators decided not to detonate it. Serov's name did not feature in their final report—at least, not as a suspect. Rather, he was one of those to whom the report was addressed. The report made Serov responsible for deciding whether to retain the perpetrators. One supposes that he must have recognized his own part in the Mill. Perhaps, alone in his office, he privately reviewed his own continued employment as head of the KGB and decided he could live with it.

We cannot take this question outside

In the Soviet system there was injustice. To compensate, there was justice. Soviet justice took many forms: poetic justice, delayed justice, and secret justice. We can see all the various kinds of Soviet justice and injustice in the tale of Stanislav Bronikovsky.

First, there is injustice: Stanislav was killed by order of a committee that was established to cut through the requirements of due process. He was killed in secret after the most fleeting consideration—or none at all. He was killed because, having identified him as a potential enemy, the state deliberately and successfully entrapped him.

After a while, there is poetic justice: Goglidze and some of the other key figures in Stanislav's death were eventually killed in a similar way, not for the crimes they had actually committed, but on evidence fabricated by their enemies, who found it convenient to remove them.

Much later, there is delayed justice. Once Stanislav's killers had left the scene, it became possible to review their crimes, identify those who had abetted them, and exonerate the victims. Justice in this form was still incomplete. For one thing, it was secret, leaving no public record. For another, while it identified many of the perpetrators of the Mill, those who were still living suffered only minor consequences, or none at all.

The living included Peter Fedotov and Ivan Serov. Fedotov was the Moscow official who watched over the Mill every step of the way. By 1956 his career was in decline, and he had been sidelined in the KGB. In 1959, Fedotov suffered further humiliation: he was retired, stripped of his military rank, and expelled from the party. This was apparently because of his part in the Great Terror of 1937 in Soviet Armenia; it had nothing to do with the Mill. But he was never brought to trial for any crime. He died in 1963, still at liberty.

Serov, who gave his approval to the Mill at the outset, suffered no consequences at all. In 1958 he moved from the KGB to become head of Soviet military intelligence. His glittering career did not come to an end until 1963, when he was demoted and lost some medals. This was partly because of a real spy scandal, the exposure of his friend Oleg Penkovsky as a traitor who informed the West about Soviet nuclear weapons and their deployment to Cuba. Penkovsky was tried and shot; Serov's career suffered terminal damage. Khrushchev's own position was weakening anyway, and now it suited Khrushchev's enemies to drag up some murky episodes from Serov's past. Still, Serov lived on to retire and to die peacefully in 1990, a year before the Soviet collapse. No justice for him, either.

Justice for Stanislav was secret justice. The party report on the Mill was classified "top secret" and stamped "special file," meaning that it was intended to be seen only by a handful of people. A note written on the main report reads: "Original documentation sent to comrade Khrushchev N. S. October 5, 1956."

Secret justice could not be full justice. The purpose of secrecy was to limit justice and control its consequences. Secret justice meant that while Stanislav was exonerated, no one beyond his immediate family would ever know. It meant that Goglidze, who was already dead, could be condemned, while Serov, who was alive and well, was left alone. It meant that the party could wash its filthy laundry in private, while holding up a spotless sheet to the world.

For all his desire to break with the Stalinist past, Khrushchev did not denounce Stalin openly in 1956. The session of the twentieth party congress where he addressed the delegates was closed to the press and public. Before finishing, he said:

> We must consider the question of the cult of [Stalin's] personality in all seriousness. We cannot take this question outside the limits

> of the congress, and especially not to the press. This precisely is why we are reporting it to a closed session of the congress.[21]

The typewritten text bears this pencilled addition:

> We need to accept limits, and not feed our enemies, and not lay bare our wounds before them.

The attempt to limit public knowledge of Khrushchev's stand was a rare failure in the wall of Soviet secrecy, for the speech was soon leaked around the world. But it typified the Soviet belief that justice does not have to be seen to be done.

Although the story leaked out, the party leaders and ordinary members shared a strong incentive to contain the truth about the past, to shield each other, and to limit justice to what was expedient at the time. For who could honestly claim to be without sin? The caution that resulted is illustrated by this anecdote.

Khrushchev (to the congress):	[Investigation has found] a large quantity of documents in the NKVD archives, along with other documents, and has established cases of false and lying accusations, and flagrant violations of socialist legality, as a result of which innocent people have died.[22]
Voice from the floor:	I see. But, Nikita Sergeivich, why tell us only now? Why did you not speak up against all this at the time it was happening?
Khrushchev (sharply):	Who said that?
	Long silence.
Khrushchev (gently):	You see what I mean?

What Khrushchev could have added was: "At that time I was too busy organizing mass arrests, first in Moscow, then in Ukraine." But he didn't, and he escaped retribution along with many others—including Ivan Serov.

What changed and what stayed the same

Khrushchev made some important changes, but he did not change everything. By the time he was done, the Soviet Union was still a police state under the political monopoly of an unchallenged ruling party. And yet his reforms touched every aspect of Soviet life. They ensured that there would be no more horrors like the Mill and no more victims like Stanislav Bronikovsky. These changes became known as "The Thaw," after Ilya Ehrenburg's novel of 1954 that provided a first public acknowledgment of the harsh character of Stalin's rule.

Under Stalin, Soviet rule was violent. To maintain the regime in power, millions of people were arrested, detained, resettled, starved, enslaved, or eliminated. The violence was indiscriminate; most of these millions suffered not because they were known enemies of the regime but because they were seen as potential enemies to be neutralized before they could do harm, or even "unconscious" enemies, the category that Stalin invented for those who thought of themselves as loyal but would not be able to stop themselves from treachery when put under pressure.

Stalin died in 1953. Within a few months of his death, indiscriminate violence began to disappear. Violence was no longer the instrument of choice. Arbitrary arrest in the middle of the night became a thing of the past. The state would still order people to be beaten or killed, but only as a last resort. There was still a police state, and the methods of rule over society were still forceful. But the application of force became much more selective and more finely calculated.

The Thaw gave rise to a new system of rule. The new police state rejected the idea of unconscious enemies. It remained deeply suspicious, but it would test out every suspicion against evidence. A person could make an honest mistake and not pay for it with her life; the state would make a record of the mistake, but allow it to be redeemed. A sheep could leave the flock and become lost, and the shepherd would find it and bring it back.

Now, if the Khabarovsk KGB officers were to worry about the loyalty of a Stanislav Bronikovsky, they would surround him with informers, study him and his way of life, look more closely at the factors behind his behavior, and, if necessary, invite Stanislav to visit for a discussion in which they could share concerns. (We'll see how this worked in chapter 5.) Thus the tenor of Soviet life changed dramatically. Above all, it became safer for everyone, safer for the high officials and the ordinary party members, and much safer for the "simple" people who made up the "non-party masses."

Some things did not change, however. Between the 1930s and the 1970s, the mission of the agencies responsible for censorship, public order, and national security did not change at all. It remained preventive: to forestall any threat, even the smallest, to the incumbent regime of the ruling Communist Party. The problem of prevention remained exactly as it had been; it was the methods of prevention that changed.

The things that remained the same can be summed up in a few basic principles on which the Soviet police state operated throughout its history, from the Bolshevik Revolution of 1917 to the collapse of the Soviet Union in 1991. It was possible to work from these principles in more than one way, and this explains how police states can vary so widely around the world and how the Soviet police state could change so dramatically from one decade to the next. But the principles themselves did not change.

What are they? There are seven of them, and we will find them at work in every story that is told in this book, for no dictator can afford to ignore even one of them.

First Principle: *your enemy is hiding.*
Second Principle: *start from the usual suspects.*
Third Principle: *study the young.*
Fourth Principle: *stop the laughing.*
Fifth Principle: *rebellion spreads like wildfire.*
Sixth Principle: *stamp out every spark.*
Seventh Principle: *order is created by appearances.*

First Principle: Your enemy is hiding

The first principle is: *your enemy is hiding.* It's because the enemy is hiding under cover that every dictator also needs undercover agents—a secret police that can track down enemies and flush them out from their hiding places.

We owe this principle to the political scientist Ronald Wintrobe, who identified what he called the dictator's dilemma. Every dictator has enemies, but who are they? The more powerful the dictator, the more people fear him. Those people conceal their true feelings and put on a show of loyalty and devotion. They do this because their feelings are mixed or hostile and must be concealed for safety. Knowing this, the dictator must suspect everyone, even those who seem to be his most committed supporters (and, for this very reason, even committed supporters may feel the need to show more loyalty than they feel).[23]

Stalin recognized that his enemies wore a mask; he called them "wolves in sheep's clothing." The more they looked like friends, he realized, the more dangerous they were, because the appearance of friendship induces complacency. That's what Stalin had in mind in 1937 when he asked:

> Wherein lies the strength of the present-day wreckers, the Trotskyites? Their strength lies in the Party card, in the possession of a Party card. Their strength lies in the fact that the Party card enables them to be politically trusted and gives them access to all our institutions and organizations. Their advantage lies in that, holding a Party card and pretending to be friends of the Soviet power, they deceived our people politically, abused their confidence, did their wrecking work furtively and disclosed our state secrets to the enemies of the Soviet Union.[24]

The idea that people hide behind a mask of loyalty turns out to be a shared obsession of dictators and repressive regimes. Indeed, that's what the word "repression" means: to subdue intrinsic feelings and cover them with a mask. The dictator wears a mask of power; he relies on secrecy to hide his decisions and actions. In turn, he forces the citizens to wear a mask of loyalty. But behind the masks, enemies lurk.

Suspicion was a rational response to the dictator's dilemma. Stalin's suspicious attitude is sometimes disparaged as "paranoia," with the implication that he took it too far, seeing the world around him as full of nonexistent conspiracies. But Stalin did not show any symptoms of mental illness, such as uncontrollable feelings of anxiety or hopelessness. In all things, his behavior was patient, purposeful, calculating, and controlled.[25]

Stalin was suspicious of others, not from paranoia but because he could not afford to be complacent. His particular view of the world might not be one that you'd expect to share, but it is more common than you might think. It is mirrored, for example, by many citizens of more open societies who believe that—for the sake of private profit—government officials and private corporations will readily collude against the public good behind closed doors and that the reason we do not know more about such activities is that there is a coverup.[26] Replace "private profit" by antipathy to communism and "government officials and private corporations" by "foreign enemies and domestic traitors" and you have Stalin's core beliefs about the world.[27] Rather than wait for the evidence to bear out his beliefs, Stalin preferred to rely on revolutionary instinct. "Experienced conspirators," he noted, "don't leave behind a trail of documents in their work."[28] Sometimes you just had to beat the truth out of people.

These views of the world see conspiracy as a driving force in public life. One might regard them as biased or unbalanced, but it is impossible to say that they are categorically wrong, for such conspiracies do occur. Politicians do sometimes take bribes to pervert public processes for corporate gain. Citizens of one country do sometimes act in the interests of another. No Bolshevik could brush such a view of the world aside, because of what was at the time a quite recent case, terrifying in its implications. In Russia in 1917, a foreign enemy (Germany) and domestic traitors (the Bolsheviks) *had* colluded to bring about the overthrow of the existing government. Seen in that light, Stalin's suspicions look reasonable.

In order to manage his suspicions, Stalin continually tested those around him. One way for Stalin's servants to prove loyalty was to learn about Stalin's suspicions, share them, and test them for themselves in their own environments. When Khabarovsk NKVD chief Goglidze set out to test Stanislav by pushing him across the fake border into "China," he was proving his own loyalty to Stalin by doing exactly what the Boss hoped for.

Second Principle: start from the usual suspects

At first glance, the task of the secret police looks hopeless. If everyone tries to look the same, how can the enemies be separated from the friends? No matter how hard this seems, the secret policeman has a clear point of departure in our Second Principle: *start from the usual suspects*. The usual suspects have something they cannot hide: their pasts. Check out each person's past: each person's social origins, family background, and previous political and social connections. Evidence from the past will not discriminate perfectly between present loyalty and disloyalty, but it is a start.

Although Stalin and his ruling circle did not know exactly who the enemies would be, they knew well that there were broad classes of people who could be expected to show an average propensity to disloyalty. From its very beginning the Soviet regime used historical records, surveys, censuses, and police registration to catalog and classify the population by markers of political and social unreliability.[29] By the 1930s the NKVD had card indexes listing 10 to 15 percent of the population (which can be taken to represent 20 to 30 percent of all adults), classified by the degree of social danger that each person represented. By using such categories, Paul Gregory has argued, the secret police could quickly isolate or eliminate people based on who they had been, rather than go to the trouble of establishing what each person was actually doing or intended to do. Many would be innocent, but it was less important to protect the innocent than to protect the regime.[30]

Who were the usual suspects? The composition of the usual suspects varied and at different times included everyone who had once been associated with non-Communist parties or prerevolutionary governments or police service; party members who had ever shown sympathy for the positions adopted by Stalin's rivals; religious congregations, especially those that crossed international borders, such as the Roman Catholic Church; independent farmers whose homes and livestock had been confiscated; people whose ethnic origins could be traced to a foreign country (including Poles, Germans, Jews, Greeks, and Chinese, even if their families had left the ethnic homeland many generations before); people with foreign language skills or who had lived abroad; people who collected foreign stamps; people who were interested in space travel, a subject with clear potential for infringing on both national frontiers and military secrets; and people who had been previously detained by the security police for any reason.

By 1943 Stanislav Bronikovsky already belonged to at least two of these classes of people: he was a Pole, and he had once before been in the hands of the NKVD. These are the things that made him a usual suspect.

Having identified the usual suspects, Stalin's policy became to cut a broad swath through them. It did not matter to him that the usual suspects would include many innocent victims, because protecting the innocent was not important. A Chinese maxim advises: "One would rather kill a thousand people wrongly than allow one guilty person to escape unpunished." Stalin himself recommended the ratio of twenty to one: "Because it is not easy to recognize the enemy, the goal is achieved if only 5 percent of those killed are truly enemies." Nikolai Yezhov, who implemented the Great Terror, applied the ratio of ten to one: "Better that ten innocent people should suffer than one spy get away. When you chop wood, chips fly."[31]

After Stalin, the Soviet state would change its treatment of the usual suspects. It would treat them with more attention to detail and much more discrimination. But the principle of the usual suspects remained the same: as a priority, the state needed to work out who they were and get to know them.

Third Principle: study the young

The usual suspects are a beginning. They are the enemy you know. But the most dangerous enemy is said to be the one you don't know. Who was the unknown enemy?

The usual suspects deserve suspicion because they belong to particular classes of people that you can identify: there is something you know about each of them. But there is also another class of people that you should suspect exactly because you know nothing about them. Well, you know nothing for sure, but you can still guess that they are full of vigor, they love excitement, and they have a propensity for rebellion. Moreover, their ranks are being continually replenished. This is because they are young: teenagers and young people, between ages sixteen and twenty-five.

Consider the usual suspects: many of them already have a record or reputation of some sort, and to have acquired that record they must have reached a certain maturity. Usual suspects can be in their thirties or older. In contrast, young people are too young to remember the old days, too young to have experience of the outside world, too young to have acquired a police record or a reputation for political resistance. They are young enough to be impressionable and too young to be afraid. Although they are products of the new society and although their experience is limited to its schools and its media, it turns out that young people are especially likely to provide a hidden channel for dissenting values to reemerge.

How do young people become secret carriers of protest? For economists Avner Greif and Steve Tadelis, the answer begins with the clash of ideas between home and school.[32] Under a dictatorship, the government schools, textbooks, and newspapers teach official standards of good and evil, right and wrong. But young people are also influenced by what their parents tell them at home. What does the parent choose to tell the child? When a repressive regime sets out to impose its moral standards on the child, the family must choose between teaching the child to resist and uphold family values or adopting a position of silence that leaves the child open to official influences.

Studying this choice, Greif and Tadelis note that parents who conform to regime values themselves do not have a problem: their children will hear the same at home and at school. But among those who do not conform, the loving parent is torn. You want your child to share your sense of right and wrong, but you also want her to be safe. If you cannot have both, you must choose.

Still, if the risks of dissent are not catastrophic, and if there is a degree of trust within the family, Greif and Tadelis argue, there can be a middle way. This is the path of hidden morality. Dissenting parents can teach the children: That is what you must say at school, and this is what we believe at home; be careful, and don't mix them up. As a Jewish woman recalled her parents' instruction in Odessa in the 1950s: "It was a given . . . You are not to repeat . . . Only to your family members and your friends."[33]

The result can be a generation of young people who "carry" dissenting values. There is no outward sign or symptom, but behind the serious, obedient brows of these young people lies hidden a store of incendiary beliefs. These beliefs will remain under cover until the moment when those who carry them lose their fear of showing them in public. When that time comes, the spark will become a flame.

The work of Greif and Tadelis gives us our Third Principle: *study the young*, because you have no idea what they are really thinking. They are too young to have proved their loyalty. They can turn out to be the most dangerous enemy, the one you do not know.

Fourth Principle: stop the laughing

Everybody needs to laugh, to be entertained, to forget their troubles, and put their worries in perspective. There's a demand for laughter; those who supply it are generally rewarded by social approval, so laughter will be supplied. For the same reason, laughter is social. If I crack a joke and you chuckle, we have shared something intimate: our sense of humor. When laughter is social, it often takes sides in society. Then, laughter is not neutral and it is not always polite. We laugh *with* our friends, but we laugh *at* those who have wronged us, or those we find pompous or contemptible or different.

When people laugh, will they laugh at the regime and its representatives? Many people have limits; life has made them sensitive so that some subjects eventually lose their comic appeal. But younger people are not yet burdened by experience and love to play with words and meanings, so they will usually laugh at anything at least once, even at symbols of power. And some people never lose that playfulness, even in old age.

What are capitalism and communism? "Capitalism is the exploitation of man by man!" And communism? "The other way around."[34]

Lenin has died but his cause will live for ever! "Hmm. Can we change that around?"[35]

Is the ruling order weakened when its funny side is exposed? This question has been much debated. George Orwell maintained that "every joke is a tiny revolution."[36] But no one has yet found data to prove that kings or dictators can be laughed out of office. Perhaps humor is the weapon of those who have no weapons;

perhaps there can be "humor that has ceased to struggle."[37] Some people have argued that humor can be an obstacle to change, because it helps people to endure what they cannot resist. In this view laughter provides only comic relief, a harmless safety valve that merely releases frustration and resentment.[38]

For the secret policeman, such debates are irrelevant. The debaters miss the point. It doesn't matter whether people who share a joke are just letting off steam. The point is that humor is a currency: it allows people to exchange feelings. It's not the joke as such, which presents itself disarmingly, pretending to be harmless.[39] The harm is in the laughter that responds to it. If I crack a joke and you chuckle, you're telling me something I might not have known before: you think like me—I am not alone.

To put it another way, if I tell you a joke, the harm is not in the joke but in the sharing: I share something with you, and you share your response with me. Here the result can be the formation of an illicit bond, an underground network of consumers and suppliers of jokes. This network has no register of members and it has no structure that has been authorized by the party or the government, no forum where the party members can exercise a leading role, and no leaders who can be held to account for the actions of the followers. In fact, it's thoroughly suspicious, demands investigation, and ought to be suppressed.

So there it is. Everyone needs to laugh. You can laugh at the enemy—the foreign enemy and the enemies within. You can laugh at the thief, the slacker, and the black-market trader. You can laugh at the pen-pusher, the bribe-taker, and the petty bureaucrat. But you may *not* laugh at the system, nor at the ruling party, nor its leaders, nor their policies. Such jokes are a flame that draws people together for warmth. The laughter that answers the jokes is the signal of their community around a hearth that should not exist and cannot be tolerated. Hence the Fourth Principle: *stop the laughing*.

Fifth Principle: rebellion spreads like wildfire

What keeps the secret policeman awake at night is the fear of a rebellion that comes out of nowhere. Everything is tranquil and sleepy. Then a tiny spark takes hold and spreads, so that suddenly the whole meadow is ablaze. Writing about "Sparks and Prairie Fires," the economist Timur Kuran observed that the overthrow of the old regime always comes as a surprise.[40] Kuran gave three examples. The French Revolution of 1789 came as a complete shock to Frederick the Great, just over the border. On the eve of revolution in Russia in 1917, a British diplomat wrote to London: "Some disorders occurred to-day, but nothing serious." In 1979, Iran's queen was baffled by the turn of events: "For heaven's sake, who is this Khomeini?" Kuran's insight is confirmed by more recent events, including the sudden collapse of the Berlin Wall and the unexpected uprisings that made up the Arab Spring.

Why does revolution have this abrupt character? How can a random spark turn so swiftly into something that changes history? Kuran argued that under the dictator there live many who have chosen the path of conditional loyalty. They give their allegiance to the dictator, based on the belief that everyone else is doing the same. Each one feels alienated from the regime but keeps it to himself (First Principle), with the result that each believes he is the only one. This can be for more than one reason. It might be because you don't really know whether you like the government, but everyone you know seems to be a supporter, and it would be foolish to ignore them. Or you might fear that if you take a contrary position they will not wish to know you. Or you might just figure that it would be pointless to stand out from the crowd and be a lonely martyr for a lost cause. These motives are distinct, but they point in the same direction.[41] The combined result is that these individuals live a lie, their everyday speech and actions being opposite to their inner convictions.

That people could live like this every day of their lives is shown by a story from postwar Hungary, told by the historian Melissa Feinberg:

> Two sisters . . . had both been loyal Communists. Each claimed that after hearing some of the truth about the [show] trials she was becoming disenchanted with the regime she had so strongly supported a few years before. But each was convinced that the other sister was still a true believer, even though they were very close and lived together in the same apartment![42]

When people live like this, the spark is a moment of discovery, an unexpected flash of illumination. When one person stands up in the light, one, ten, or a hundred others can suddenly see: "I am not alone!" It galvanizes mass resistance. Thus every spark is a rebellion, and our Fifth Principle warns: *rebellion spreads like wildfire.*

Sixth Principle: stamp out every spark

A spark can land in brushwood and suddenly blaze up across the prairie. How can you fight a fire like that? For the secret policeman, there is still hope. You can prevent the fire of rebellion from taking hold, but only by following our Sixth Principle: *stamp out every spark.* The reason is that, while a spark can become a wildfire with immense speed, it does not do so instantaneously. You can beat it, if you respond within the instant.

Sociologist Mark Granovetter's framework explains the capacity of a police state to prevent the fire from taking hold.[43] Imagine all the possible troublemakers in a society lined up in order from the most reckless (or incendiary) to the most cautious or timid. How does rebellion spread? It begins with the most reckless person, one who is willing to be a hero and march down the street even if no one else does. Then there is the next most reckless person, who will not act on his own but will join the march if at least one other person is in front of him. After that one in line is the third most reckless person, the one who will march if two other people are in front . . . and so on down the line till you get to someone like me: a conformist who will generally join a march in a good cause only if around 100,000 other people are there before me. In this sense, at least, I am fairly normal, so while there are very few heroes, there are lots of people who are about as cautious as I am.

This chain tells you several things. One is exactly how rebellion spreads: the spark is provided by a hero (or fool), who is then joined by a few particularly brave (or foolish) people, and then the fire spreads rapidly as wider and wider circles of more and more normal people join them. And of course all this can happen very quickly (see the Fifth Principle). It can happen more quickly, perhaps, if everyone is connected by being gathered in a big workplace like the Gdansk shipyards where Poland's Solidarity movement was born; or by being crowded into Revolution Square in Bucharest where a lone heckler sparked the sudden collapse of Nicolae Ceauşescu's power; or, nowadays, by following each other on Twitter or Facebook.

A second thing is just how random revolution can be. Suppose, for example, that one day there could have been a revolution, but the second-most-reckless person had a hangover and stayed home. The result is that instead of a revolution you have the first person marching down the street and everyone else looking at him and thinking: "He's crazy and I'm not getting involved." In other words, there are bound to be many random sparks that didn't set the world alight, because the brushwood happened to be damp that morning.

And a third thing: now we see just what the secret policemen must do. They start without any idea of who exactly is the most reckless person, and the reason for this will be that he's probably young and so lacks a record (see the Third Principle). They may well be unable to prevent him from starting his lone demonstration in the first place. But they can watch and wait. If they can grab him in the first moments—before the second guy comes along to join him—or if they can grab the first two before the third one joins, they can still stop the thing from spreading. Their job will be done. There was a spark, but it existed only for an instant. It was stamped out, and no fire took hold.

Seventh Principle: order is created by appearances

The ruler can employ professional fire-watchers, but people are human and perpetual vigilance is an impossible standard to maintain. It seems that any authoritarian regime faces a high risk of conflagration at some point. How can the regime best assure its security?

Forty years before the opening of the Russian archives, when Stalin was barely in his grave, Alex Inkeles and Raymond Bauer put their finger on this issue.[44] Soviet leaders, they wrote, did not expect to win the hearts and minds of the masses of ordinary people. Although they made efforts in this direction, they also knew that many of their policies could be expected to create hidden hostility among large sections of the population (see the First Principle: *your enemy is hiding*). This led them to assume that every ordinary citizen was at least potentially disloyal.

While the Soviet rulers could not know anyone's innermost thoughts, and did not expect to change those thoughts directly, all their efforts went into controlling outward behavior. This meant giving the citizen "no viable alternative except to conform." Whatever people thought, the regime required them at least to put up the appearance of loyalty by behaving in conformity with political and legal norms.

Each person's appearance of loyalty, in turn, had a striking effect on others. By conforming, each one mirrored the conformity of those around them. The result was "an exaggerated picture of actual loyalty." While many of them continued to give shelter to dissenting or rebellious thoughts, each one would feel (like Feinberg's sisters): I am alone.

In turn, this could change those thoughts. Believing they were alone in their alienation, knowing that they had no choice but to live in this society and get along, they might doubt their own disloyal beliefs. Thus, the regime's insistence on keeping up appearances fostered actual loyalty. Put another way, the ruling order was stable because everyone believed it was stable—not only its own citizens, but most Western observers at the time (including me).

But this was also a weak point of the system. When the first person with enough youthful optimism and irrational courage to stand up and differ did so, all around were others who were suddenly reminded of their own true feelings, long suppressed and undermined by doubt. In that moment they understood for the first time: I am not alone.[45]

Common sense suggests that the way a society looks is determined by how it works. Our Seventh Principle of the police state flies in the face of common sense, because how it works is actually determined by how it looks. *Order is created by appearances.* This explains why every ruling Communist Party not only claimed the unity of the people around the program of the Party and its leaders, but required the people to demonstrate this unity over and over again. Their ruling order depended on a fragile equilibrium of appearances that kept the flicker of nonconformity hidden in each person's mind—hidden from the regime and hidden from others. In this way, the appearance of order created its own reality.

There was more than one way to create the appearance of order. Stalin's way was to sweep away the potentially disruptive people like Stanislav Bronikovsky by killing them. His successors would look for more humane methods of tidying up society, killing only in the last resort.

Thus, the methods changed. But while the methods changed, the keeping up of appearances remained the first priority as before. Keeping up appearances worked by making a collapse of order unimaginable, and this worked until it failed. When order failed it was bound to fail suddenly, catching everyone by surprise. Then, what would never happen became something that had happened already and now looked inevitable in hindsight.[46]

CHAPTER TWO

Truth Hurts

In January 1937, the world was gripped by reports of a major trial in Moscow. On the last day of the month, verdicts were handed down in the cases of Yuri Pyatakov, Karl Radek, and fifteen other former oppositionists who had held high positions in the party and government. Until his arrest, Pyatakov was in the forefront of Stalin's industrialization program as a leading official responsible for heavy industry. Radek was once secretary of the Communist International, the umbrella organization of the world revolution. More recently, he had worked for the government newspaper, *Izvestiya*. All were charged with horrendous acts of treason, espionage, sabotage, and terrorism. At the core of the plot was a supposed conspiracy with Hitler's Gestapo and the exiled revolutionary Leon Trotsky to provoke a war in which Germany and Japan would attack and defeat the Soviet Union. All the defendants confessed their guilt. Behind the confessions lay solitary confinement, intimidation, false promises, and torture. All were found guilty, and most were sentenced to be shot. There was no appeal; Pyatakov was executed the next day.

As a reward for his cooperation, Radek got a light sentence: ten years. This gave rise to a famous joke. Three prisoners meet in a cell and share their stories. The first says: "I got ten years because I criticized Radek." The second says: "I got ten years because I praised Radek." The third says: "I'm Radek." Radek did not outlive his sentence. He was killed in 1939, still in prison, on the order of Stalin's security chief, Lavrenty Beria.

An ambiguous blotch

In Moscow the nights were still frosty. By day, the sun shone and the temperature rose. The packed snow melted, exposing the rubbish that had piled up through the winter for the street sweepers to clean away. The trees were still bare, but spring colors would soon return to the streets and parks.

On Friday, April 9, 1937, Katya Novikova was out sick.[1] She was a middle-ranking official of Glavlit, the office of censorship in Moscow. The next day, which was a Saturday, she was back in the office. She was still tired, and now she faced the backlog of work that had piled up during her absence. In the rush, a familiar-looking face thrust a familiar-looking document at her. She signed it and moved on to other things. The moment was gone in a flash.

The consequences became public exactly four weeks later. On Saturday, May 8, a brief notice appeared on an inside page of the party newspaper, *Pravda*.[2] When Katya read these words, the ground began to slip beneath her feet.

from the latest mailbag

A SUBVERSIVE MONTAGE

At the time of going to press, Presscliché [a government photographic agency] has distributed a picture to newspapers under the caption "Truth hurts." Fortunately, in many newspapers this drawing has not seen the light of day. The editors have preferred to leave their paper without illustration than to print a subversive montage.

Some idiots and fools, however, have printed the counterrevolutionary cartoon for all to see. Thus for example did comrade Barannikov, deputy director of the Danilov district newspaper *Collective Farm Banner* (Stalingrad region). Most journalists of the local press had more political sense than Presscliché director comrade Abramov, and they rejected the ambiguous blotch. Staff of the local newspaper *Talačyn Collective Farmer* (Belarusian SSR) comrades Boikachev and Kipper have sent *Pravda* a copy of the print they received. The authors quite reasonably point out the libelous, anti-Soviet character of the drawing. They demand that the picture should be withdrawn and those responsible for distributing the pernicious print should be punished as they deserve.

Usually, Soviet censorship worked

Glavlit, where Katya worked, was the office of Soviet censorship. Censors were the secret policemen of the word and the image; they scrutinized every publication, every broadcast, every photograph and cartoon. Their first duty was to prevent the unauthorized disclosure of government and party business, all of which was secret by default. Their next duty was to suppress all the heresies and hidden meanings that they or anyone else could imagine.

The Bolsheviks introduced censorship in November 1917 as one of the first acts of the revolution (the "Decree on the Press"). In the first years, many agencies competed at many levels to operate censorship. Glavlit, the Chief Administration for Affairs of Literature and Art, was established in 1922 to pull all the functions of censorship together into a single, unified agency. Its official title changed a few times over the next seventy years. Still, no one ever called it anything but Glavlit, even in official government and party documents.

Soviet censorship was impressively complete. In democracies, most business is done in public and that which is done behind closed doors is commonly leaked to the press because there is a demand to know other people's secrets and those who are party to them have many incentives to break trust and supply them. The reader may find it hard to imagine anything else. Yet the number of important Soviet secrets that was leaked to the public in the lifetime of the Soviet state, other than through espionage or by defectors, was extremely small; Khrushchev's secret speech of 1956, in which he denounced Stalin (as discussed in chapter 1), is a rare exception.

How well did Glavlit go about its work? One of its duties was to prevent the disclosure of secret government business, and Glavlit was a government agency, so its work was entirely secret; in other words, the censorship had to censor the facts of its own business. For this to succeed, Glavlit itself had to drop out of the public view. The frequency with which Glavlit was mentioned in published works of the time gives us a simple measure of how completely this was done.

The Google Books Russian corpus includes more than half a million books published in Russian between 1900 and 2008. Figure 1 shows both the absolute number of appearances of the word "Glavlit" in these books in each year, and also the number of uses of "Glavlit" relative to the total of words in the corpus. The absolute and relative uses of "Glavlit" look different over time because in the 1990s ten times as many Russian words were published each year as in the 1920s. The figure shows that the word "Glavlit" was unknown before the revolution. Its usage increased rapidly after Glavlit was established, peaking in 1927. After that it declined with equal rapidity before disappearing

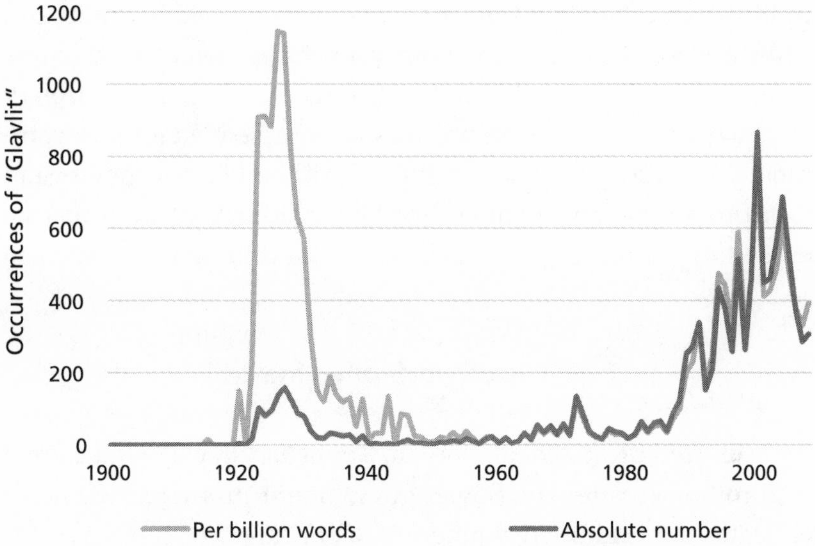

FIGURE 1: The frequency of "Glavlit" in half a million Russian books, 1900 to 2008

This figure shows the results of searching for "Glavlit" in the Google Books N-gram Viewer. The search uses the Google Books Russian-language corpus of 2012 from 1900 to 2008 and "Glavlit" in Cyrillic characters, switching off both case-sensitivity and year-to-year smoothing. Over these years the Google Books Russian-language corpus includes more than 63 billion words from more than 555,000 books.

Source: The Google Books N-gram Viewer can be found at https://books.google.com/ngrams/. For a description, see Michel et al., "Quantitative Analysis of Culture Using Millions of Digitized Books," *Science* 331, no. 6014.

entirely from public discourse. By 1937, the year of our story, "Glavlit" was barely mentioned. Glavlit was working!

The figure shows something even more startling in the period *after* our story. In the 1950s "the Thaw" set in following Stalin's death, and with it censorship was partially relaxed to allow publication of information that was discreditable to Stalin and some of his associates. But, while censorship was relaxed in one direction, it became still more restrictive in another: mention of the institutions of censorship was suppressed even more completely than before. It was not until Mikhail Gorbachev began to promote greater openness in 1987 that Glavlit could be discussed in public.

The censor's dilemma

An educated professional woman, Katya Novikova owed a great deal to Soviet rule. The Soviet government promoted women's education, encouraged women to work, and created work for them on a tremendous scale. Between 1928 and 1940, nearly half a million women entered government service.[3] Without the social and economic transformation of Soviet society, most of these women would have been condemned to illiteracy and sweatshop labor. In government service, women were less likely than men to rise to positions of higher rank, but the work that they did was often responsible; it demanded commitment to party values and conscientious attention to detail, and it conveyed a sense of trust and empowerment.[4]

Among the women who entered the service of the state in these years is Katya. We find her in April 1934, listed among the Glavlit employees as a political editor with a monthly wage of 350 rubles.[5] This is a good salary. She gets substantially more than the librarian, and more than twice what the typist gets. The head of Glavlit is too high-up to be credited with a salary, but even his deputies get only small increments over Katya. Of course, pay is not the most important thing. More important than pay is the privileged access to the scarce foodstuffs and household goods, the health care and vacations that come with position. As a responsible worker at Glavlit, Katya will get her share of these things.

Katya works in the department that deals with the local press. She is sufficiently engaged in her work to write about it. "To master the equipment of one's business is a combat assignment of the chiefs of the local offices of Glavlit," she declares in 1934 in Glavlit's *Bulletin*.[6] The bulletin is classified "secret" and cannot be read by the public. It circulates only in-house, among the employees. Although it is secret, and written for censors, it too will have been censored. In the Soviet state, access to information is based on need-to-know; there is no right-to-know.

As a censor, Katya must juggle many responsibilities. Her task is preventive: to suppress the disclosure of facts, ideas, or attitudes that might help an enemy. This sounds straightforward, but it is not. The censor's problem starts from the First Principle (from chapter 1): *your enemy is hiding*. In a repressive society where everyone seeks to put on the mask of loyalty, anyone can turn out to be an enemy behind the mask, including new and established journalists, novelists, and artists. Every item must be scrutinized. Even scripture can be given a subversive meaning when it is quoted selectively or taken out of context. For this reason, a special regulation of 1935 states that even the writings of Lenin or Stalin may be reproduced in the media "only by special permission of Glavlit."[7]

According to one anecdote, a censor is asked: "What books do you allow?" The censor replies: "The ones we can't stop. Like the phone book."[8] If only it were so simple. Employed as a censor, you want to say "no" all the time. If you let suspicious material through and you could have prevented it, they will say that you are helping the enemy. Perhaps (they will say) you are an enemy yourself.

But you can't say no all the time. The people need something to read. The party needs the people to be educated and entertained.

If you prohibit everything, you will stop the people from learning about the policies of the party. If all you give them to read is the phone book, you are not doing your job. The Fourth Principle is in your hands: *stop the laughing*. But people still need something to laugh about. If you cross out every joke for fear of missing some double entendre, you will deprive the people of their entertainment. And they will say (again) that you are helping the enemy.

As a censor you must take care, but you can also overdo caution. You have to take some risks. One risk is to find secret signals and coded meanings in everything you read, and forbid it, only to be condemned for timidity. An opposite risk is to miss the secrets and downplay the codes and let dubious material be published, so that you will afterward be condemned for negligence (if nothing worse). One is a rock and the other is a hard place. The risks cannot be eliminated, but somewhere between them is a balance to be struck that at least lets you keep the risks to a minimum. Where is that middle way? There is the censor's dilemma.

A riddle asks: "What do a censor and a bomb disposal officer have in common?" Answer: "They both get to make one mistake in a lifetime."[9] Whatever decision you make, it can all go horribly wrong. This is Katya's story in the Presscliché affair of 1937.

A winning entry

Presscliché was a unit of Soyuzfoto, the photographic department of the official news agency TASS; *klishe* is the Russian word for a stereotype block used for printing photographs. Early in 1937, Presscliché ran a nationwide photomontage competition. The judges picked a winner, a collage on a political theme by an artist called Ilinsky.

Ilinsky's central image was a front page of *Pravda*, the party's daily newspaper. He used a mock-up rather than an actual issue. This was made out of a few stories that the artist had selected from the hundreds prompted by the Pyatakov-Radek trial. All the stories had actually appeared in the columns of *Pravda*, but not on the same day.

FIGURE 2: "Truth stings the eyes" by Ilinsky

Source: Hoover Institution Library & Archives, Archives of the Soviet Communist Party and Soviet State Microfilm Collection, 1903–1992: Russian State Archive of Contemporary History (Rossiiskii gosudarstvennyi arkhiv noveishei istorii—RGANI), 6/1/74: 160.

We can make out three major stories. Just below the *Pravda* banner on the left, the headline reads, "Enemies of humanity." To the bottom right another headline deals with "Lying antics of German newspapers." Above it on the right are the words "The peoples of the USSR are invincible." The first of these stories appeared on February 1, 1937, the day of Pyatakov's execution, when *Pravda's* leading article denounced:

> ***Enemies of humanity, arsonists of war***
>
> The threat of war has hung over Europe, over the Far East, and over the entire world . . . In the vanguard of the fascist aggressors stand their agents: the Trotskyist traitors . . .

The story about "Lying antics of German newspapers" came out a few days later. On February 7, *Pravda* reported: "The German fascists are clearly maddened by the fact that the Gestapo's Trotskyist agents have been exposed and neutralized by the Soviet people."

The third headline was the earliest; it comes from the middle of the trial on January 27. Soviet radio was broadcasting the proceedings daily across the country. The defendants were daily confessing to outrages they had committed against the party and the country. That day, under the headline "The peoples of the USSR are invincible," *Pravda* reported a resolution of listeners at the Voroshilov Naval Academy in Leningrad: "We demand capital annihilation of the entire fascist gang." Just to confirm where things were going, an adjacent story from the same day was headed: "Shoot the rabid Trotskyist bandits."

In Ilinsky's composition, the mock-up of *Pravda* is complemented by two other images. Above the news rises a portrait of

Stalin: stern, calm, full of authority, gazing into the distance beyond the headlines with a benign smile.

To the side of the news is drawn a grotesque creature: part human, part farmyard animal, dressed as a Nazi storm trooper, with doggy ears that twitch through holes in a coal-scuttle helmet. Huge, hobnailed jackboots and a fascist ax at its belt complete the image of the beast. Stalin's gaze has flushed it out from the shadows. Snarling with fear and rage, the creature is in flight, scampering up and away.

The importance of being clear

So far, so good. The fatal element in the collage was surely the last: its title. Ilinsky called his creation, in Russian, *Pravda glaza kolyot*: "Truth stings the eyes," or just "Truth hurts."

What did that mean? Right out in the open was a clear double meaning: the Russian word *pravda* means "truth," and *The Truth* was also the name of the party newspaper. This double meaning was perfectly clear; it could hardly have raised any eyebrows. The headlines in *The Truth* were telling the truth, the cartoon suggested, and the truth was hurting the fascist beasts who had been put on display in the Moscow show trial.

But could there be some *other* double meaning, one that was concealed within the clear one? Most likely, the question that could be raised was: *Who was it*, exactly, that was hurt by the truth? The truth hurt Germany, obviously, whose plans and secret agents had been exposed in the show trial just concluded. But was *Pravda* hurt by its own truth? Nikolai Bukharin, who would be the principal defendant in next year's major show trial, had edited *Pravda* from 1918 to 1929, and had only just stepped down as editor of *Izvestiya*. Soon he would be tried and executed as another traitor. Or was *the Soviet Union* damaged by the show-trial revelations?

Most dangerously, perhaps, had *Stalin* been damaged by the "truth" about the treason of his close comrades in arms? These were men he had accepted, promoted, and worked with in the highest positions of the party and state. At a meeting held immediately after the trial, March 3–5, 1937, Stalin told the party Central Committee:

> Some of our leading comrades, at the center and in the districts, not only failed to discern the real face of these wreckers, diversionists, spies, and assassins, but proved to be so careless, complacent, and naïve that not infrequently they themselves helped to promote agents of foreign powers to responsible positions.[10]

This comment surely suggests a question: Had *Stalin* been "careless, complacent, and naïve"? Should Stalin apply his own criticism to *himself*? Had *Stalin* "helped to promote agents of foreign powers to responsible positions"? If the truth hurt, was it hurting *Stalin*? The thought could have crossed anyone's mind. But would anyone be so foolish, so bent on self-destruction, as to even hint at such a thing in a public forum?

By the 1930s, Soviet censorship was already fairly effective in preventing the publication of party and government secrets and ensuring that only authorized works and statements were available to the public. The historian Jan Plamper, who has studied the operation of censorship in the Soviet Union in the 1930s, suggests that a new problem now arose: how to ensure that government and party publications were clearly understandable in just one way—the correct way.[11]

The result was a crackdown on double meanings and unfortunate juxtapositions that might expose official messages to mockery or contradiction. The authorities wanted everyone to understand that playing on words and images was no joke. A lack of serious intent could not be a defense. In Plamper's examples, to tolerate an ambiguity was called "negligence . . . if not wrecking," not just any mistake but a "so-called" mistake, suggesting intentional sabotage.

The struggle with underground humor (as in the Fourth Principle: *stop the laughing*) was one battle in this wider war on double meanings. For many jokes are just double meanings that turn out to be funny because they catch you by surprise when a truth deeper than the surface meaning is suddenly unveiled.[12] The war on double meanings gave the censors plenty to do, because Soviet language gave so much opportunity. For example, in the Soviet Union there were two national daily newspapers for readers to choose. One was *Pravda* (The Truth), published by the party. The other was *Izvestiya* (The News), published by the government. Inevitably a joke followed: "Ah well, there's no truth in 'The News' and no news in 'The Truth'."

Intolerance for ambiguity might be a common feature of totalitarian regimes. It was something that Hitler shared with Stalin. Speaking at an art show in Munich at about the same time, Adolf Hitler commended the aphorism: "To be German means to be clear."[13]

Libelous and anti-Soviet

The documents in the case do not expand on why the party officials found the winning collage so objectionable. More than likely, just to write down the double meaning would have been dangerous in itself.

The author of the report was no fool. He would prove himself to be an accomplished survivor. In 1937, not yet forty years of age, Peter Pospelov was a relatively junior member of the Party Control Commission. Under Stalin he rose up the party ladder to become a senior ideologue: editor of *Pravda* and director of the

Institute of Marx-Engels-Lenin, a safe pair of hands for the party's history and doctrine. After Stalin's death he helped Khrushchev establish the scale of Stalin's assault on the party membership, and under Khrushchev he joined the second circle of power as a candidate Politburo member. He died peacefully at the age of 81.[14]

This man could be flexible as well as solid. His verdict of 1937 was as clear as it needed to be, and was copied shamelessly from *Pravda*'s original exposé of May 8. The "ambiguous" montage, Pospelov confirmed, was "libelous and anti-Soviet." And that was all the attention that he gave to the artist and his art.

The rest of the report explains just how the joke slipped past the censor, to be published in a number of local and factory newspapers. How did that happen? We see the process of censorship at work: there is a story of rush, delay, and negligence. There were many chances to stop the artist's work from entering circulation because many people had to give their approval. What went wrong?

A time line of errors

Sunday, March 21: comrade Mokeyev. Presscliché chief Abramov handed Ilinsky's drawing into the Central Committee press department. There, Mokeyev was in charge of local and factory newspapers. Mokeyev was first to approve the drawing. This allowed it to go onward in two directions: upward into Soyuzfoto (Presscliché's parent organization) and sideways into Glavlit.

Wednesday, March 31: comrades Slavolyubova and Yevgenov. Slavolyubova was an editor at Presscliché. Yevgenov sat upstairs from her as chief editor of Soyuzfoto. Both approved the drawing on March 31, although Yevgenov recalled later that he found the drawing "confusing." In other words, Yevgenov sidestepped the responsibility that was rightfully his, and passed the burden onto the next stage. He could have stopped the process in its tracks, but he missed the chance.

Wednesday, March 31: comrade Novikova (Katya). At Glavlit, Katya was one of the censors responsible for Soyuzfoto. Katya also had reservations. She disliked the drawing, but she too did not take her opportunity to put a stop to it. Instead, she did two things, both fateful. She signed one copy, giving it the censor's preliminary approval. Final approval required a second, independent signature from one of her colleagues. At the same time Katya resolved to seek "clarification" with her colleagues in Glavlit. Like Yevgenov, in other words, she relied on someone else making the final decision. But her chance to get that decision came and went. As the official account notes, " she did not clarify anything; apparently a party meeting began in Glavlit where she took part, but no clarification was obtained."

Thursday, April 1: comrade Abramov. Presscliché chief Abramov now seized the initiative. Since no one was stopping him, he ordered the printer to set up the drawing on a printing block. Printing began on April 3 and ran to 2,800 copies. At this point the copies were made, but they could not be distributed to the press for publication without final approval. This was waiting for a second censor's signature, which was still missing. Who would provide it?

Friday, April 9: comrade Chugunov. On that day, Presscliché secretary Kuznetsova attended a censors' meeting in Glavlit with two copies of the drawing. But Katya was out sick. In her absence, responsibility passed upward to her group leader, comrade Chugunov.

Chugunov knew that others were doubtful of the political correctness of the drawing. Afterward, he claimed to have shared their doubts all along. At the time, however, he was swayed in favor by the fact that it had been endorsed in the Central Committee (by comrade Mokeyev on March 31). Chugunov could still have stopped the whole thing on his own authority but, as the report puts it, he "did not display the necessary firmness as a censor." Instead, he told Kuznetsova he would consult *his* superiors. (That is, he too did not want to be responsible for deciding the matter and hoped to pass the burden upward.) He kept one copy for this purpose, leaving the other with Kuznetsova. As yet, there was no final approval.

Saturday, April 10: comrade Novikova again. The following day, impatience clashed fatally with procrastination. Presscliché chief Abramov felt sure that the censor was holding back a masterpiece. The censor was behaving ignorantly and he, the intellectual, knew better. On that fateful day he sent his secretary Kuznetsova back to Glavlit with the unsigned copy that remained in her possession.

At Glavlit, Katya was back at work after her sickness. Kuznetsova found Katya and thrust the copy in front of her. Without stopping to think, Katya signed it for publication.

Katya's signature had the look of a final decision, but it was not valid. Two independent signatures were required for final approval. Inadvertently, Katya had now signed the drawing twice, the first time being ten days previously, on March 31. Another copy, still unsigned, was in the hands of Chugunov. If Katya had asked about it, the absence of the other copy could have warned her that something was not right. But she did not ask, and Kuznetsova did not tell.

Then Katya forgot about it. The same day she signed the second copy, Chugunov held a group meeting and there was a row.

Katya denied that she had authorized publication. Chugunov believed he had prevailed in suppressing a counterrevolutionary cartoon. No one paid any attention to what was going on outside the room. There, events were already spiraling out of control. For, while they hissed at each other, Abramov was scattering two thousand copies of "Truth hurts" across the length and breadth of the world's largest national territory.

The reckoning

Three days passed before Chugunov could get his boss's attention. With the latter's sanction, on April 13, Chugunov ordered the suppression of "Truth hurts." But this action was beside the point. Abramov tried to recall the drawing from its many addressees across the country, but he was too late. Some local papers (we don't know how many) had already published the forbidden picture for the enjoyment of their readers.

What had gone wrong? It turns out that half a dozen officials worked together to bring disaster upon themselves and their employers. They let through an artifact that at least three of them—Yevgenov, Chugunov, and Katya Novikova herself—acknowledged as politically doubtful. How did this come about?

The reasons begin from the censor's dilemma. You want to say no, but *you can't say no to everything*. The public has to have something to look at. If you reject everything, you will not have done the job that the party wants you to do.

Given the censor's dilemma, it helped to delay decisions and share responsibility—especially with superiors. Katya Novikova did this first (on March 31) and Chugunov did it again (on April 9). They avoided taking up clear positions and played for time in order to consult with colleagues. And this could well have worked, except for two other factors: some others behaved badly, and there was also bad luck.

The behavior of others left the censors badly exposed. Abramov clearly felt he could enhance his reputation by being a little daring. (And in the spring of 1937!) Kuznetsova probably thought she had done her boss a favor by her little deception of Novikova. And Mokeyev, Slavolyubova, and Yevgenov, who worked for the party but were not censors, all signed the picture off first. Yevgenov did so in spite of reservations, or so he claimed afterward. Most likely, each believed his or her own signature would not be decisive. The final responsibility would lie with Glavlit. So they passed the buck to the censors, who did have to decide, and also did not find it easy.

Finally, there was plain bad luck. If Novikova had not been ill, if she had not been momentarily out of the loop, if Kuznetsova had not grabbed her on her first day back, the one day when she was not properly focused on the one thing that really mattered, she would never have signed the picture off unthinkingly. She meant no harm; she was just unlucky. But that is how it is with tyrannical power: it treats the disloyal and the hapless the same.

"Truth hurts" became the occasion for a wider reckoning with Presscliché and Glavlit. Party Controller Pospelov recommended a shake-up. Because this was the outcome of a party inquiry into wrongdoing by party members, he recommended party reprimands for Chugunov, Mokeyev, and Katya Novikova. But because the party controlled the state, he could also specify disciplinary measures against the state's employees. Abramov was demoted, and Katya was dismissed. Thus her career as a censor came to an abrupt end, although (or perhaps because) her predicament had been one with which anyone could sympathize.

Was this the end of the affair? Probably not. For this was the spring of 1937, the year of the Great Terror, when tens of thousands of party and government officials, scientists, writers, and others who had attracted the authorities' attention by accident or design were put on public trial on fabricated charges of spying, wrecking, and killing on behalf of the foreign enemy. And that was just the public dimension of the Great Terror. In secret, in the autumn and winter, hundreds of thousands were quietly rounded up and executed with little or no process. Suspicion was enough, and any of those involved in the Presscliché affair had done enough to attract it.

Glavlit's turn for purging came around in the autumn of 1937. At the Central Committee, Lev Mekhlis was in charge of the press department. This was the same press department that employed comrade Mokeyev, who had been first to swallow his reservations and sign off the offending cartoon. Having worked closely with Stalin over many years, Mekhlis was also a member of the party's powerful Organizational Bureau, the committee that approved government appointments and deployed party members. From these positions he launched a campaign against the national and local personnel of the state censorship office.

In October 1937 Mekhlis wrote to Stalin and other leaders attacking the local censors for allowing the publication of military secrets and "counterrevolutionary attacks." In a second memorandum the next month he accused the Glavlit leadership of seeking to recruit "politically doubtful people" and of developing a culture of "mutual protection, suppression of criticism, and bootlicking." He reported that his department had already begun to clear out the middle ranks of Glavlit—which surely included Katya Novikova. The incumbent head of Glavlit was soon arrested, and others with him.[15]

With 1938, Glavlit had a new chief. In April the new chief reported to Premier Vyacheslav Molotov: "The Glavlit organs have been choked by Trotskyist-Bukharinist, bourgeois-nationalist spies and traitors. Suffice it to say that in 1937 and 1938 of the total of 144 staff of the central apparatus the NKVD has removed 44."[16]

What happened to Katya? I wanted to know. Today there exist many directories of people arrested and condemned in those years, and I searched as many as I could without finding her. But all such lists are incomplete, so I learned nothing. All that can be said is that from this time the actors in our story no longer appear in the public record. That in itself doesn't mean they were all arrested. To lose your job in the spring of 1937 might be a safer outcome than keeping it until the autumn when Stalin stepped up the pace of arrests and executions. I also wondered what happened to the artist Ilinsky, whose composition caused all the trouble. He too vanished without a trace.

A message for everyone

There was one more message in the Presscliché affair. This one was for the public, and it explains why the story was advertised in *Pravda*. Why was the whole thing not hushed up? There was something about the Presscliché affair that *needed* to be said—but what was it?

> Some idiots and fools [reported *Pravda* on May 8] have printed the counterrevolutionary cartoon for all to see . . . Most journalists of the local press had more political sense than Presscliché director comrade Abramov, and they rejected the ambiguous blotch.

You were an idiot and a fool, in other words, if you believed that what was not prohibited was permitted. The "idiots and fools" were those who delegated their duty of vigilance to the censor. Even the censor could not be trusted. When the servants of the state were fallible, you had "political sense" only if you stood ready at all times *to censor yourself*.

CHAPTER THREE

Heretics

The disengaged scholar dreaming in an ivory tower is a familiar image. In the Soviet Union, universities and colleges were not places where disengaged scholars could dream easily.[1] The ruling party of the Soviet state set clear objectives for them. In teaching, they were to recruit and educate the new Soviet middle class and train its new members in professional competence and political loyalty. In research, they were to benefit the state by adding economic value and winning the prestige associated with world-leading discoveries. These things were too important and too urgent for anyone to be left alone with his own thoughts.

The party carefully monitored the life and work of Soviet universities and colleges and managed them actively. But this was not easy; anyone who has had to direct the work of scientists and scholars knows that they are close to unmanageable. Scholars are driven, skeptical, argumentative, and too clever with words for their own good or anyone else's.

The scholars and their managers tended to be very different types of people. College professors and their students were selected for their ability to manipulate the multiple meanings of words, numbers, symbols, and shapes in complex ways. The managers were always less educated; they would respect education and competence but they would never be as intellectually agile as the scholars they supervised. They were selected for ambition, work capacity, shrewdness, and loyalty. Complexity of thought or a capacity for self-reflection could be a disadvantage.

It was a recipe for suspicion. What were these educated people *doing* in the laboratory or classroom when they looked as if they were working? What were they *saying* when they used long words (or foreign words) that were far outside the vocabulary of everyday life? (Remember the First Principle from chapter 1: *your enemy is hiding*.) What sophisticated ideas were they putting into the heads of the young? (Third Principle: *study the young*.) And what would the young do with these ideas when they left college and joined the "real world" of technology, business, and power? (Sixth Principle: *stamp out every spark*.)

With hindsight, such suspicions look more than reasonable. What guarantee was there that some bright young Misha, some outwardly conformist college graduate, would not one day climb the ranks of the party, penetrate the inner sanctum of the Politburo, start thinking for himself, and pull the whole system down around his ears? Wasn't Mikhail Gorbachev himself a member of the Moscow State University law faculty's graduating class of 1955? Thirty years later he found himself the new general secretary of the ruling party. Unexpectedly, he set about injecting transparency and democracy into the Soviet political system. The injection proved fatal, and in 1991 the system collapsed.

What was it like to breathe the atmosphere of a Soviet college? Here are some stories from Stalin's last years—the late 1940s and early 1950s. Times were changing. The Great Terror was ten years past. The agony of the war had intervened. Stalin had counted his losses. In the 1930s, suspicion alone was enough to send millions to prison or the execution cellar. After the war, this was no longer the case. From now on, suspicion unfounded in fact would no longer be enough reason to write off the career or life of a citizen.

But suspicion could not be ignored, because enemies did exist. The country was still ruled by fear of the "unconscious" enemy—the unreliable people, superficially loyal, who would turn against the party under pressure and put everything at risk. Every allegation that reached the authorities and that offered some small chance to uncover such enemies required careful, specialist investigation before it could be proven or laid to rest. One such investigatory authority was the Party Control Commission, charged with looking into wrongdoing by party members, from whose files these stories are drawn.

Aiding and abetting the enemy

Konstantin Rybnikov was a mathematical physicist. Born in 1913, he graduated in mechanics and mathematics from Moscow State University before the war. In wartime he served in the Red Army. On demobilization, he was appointed lecturer in the mathematics department of Moscow University's physics faculty. A party member, he was twice elected secretary of the faculty party bureau—the lowest rung in the ladder of Soviet rule. By then Konstantin was definitely giving more time to politics than physics. In 1948 he moved to the personnel administration of the party Central Committee as an "instructor," and then to the Central Committee's department of propaganda and agitation. An instructor was a fairly high official: not a party boss, but someone who could fix things and handle troubleshooting on the boss's behalf.

Konstantin's description in the paperwork lacks color. What sort of person was he? We can be sure he was clever. Equally, he was not the sort of clever person who naturally seeks refuge in science from the foolishness of society and politics; if so, he would not have tried himself out on a party promotion track. In the end, however, he was better at math than politics. His political career did not last. In 1955 he was back in Moscow University, no longer in physics but as a professor in the mechanics and mathematics faculty from which he had graduated in 1936. He served there for many years in charge of a center for the history of mathematics. His books are still on the faculty reading lists.[2] So he made a decent scholar in the end.

Konstantin's troubles began at a gathering of the university's party activists on January 19, 1950. A high-ranking party boss had just been disgraced, and meetings were being held all around the city to criticize him. This was one of those meetings. The target was Georgy Popov, the boss in charge of Moscow and its surrounding province. The Central Committee had just condemned him for exceeding his authority and suppressing criticism. After these events Popov was demoted and Stalin appointed Nikita Khrushchev to take his place.[3]

Among historians, the campaign against Popov has two versions.[4] Each version is plausible and both are consistent with Stalin's divide-and-rule approach to power. In one version, having destroyed what he saw as the "Leningrad faction" in the party, Stalin wanted to balance the vacuum in Leningrad by squashing any ideas that the Moscow city party might benefit from Leningrad's misfortune. For Stalin, squashing ideas began with squashing people, so: get rid of Popov. Another version is that Stalin wanted to offset the growing influence of Georgy Malenkov and Beria by bringing Khrushchev back to Moscow as a counterweight. This required an opening for him, which would be created by getting rid of Popov. In both stories, Popov was an incidental casualty, not the final objective. That Popov was only demoted and not arrested tends to support this idea.

For those summoned to the university meeting, the main purpose was to show unanimous support for the wise policy of the party Central Committee, which in turn was obediently following Stalin's direction. On the agenda was a Central Committee resolution, snappily entitled, "On mistakes in the work of the MK (Moscow provincial party committee) and MGK (Moscow city party committee) of the VKP(b) (communist party) and comrade G. M. Popov." As you might expect, not everyone was disciplined enough to keep to the point. Discussion soon spilled out into other matters. Another professor, Nikolai Lednev, accused Konstantin of "aiding and abetting the class enemy" and "adventurism." There's no suggestion that Konstantin had any direct connection to Popov. Most likely, in the already poisonous atmosphere, Lednev just felt empowered to raise completely unrelated matters.

Konstantin was not actually present when he was criticized. He found out what Lednev said about him only afterward, by reading the minutes. "Aiding and abetting the class enemy" and "adventurism": these were terrifying words. Left unchallenged, they were a guilty verdict on charges amounting to treason, enough to end his career and even have him arrested. Konstantin appealed to the Party Control Commission to clear his name.

Further allegations

The first thing the investigators did was to call in Konstantin's accuser. Nikolai Lednev was living proof that being clever does not make you sensible. One of his students recalled him at this time:

> Mathematical analysis lectures are by Nikolai Andreyevich Lednev—a Moscow University legend. He came to Moscow barefoot and worked as a janitor, but showed rare mathematical talent

> and is now a professor. Lednev [. . .] looks like a thug, badly dressed, with a violent tic. He openly despises us. He lectures with erudition, deliberately making it difficult for us to understand. Delighted when he shows us up. A real nugget.[5]

When his accusations were challenged, Lednev temporized. He denied he had used the words that appeared in the minutes: "aiding and abetting the class enemy" and "adventurism." These words, he said, had been put into his mouth by the stenographer, who had not given him the chance to correct them. Then, he went on to make different, more detailed allegations. These went back to 1946 and 1947, when Konstantin was secretary of the physics faculty party bureau.

There were two main charges. First, he said, Konstantin had recruited another physicist, Sergei Konobeyevsky, into the party, and helped to promote him to the position of faculty dean. The issue here was that Konobeyevsky, according to Lednev, was a "bourgeois cosmopolitan" and a "protégé of Academician Kapitsa." Second, he alleged that Konstantin stole from a consignment of potatoes intended to feed the physics faculty.

Let's start with potatoes. In 1947, the memory of World War II was still raw. In that most destructive war of modern times, the greatest losses of human life and wealth had taken place on Soviet territory. Soviet war deaths totaled around 25 million, including one in eight of the prewar population. In the interior of the country for much of the war there was not enough food to go around. Millions of civilians died of hunger and hunger-related causes.[6] For the survivors, every calorie counted.

When the war ended the Soviet food supply actually got worse for a time. In 1946 the southern regions were hit by drought and harvest failure. The Soviet Union's last great peacetime famine took at least a million more lives, most of them in the months before the 1947 harvest.[7] Although Moscow was considerably protected against shortages, in the first half of 1947 the daily consumption of a male blue-collar worker in the city fell to 2,135 calories. This was well below the 2,900 calories normally required by an adult male (such as a college professor) engaged only in light to moderate physical activity.[8]

In short, food in 1947 was a matter of life and death and stealing it was no joke.

A dream of potatoes

Potatoes featured in many Soviet anecdotes. In one story, a collective farm boss bragged to Stalin: he had harvested enough potatoes that, if piled up, they would make a stairway to heaven. Stalin stopped him short: "But heaven does not exist!" "OK. The potatoes don't exist either."

Nonexistent potatoes were also no joke. Here is a true story.[9] In 1960 the potato crop failed in western Ukraine. This was a disaster for three groups of people. The collective farms of western Ukraine would fail to meet their plan for harvesting potatoes. The state trading agency would fail to meet its plan for buying the potatoes from the farms at a low price and selling them on to the workers at a higher price, with the profit going to the state as revenue. The workers of the industrial cities in eastern Ukraine, whom the missing potatoes were supposed to feed, would go hungry.

A disaster loomed. It sounds bad—but don't underestimate human ingenuity. They came up with a solution. As a result, two out of those three groups were perfectly all right in the end.

In the autumn of 1960, the farms sold the *planned* amount of potatoes at the low state purchasing price to the state trading agency: 600,000 tons. But only 450,000 tons actually changed hands. The missing 150,000 tons (which never existed) were recorded as "awaiting delivery." Now the farmers were in the clear, because they had receipts to prove that they had fulfilled their plan for harvesting potatoes!

The state trading agency delivered 450,000 tons of actually existing potatoes at the much higher state selling price to the hungry workers in the eastern Ukraine. This left a gap: their sales plan was for 600,000 tons, so 150,000 tons were still to be sold. They filled this gap by selling 150,000 tons of *potatoes that did not exist* back to the original farmers, all at the high state selling price. The paperwork would show that, in total, they had bought 600,000 tons at the low price and sold the same amount at the high price. Now the state trading agency was also in the clear because it could show receipts for the planned amount of sales and profits!

That left two problems. One problem was a huge hole in the financial accounts of the collective farms: they had had to lay out a small fortune to buy back the 150,000 tons of non-existent potatoes at the higher price. But who cared? It was only money, which the state could print freely.

And one problem was left: in the following spring, the workers of eastern Ukraine went hungry, because they could not buy potatoes that had not been delivered or eat potatoes that had never been grown. Hunger has lasting consequences: hungry people get sick and have shorter, less productive lives. Hungry children fail to thrive. But who cared? This was nothing new, for Soviet families were already well-used to shortages of all kinds.

Guilt by association

That's enough about potatoes. Konstantin also faced more dignified charges. His name had been linked with that of "Academician Kapitsa," whoever that was. And what was wrong with that?

Alongside the leading actors—people like Konstantin Rybnikov and his opponents—the stories in this chapter have a number of characters whose role is symbolic. They play no part in the action. Rather, they are like flags that are pulled out of the cupboard from time to time, sometimes to run them up the flagpole, sometimes to trample them underfoot. The Academician Peter Kapitsa was one of these.

Kapitsa was a unique figure in Soviet life. Born in 1894, he left Russia in 1921 and settled in Cambridge, England, where he did the work on low-temperature physics that won him a Nobel Prize in 1978. From England, Kapitsa visited Russia regularly. On a visit in 1934, he was denied an exit visa and forced to remain. Unwillingly resettled in Moscow, he became a leader of Soviet science.

Given his time abroad and his network of foreign contacts, in 1937 Kapitsa could easily have been arrested as a spy and imprisoned or shot. It helped him that Stalin evidently valued him enough to keep him safe. And Kapitsa had some limited influence over Stalin. In 1938, when another physicist was arrested, Kapitsa saved him by writing immediately to Stalin. By the end of the war Kapitsa had become one of the key figures in the Soviet project to create an atomic bomb.[10]

The Soviet bomb project was wrapped in secrecy and buried in security. Stalin gave oversight of atomic energy to Lavrenty Beria, his interior minister and chief of security. Kapitsa spoke out in favor of international scientific cooperation and against secrecy; he also wrote to Stalin accusing Beria of incompetence. In December 1945, Kapitsa was suddenly removed from the atomic bomb project; this was at his own request, but it was still unexpected because it came after a long delay. In August 1946, he was dismissed from all other official positions. He was not arrested and, as an academician, he had a home and could continue to draw his salary. Professionally, he was cast into limbo and stayed there until after Stalin's death.

Kapitsa had done so many things to merit oblivion. In fact, Beria asked Stalin for permission to arrest Kapitsa. The fact that Kapitsa was only dismissed shows that he still had Stalin's protection.

How did Moscow University's physics faculty fit into this complicated picture? It didn't fit at all, and this became a problem. Before the war, there were two centers of Soviet physics, one at Moscow University and the other in the Academy of Sciences. The atomic specialists gathered under the roof of the academy. Kapitsa, for example, was elected to the academy in 1939. When the secret work began on the atomic bomb, the university physicists were left out. Unable to compete in scholarship, some of the university physicists responded by shifting the rivalry away from research quality to political correctness. They argued that the theories of relativity and quantum mechanics must be wrong, because it was not easy to reconcile these ideas with the teachings of Marx and Lenin. Gradually, the university lost its more talented scholars to the academy. More often than not, those who filled the vacant university posts shared the pseudoscientific views of those who appointed them.[11]

The outcome was bitter conflict between the university and the academy. In 1944, some leading physicists wrote to Stalin's deputy, Vyacheslav Molotov, to draw his attention to the shortcomings of physics at Moscow University. The letter asked Molotov to appoint new leaders to the physics faculty. Kapitsa added his signature.

In the summer of 1945 the Academy of Sciences set up a committee of inquiry into the Moscow University physics faculty. As a result, in May 1946, Sergei Konobeyevsky was appointed faculty dean.[12] Konobeyevsky was a specialist in X-ray analysis and one of the few Moscow University physicists with an international reputation. In 1939, for example, he was admitted to membership of the British Non-Ferrous Metals Research Association. In December 1946 he also became a corresponding member of the Academy of Sciences. In short, although Konobeyevsky's career had been in the university, his scholarship was aligned with world science and the academy. That is why he was Kapitsa's man.

Established in 1920 to promote scholarly research, the British Non-Ferrous Metals Research Association (or BNF for short) has a distinguished place in the history of science, atomic research, and the Cold War. If the nineteenth century was the age of iron, the twentieth century was the age of non-ferrous metals: copper for conductivity; aluminium for lightness; tungsten for solidity; manganese, molybdenum, titanium, and vanadium for toughness; chromium, nickel, and zinc for resistance to corrosion; uranium and plutonium for mass destruction. If you could wave a wand and magically remove non-ferrous metals from the modern battlefield, tanks and trucks would shudder to a halt, guns would fall silent, and planes would fall from the sky.

The BNF is symbolic in the same way that Kapitsa had become a symbol. When others heard that a Soviet scientist such as Konobeyevsky was a member, they immediately divided over how to interpret it. To some it was a good signal: Konobeyevsky was famous abroad and the world thought well of a Soviet scientist. For others, the signal was set to danger: what was Konobeyevsky really up to when he was mixing with the foreigners? Whether he wanted to or not, wasn't it inevitable that he would end up taking instructions from the enemy or giving away our secrets?

To sum up, when Konstantin's accusers linked him to Konobeyevsky, and Konobeyevsky to Kapitsa, they were basically saying: Konobeyevsky and Kapitsa are probably spies and Konstantin Rybnikov has been helping them.

None of these people were aware that the BNF really was a channel for espionage. Today we know that secrets were flowing through the BNF from west to east, exactly opposite to the direction imagined by Konobeyevsky's critics. The BNF was penetrated by Soviet foreign intelligence through Melita Norwood, who joined as a clerk in 1937 and remained as its secretary until 1972. The historian Christopher Andrew describes her as "the most important British female agent in KGB history and the longest serving of all Soviet spies in Britain."[13]

The cosmopolitan

One more thing: according to Lednev's charge sheet, Konobeyevsky was not just Kapitsa's man but a "bourgeois cosmopolitan." Bourgeois cosmopolitan: what did *that* mean?

To be *cosmopolitan* means that you are a citizen of the world, at home in every country. This can sound like a good thing until somebody turns it around into an accusation: if you are equally at home everywhere, then where is your loyalty? Whose side will you take when the fighting starts? And to be a *bourgeois* cosmopolitan would then ascribe you to the international capitalist class, the enemy of the working people of every country.

Right after the war, "bourgeois cosmopolitanism" meant little or nothing. This began to change in 1948 as Stalin prepared a nationalist campaign with strong anti-Semitic overtones. The nationalist message of the campaign was: homeland first. It was directed explicitly against "bourgeois cosmopolitans" who failed to give priority to the Soviet homeland and to Russia, its interests and achievements, over all other nations.

In many explanations of the new policy, the cosmopolitans were also described as *rootless*; this conjured up the image of the wandering Jew. Many of those attacked were Jews, and official statements emphasized Jewish-sounding family names. The anti-Semitic aspect may have been stimulated by Stalin's second thoughts over the foundation of the state of Israel. Israel declared its independence of the British protectorate in May 1948. Soviet recognition followed quickly. But Stalin soon came to regard Israel as an alternative magnet for the loyalty of Soviet Jews, especially after Israel's first ambassador, Golda Meir, was mobbed by enthusiastic crowds at a Moscow synagogue. There were many dismissals and some arrests. Most prominent of the victims was the Jewish wife of Foreign Minister Molotov; she had made a point of welcoming Ambassador Meir. Stalin forced Molotov to divorce her and to sanction her detention in a labor camp. Molotov chose to do these things rather than join her there.[14]

In short, one reasonable interpretation of the charge that Konstantin had sponsored a "bourgeois cosmopolitan" is that Konobeyevsky was Jewish or was thought to be Jewish. But apart from the matter of his ethnicity, Konobeyevsky was also well-qualified for the charge of cosmopolitanism by the facts of his foreign scientific associations and his alignment with leading Jewish physicists.

Put yourself in the shoes of the people who felt threatened by Konobeyevsky. You love your job at the university. You're lucky to have it—and you know it. You're good at physics, but not that good. You can do mechanics, but quantum mechanics is just a foreign fashion or, worse, a deliberate distraction. And now, that bastard Kapitsa has put some Jew in charge to make trouble for you. Well, we'll see who can make trouble!

Exoneration

The final report on comrade Rybnikov went from the Party Control Commission to the pudgy-faced Georgy Malenkov. At this time Malenkov was a Central Committee secretary and one of the most powerful men in the country after Stalin himself. It's of some interest that what went on in the physics faculty of Moscow University was thought important enough that Malenkov needed to know.

On the first charge, that of aiding and abetting Kapitsa's man Konobeyevsky, the investigators exonerated Konstantin. When Konobeyevsky was appointed dean, Konstantin was not involved. He was not important enough for that. Not only did he *not* help appoint Konobeyevsky, the investigators found, Konstantin helped to get rid of him a year later.

As for Konobeyevsky's recruitment into the party, which Konstantin had supposedly procured, this was a nonevent. Konobeyevsky was not a full party member. He was a candidate (probationary) member. On his appointment to faculty dean in 1946, he applied for full party membership. His application came to the university party committee—and was refused.

The pretext for refusing Konobeyevsky admission to party membership was his link to the BNF, the British Non-Ferrous Metals Research Association, whose secretary was a Soviet spy. When they heard that Konobeyevsky was in contact with foreign scientists, his sponsors for party membership got cold feet. Either they suspected he could be sharing important Soviet research findings with the West, or they were scared somebody else might suspect them of not being sufficiently concerned about the possibility. At that time, Moscow University's party hacks could have no idea that the BNF was a conduit for Western secrets to reach the Soviet Union, not the other way around.

By this time, Konobeyevsky had left the university. He was transferred to Research Institute no. 9, formerly the Institute of Special-Purpose Metals. The "special-purpose" metals were uranium and plutonium, and the institute was part of the Soviet atomic bomb project.

So Konobeyevsky helped to produce the raw material for the first Soviet nuclear weapons and reactors. In 1948 he was allowed at last to join the party. Defending the decision, the record notes that "although he was a member of the English research society for a short period, Prof. Konobeyevsky did no work in it and did not compromise himself in any way." In 1949, he was rewarded with an Order of Lenin.

In the end the party investigators could find no substance in the more lofty charges against Konstantin. But they still had to resolve the question of dirty dealing over potatoes.

Here are the facts: in the hard times after the war, the collective farm "Trud" (Labor) near Zaraisk, a hundred miles south of Moscow, was assigned to feed Moscow University's hungry physicists. In 1947 the faculty trade union branch's officers made an expedition to Zaraisk and came back with four and a half tons of potatoes "free of charge." The potatoes were sold to the faculty staff. Konstantin came out of the allocation somewhat ahead of others, with thirteen sacks at seventy-five rubles each.

How much was that? Assuming a sack is fifty kilos, Konstantin had bought 650 kilos—more than half a ton, or one-seventh of the total consignment. This was surely more than his fair share. At less than ten rubles a kilo, he was also paying a good price; the semi-free-market price of potatoes in the first part of 1947 was twenty-seven rubles a kilo (the official ration price was ninety kopecks, but most likely you could not buy them anywhere at that price).[15] The sheer quantity meant that he was also paying out a great deal of money, almost one thousand rubles in total. We don't know Konstantin's salary, but this was one and a half times the average monthly Soviet industrial wage of 626 rubles in December 1946.[16]

A question any policeman would ask is whether Konstantin had bought so much in order to resell it. In Soviet law, "speculation" was a heinous crime. Farmers were the only people allowed to sell for a profit, and it had to be their own produce from their tiny private allotments. Konstantin, who was not a farmer, had the right to buy potatoes but not to sell them. Some countries make a similar distinction between users and dealers in narcotics. If you are found with a small quantity of drugs, the law assumes that they are for personal use, and there is no penalty, or just a caution. If the quantity is large, the law will punish you severely as a dealer. So the question became: with that quantity of potatoes, was Konstantin a user or a dealer?

Was it even possible to eat more than half a ton of potatoes? Anyone accustomed to a modern varied diet would be appalled by the prospect. Just after the war, however, most urban Russians did not eat a varied diet. They lived off bread, potatoes, and cabbage, with scraps of meat, fat, herbs, and fruit for variety if they were lucky. A family of four that got just half its calories from potatoes would chomp through Konstantin's haul in about fourteen weeks. At this point the potatoes would still be just within their storage limit.[17] Put another way, Konstantin's purchase looks opportunistic but not abnormal for a time when food was hard to come by and it could be dangerous to pass up a good opportunity. On a balance of probabilities, he was a user, not a dealer.

More important than opportunities for private sale might have been the chance for Konstantin to have surplus potatoes to exchange, not for money but for favors. Trading in goods was illegal, but everyone traded favors. In the Soviet system not everything could be had for money. Access to scarce commodities and opportunities often depended on building long-term relationships with the people who controlled them. These relationships were built on mutual favors.[18] In a hungry city, the offer of a few sacks of potatoes might open the door to a new flat or a new career. Money was not involved; the parties to the exchange could feel the warm glow of mutual aid, not the chill of corruption.

However you looked at it, the investigators concluded, Konstantin's sin was one of omission more than commission. He had not carefully checked the work of the procurement expedition, and he had not scrupulously assured himself that everyone had had their fair share before he took his. This part of the report reads as if the investigators had decided they could not exonerate Konstantin entirely, but they would soften the charge so that it could do no damage. They were saying effectively that persons unknown had decided to give Konstantin a large quantity of potatoes and he had not asked for this and had carelessly overlooked the considerable margin by which it exceeded his entitlement. Perhaps someone had done him an unwanted favor. They noted that the matter had already been reviewed in the party bureau and no action had been taken. Konstantin's record was good otherwise. The conclusion that went to Malenkov for approval was that Konstantin's case could be closed.

In the end, all of Konstantin's sins were forgiven and forgotten. As for Georgy Malenkov, he would quickly forget all about Konstantin and stop worrying about a few potatoes that had once actually existed but were long since eaten. In the summer of 1951 Malenkov had more important things on his mind, such as bringing Sergei Goglidze back to Moscow from Khabarovsk (in chapter 1), prosecuting the MGB affair, and destroying Minister of State Security Viktor Abakumov.

As for Konstantin, it seems that he lost his taste for politics and returned to the reassuring world of mathematics where two plus two equals four always, not just when authorized by the party Central Committee and its secretaries.

A dangerous science

Sometime around the winter of 1952 or the next spring, an anonymous denunciation reached the Party Control Commission. Like a shotgun casing full of pellets, the letter was crammed with accusations. Perhaps the author hoped that at least one would find a target. The letter denounced numerous failings of the Kiev agricultural institute. At the center of its aim was a middle-aged plant scientist, Professor Demidenko. According to the letter, Demidenko alone was guilty of four separate crimes. Several other people connected with the institute were also accused of multiple violations committed separately or together. Each charge would need to be carefully examined.

Demidenko's charge sheet illustrates the hazards of the time. It was alleged first that, when listing the leading scholars in the field of agricultural science at a meeting in 1948, Demidenko *had failed to include the name of Stalin*. The letter claimed, second, that Demidenko had been "smuggled" into corresponding membership of the Ukrainian Academy of Sciences, implying some kind of favoritism or underhanded dealing. A third accusation was that Demidenko had once been expelled from the Timiryazev Agricultural Academy as a kulak. In other words, his family background was among the prosperous farmers whom Stalin had resettled in the 1930s, making him a "usual suspect" (recall the Second Principle: *start from the usual suspects*). The last allegation was that he had obtained party membership by deception: he had not been honest about his past (First Principle: *your enemy is hiding*).

Saved on technicalities

On the first charge, that of not mentioning Stalin, the investigators asked Demidenko what he had actually said. Demidenko told them he had listed a number of leading plant scientists including "Michurin, Vil'yams, Dokuchayev, Kostychev, and Lysenko" (but not Stalin). The investigator also tracked down a critic and a defender. The critic had spoken up at a party gathering, attacking Demidenko for failing to recognize Stalin as a "coryphæus"—a word of Greek origin meaning "leader of the choir"—of agricultural science. The defender was the institute director himself, who had spoken up for Demidenko at the same meeting.

Demidenko escaped this charge on technicalities. One technicality was that there were no verbatim records of any of the meetings to prove who said what. Another technicality lay in the distinction between agricultural and plant science. Demidenko had listed the "choir leaders" of *plant* science—not agricultural science. Agronomy is the science and technology of plant cultivation. Agricultural science is broader, and includes the science of animal husbandry in addition to plant science. If Demidenko had spoken of agricultural science, and failed to acknowledge Stalin as a leading agricultural scientist, he would have been in real trouble. Because he had limited himself to plant scientists, and Stalin had not concerned himself personally with plant science as such, Demidenko would get away with it.

But what did Stalin have to do with science? If agricultural science had been on the agenda, why should Stalin have been nominated as its leader? Stalin had never put on a white coat or carried out a laboratory or field experiment in his life. He had probably not been on a farm since the Civil War. Despite this, he *had* played a decisive role in agricultural science in the Soviet Union. His revolutionary insight, based on Marxism-Leninism, told Stalin that modern genetics is wrong. Stalin had given the authority of the Soviet state to an alternative view, which was followed by all the scholars that Demidenko had listed as leaders of plant science: "Michurin, Vil'yams, Dokuchayev, Kostychev, and Lysenko."

All were symbolic figures. They're irrelevant to the action in our story, other than as names that someone needed to salute. But they tell us a lot about the conditions in which someone like Demidenko had to work.

What Michurin and the others had in common was resistance to modern genetics. Modern genetics describes how wheat, say, has adapted to a temperate climate through the natural selection of genes, with random variations that aid survival continuing into the next generation, while those that hinder survival tend to disappear. Evolution is rapid in geological time, but its speed is always limited by the cycle of random variation, natural selection, and reproduction. Plant wheat in the desert, and the seedlings will die before evolution can take place.

Ivan Michurin was a Russian scientist of the pre-revolutionary generation and one of the foremost twentieth-century disciples of an alternative theory, Lamarckian evolution. The French naturalist Jean-Baptiste Lamarck argued that species evolve by inheriting acquired characteristics. The Lamarckian hypothesis was that organisms became adapted to their environment through effort. Expose wheat to the desert, and it will struggle to live. In trying to survive, the seedlings will begin to acquire characteristics more favorable to survival, which they will pass on directly to the next generation. This suggests a much faster cycle: stress, adaptation, reproduction. If the Lamarckian mechanism worked, it would be possible in a few generations to convert plant species to make the desert bloom.

Lamarckian ideas, which the rest of the world already knew to be false, kept their foothold in Soviet science for several reasons. One was the role they ascribed to effort and will. By effort and will, the Bolsheviks were changing the world—and that included nature. In fact, after World War II the Soviet Union embarked on a vast and costly program of geo-engineering, the "Stalin plan for the transformation of nature," involving the reversal of Siberian river flows and the irrigation and afforestation of the Siberian steppe on a gigantic scale. The idea that you could change nature by effort and will was entirely suited to this program, and the Michurinists were closely involved. The plan was abandoned as soon as Stalin died, but the Michurinists remained influential into the 1970s.[19]

Another factor that nourished false science was nationalism. After World War II, the party leaders in charge of science policy were looking for examples to demonstrate the superiority of Soviet science over Western science. This nearly led to a rejection of Einstein's theory of relativity in physics, but did not, because Stalin wanted the atomic bomb and came to realize that without Einstein's ideas it could not be built. The bomb was so important that Stalin did not allow ideology to spoil it.

Agriculture and the food supply did not have the same importance. Because Western genetics had gone against Lamarckism, it seemed like a good moment to create a cult of Michurin, because he was a Russian scientist who had held out against the thinking now dominant in the West. Michurin died in 1935, but he left followers. Trofim Lysenko was attacking genetic science since the 1930s on the basis that the theory of genes was counterrevolutionary. The agricultural scientists who knew better did not have a project important enough to Stalin that he would defend them. In 1948 Stalin gave Lysenko a monopoly over scientific correctness in plant evolution. Lysenko was the leader; his followers included Vil'yams, Dokuchayev, and Kostychev. With Michurin you have the full list of scholars that Demidenko saluted in his speech. Here was Stalin's contribution as a "choir leader" of *agricultural* science.

The investigation concluded that Demidenko had saluted the right flags. He had not discussed *agricultural* science; this made it unnecessary for him to recognize Stalin. In discussing *plant science* he had nodded to Lysenko and the Michurinists. And that was as it should be. The investigator went so far as to compliment Demidenko on his "ideological consistency."

The party controllers went through the other charges against Demidenko one by one. No matter how far-fetched, each allegation had to be investigated before it could be dismissed. It would have been bad if Demidenko's election to the Ukrainian Academy of Sciences had been a fix. They checked and found it had followed normal criteria and due process. It would have been worse if Demidenko had been disqualified by family background—if his parents had been kulaks, as alleged. They established that he came from a middle-peasant family; that was fine, too. They went back over his college record to ensure that he had graduated properly from the famous Timiryazev Academy in 1928: he had not been expelled. They called up the party's own records and established that his acceptance into the party as a candidate (in 1946) and full member (in 1947) had followed the normal way. It seemed that Demidenko was off the hook.

Caught out and let off

The investigators were about to close the Demidenko case when they found a problem. Demidenko had a guilty secret after all: an undeclared criminal record. In 1933 he had been arrested and condemned by the OGPU Collegium (a forerunner of the NKVD Special Assembly, mentioned in chapter 1). The charges were "disclosure of production secrets" and possession of fifty dollars in currency. At that time he went to prison for three years. Fortunately, he was amnestied after serving eighteen months.

From the party's point of view, a criminal record was not a bar to membership. But party members were expected to be open about such things, and disclose anything from their past that might be even suggestive of guilt, so that the party could consider it before taking the membership decision. This was a harsh test of a person's honesty; it meant that anyone with a suspicious family background or a criminal record was expected to declare himself to be one of the "usual suspects." You'd worked hard to redeem yourself; it was all in the past. Now you had to bring it up again, and risk reopening everything.

Demidenko failed this test when he applied for party membership, because he kept silent about his record. His silence had deprived the party of the chance to consider this information. But there was something even worse. The investigators found that his party organization did uncover the deception subsequently, in 1949, and then took no action. This created the suspicion that his party comrades had colluded in a coverup.

At this point the investigators decided to close down their own inquiry and refer Demidenko's deception to a higher authority: the Kiev provincial party committee. Following this reference, the Kiev party dug out the short autobiography that every applicant for party membership had to write to check Demidenko's wording. It was true, he had suppressed the facts of his arrest and imprisonment. But he had raised them obliquely, referring to "much grief and unpleasantness in the past." To be precise, he explained that he had received an invitation to work abroad, and went on:

> I mention this here not to boost my reputation but to emphasize the circumstances because there is no guarantee against similar circumstances arising in the future that have caused me much grief and unpleasantness in the past.

At this point the Kiev party asked Demidenko directly why he had failed to mention his arrest and imprisonment. He gave them his reason: "He considers his arrest was a mistake committed by particular employees of the former OGPU."

Putting the facts together, we arrive at the underlying story. In the early 1930s, Demidenko received an invitation to work abroad and could have been sent some dollars. Regardless of whether or not he intended to accept the offer, the secret police stepped in to preempt the matter, charging him with possessing foreign currency and revealing secrets to foreigners. But Demidenko did not accept that he had done anything wrong. Time passed. By the 1940s, sharing information with foreigners had become even more dangerous than in the early 1930s. Meanwhile, however, Demidenko had become a considerable scholar and the Kiev party officials did not wish to make trouble for him. They let the matter drop.

Arrest all the elephants

Here's an anecdote that could have been written for Demidenko. It's 1933. A herd of sheep arrives at the Soviet border. A guard stops them: "Why do you want to leave Russia?"

"It's the OGPU," they say. "Stalin has ordered them to arrest all the elephants."

"But you aren't elephants," says the border guard.

"Try telling that to the OGPU," say the sheep.[20]

More heresies

At the Kiev agricultural institute, the investigators were finished with Demidenko. But the poison pen had other victims in mind. Lecturer Baraboi of the faculty of Marxism-Leninism, for example, supposedly told the students that the driving force behind the Great October Socialist Revolution of 1917 was the peasantry (debatable, but he should have said it was the working class). He had also claimed that in the first months of World War II, Red Army morale was poor (correct, but you couldn't say that either). These mistakes had already cost Baraboi his job, so there was no work left for the investigators to get their teeth into.

Another heresy, according to the letter, was disseminated by fifth-year student Veryovka. This young person claimed that, when communism and universal abundance had been achieved, there would still be bad people and so there would still need to be a state to enforce rules and regulate society. This contradicted the teaching of Friedrich Engels and Vladimir Lenin about the gradual "withering away" of the coercive state as communism arrived. Although initially threatened with exclusion from the party, the investigators found, Veryovka now recognized his errors and was doing much better. The letter accused a teaching assistant of covering up Veryovka's mistakes. Again, the investigators found that the assistant was appointed after the lapses occurred and had already departed from the institute.

Yet another target of the letter was the director of the institute's experimental farm. He had a brother high up in the Central Committee apparatus of Soviet Ukraine's Communist Party. Here was a natural opportunity to lay a charge of nepotism. The investigators looked into it and dismissed it. They found no reason to doubt the fitness of the farm director for his work and no evidence of interference in the appointment.

Because of an anonymous letter, many people had slept badly. Many records of past lives and decisions had been exhumed. Much time had been invested in journeys, interviews, and the writing of reports and their consideration. At the end, there was a clear product: Moscow could be assured there were no enemies hiding in the Kiev agricultural institute—for now. But, like any certificate of freedom from infection, this assurance was good only on the day it was written. The day after that, some new source of error could creep in. Some hidden taint could take hold and begin to spread disease through an outwardly healthy body. There could be no complacency; vigilance must be maintained at any cost.

A prophecy

Comrade Frumkin is a forgotten prophet of the twentieth century. This got him into a lot of trouble. In 1951, his case came to the

Party Control Commission in Moscow for investigation. Frumkin was accused of adopting "a Trotskyist standpoint on matters of building socialism."

Who was Frumkin? We have few details. In Russia, Frumkin would be seen as a Jewish name. In 1951, this Frumkin should have been on his guard. Born in Russia in 1903 into a working-class family, he was a mature man by the time of our story. He joined the Communist Party in 1925. In 1935 he graduated from the Lenin Military-Political Academy in Leningrad. From there he was sent to teach in military schools in Bryansk, then Gorky.

War broke out. Two years passed until Frumkin was taken into the Red Army in 1943. He served in the political department of a rifle division, responsible for education and morale. On demobilization he became an administrator of training establishments in the ministry of trade, and then at a transport ministry college. This college was located just outside Pushkino, a small town north of Moscow. It was there that the incident took place. By the time of the investigation Frumkin had been moved on—or down—to work in the political department of the Moscow-Bryansk railroad.

The scandal broke like this. On April 11, 1951, Frumkin gave a lecture to teachers at the college where he worked. The title of Frumkin's lecture was not one that appeals naturally: "The conditions of material life of society." In the course of the lecture Frumkin remarked:

> Transitional forms of production relations can exist not only during the transition from capitalism to socialism but also, conversely, during the transition from socialism to capitalism.

This obscure remark caused uproar. As the investigator noted later, Frumkin had contradicted Stalin's teaching, which was "entirely clear." When could "transitional production relations" arise? According to Stalin, only in moving from a *lower* form of society to a *higher* form. Capitalism was a lower form, and socialism was higher. You could move only up, not down. The direction of travel from capitalism to socialism was upward: no problem. But to travel in the other direction, from higher to lower? The listeners protested. What was this "transition from socialism to capitalism"? One commented:

> Comrade Frumkin's statement contradicts the laws of historical development of society . . . it would follow from this formulation that the socialist system should be replaced by the capitalist [system].

Another asked:

> Why has so much blood been spilt in the struggle for socialism, if a return to capitalism is inevitable?

Actually, Frumkin had not said either of the things he was accused of here. He had not said that going from socialism to capitalism was *desirable* nor had he said that it was *inevitable*. He had implied that it was *possible*. But no one cared about that. If you allowed that something was possible, you had opened the door for the next person to debate its merits and for the person after that to demand it. If Frumkin was not an *actual* enemy, the mere thought that a capitalist counterrevolution was possible made him instantly into a *potential* enemy.

Already in a hole, Frumkin dug deeper. He went on to defend his error to the audience by giving three historical examples where a transition from socialism to capitalism—from the higher to lower form of society—had actually taken place. These were as follows (the explanations are my own):

"The fall of the Paris Commune." This happened in 1871. In the wake of France's defeat by Prussia in the war of 1870, the national government abandoned Paris. The city was taken over by armed militias and radical factions. An elected city council (the French word is *commune*) enacted many progressive social and economic measures. After a few months the commune was bloodily crushed by the French national army.

"The crushing of the Hungarian Soviet Republic." This happened in 1919. World War I ended in the breakup of the Austro-Hungarian Empire. In Hungary, an independent republic was proclaimed, but proved unstable. In March 1919 the communists seized power and formed a government led by Béla Kun. At war with Romania and Czechoslovakia, the government soon collapsed amid bloodshed. Hungary fell into a fascist dictatorship.

"The defection of Yugoslavia to the camp of imperialism." This happened in 1948. The communists, led by Josip Broz Tito, came to power in Yugoslavia at the end of World War II. Owing little to Stalin or the Red Army, Tito felt free to pursue independent policies in Southeast Europe, which Stalin could not accept. In 1948, Stalin accused Tito of going over to the side of the imperialists, implying that Yugoslavia could no longer be regarded as a socialist state.

The overthrow of socialism

Sitting in the archives as I skimmed Frumkin's story for the first time, I felt growing excitement. Here was a thinker—a real intellectual. Nobody told Frumkin to think originally about these things. He did it all by himself. When challenged, he came up with a good, solid argument. In history, you can use evidence to validate arguments in more than one way. The usual way is to use evidence to illustrate and exemplify. Here was a clear case of another way, to argue by counterexample. If someone tells you that X *can't* happen or that Y *can never* lead to Z, all you need to destroy that argument is to find a single case where it *did* happen that way. Frumkin had destroyed Stalin's argument by finding not one but three heavyweight counterexamples. But that was dangerous for everyone! No one could admit this. It was a moment of acute peril for Frumkin, his students, and his inquisitors.

I thought to myself that the investigators would have to find a way to disprove Frumkin's arguments—but how? What would they say? What *could* they say? For Frumkin was right!

But my excitement was for nothing. The investigators did not try to argue against Frumkin. They just declared that he was wrong. They announced: "These examples are incorrect."

When first challenged, Frumkin took half a step back. The problem, he conceded, "was not fully worked out and was for discussion." This was not what the party authorities wanted to hear. Under repeated attack over the next few weeks, Frumkin dug his heels in. During this period he was criticized at a party committee meeting in the college, and then he was reprimanded by the township party committee "for the political error that he committed and for reluctance to correct it at the proper time." (But at least they were calling it an error, not a crime.)

Eventually the matter came to the Party Control Commission. As the pressure rose, Frumkin gave in. He accepted his mistake, which he now put down to a "slip of the tongue." Stalin himself had admitted that socialism could be overthrown violently *from the outside*.[21] Frumkin now agreed that he had confused this with the possibility that socialism could give way to capitalism *from the inside*. Now that he accepted his mistake, and had received a party reprimand, the party control investigator proposed no further action.

What sort of a person was Frumkin? If we could see him today there would be nothing, probably, to distinguish him outwardly from a million other low-level functionaries. Behind an ordinary pair of eyes, however, lurked a flash of genius that led him, for a few weeks in 1951, to defend the dangerous idea that history could go in reverse. The events he foretold came about in 1991. By that time he would have been in his late eighties. There's only a small chance that comrade Frumkin lived to see his prophecy come true.[22]

A mistake is no longer a crime

When we see the pattern of these cases, and many more that are in the adjacent files, we cannot help but notice that most people who were accused were now surviving. In the 1930s, Stalin's vengeance had been truly terrifying. It struck people down, left and right, without hesitation and without mercy. It felled them for crimes they had committed that would not have been crimes in any other country or time. It destroyed them and their families for crimes they had committed, or might have committed, or somebody thought they might have committed. It punished them for crimes they had only thought of, and for crimes they had not imagined but might one day contemplate under circumstances that had not yet arisen. It ordered their killing in the hundreds of thousands, just in case.

A decade later, the country was the same, and its ruler was the same, but the atmosphere had changed greatly. Blood would no longer be spilled indiscriminately, on suspicion alone. Completely innocent people would still be killed on trumped-up charges—but no longer randomly: there would be some reason of state behind it. Guilty people would still be killed on trumped-up charges that had absolutely nothing to do with their real crimes. People would continue to live in fear. But the Soviet state was learning to be more careful of its greatest treasure: its people. The rulers couldn't go on shooting people for the smallest thing. Human beings make mistakes. As long as you were willing to admit your mistakes, to confess them honestly and come clean before the party, you could begin again. You could be forgiven. Your file would never be thrown away, but your case would be closed until you caused it to be reopened.

A few things were still unforgiveable. Misconduct in the war was one. Cowardice, desertion, serving the enemy on occupied territory in any capacity: these were beyond forgiveness. For other things you could be forgiven once, and forgiveness was still conditional on confession and repentance. Concealment of past stains, repeated mistakes, and the failure to acknowledge them would continue to put you outside the community. But if you were open with the party and worked to correct your mistakes, the party would now give you a second chance.[23]

In these small ways, Soviet society was making the first steps toward a more humane form of communism. This was a community that was learning to care for its lost sheep, and to show that it cared by not killing them at the first sign of potential departure from the flock.

That duty of care would fall upon all party organizations. Take the case of agricultural student Veryovka, who contradicted Engels and Lenin on the withering away of the state. He was guilty, the party investigators concluded, of "mistakes"—in other words, he was not guilty of crimes. The cause of his mistakes, the party investigators concluded, was "inadequate training in social sciences." Faced with his mistakes, the party's duty was not to expel the young man but to re-educate him, showing "a very attentive and patient attitude," until he understood where he had gone wrong and could put himself right.

CHAPTER FOUR

The Mafia

Men who live in retirement under the care of their wives and daughters are often in need of occupation. This was certainly true of Old Man Nikolayenko, who lived with his wife and their daughter, Valentina, and other children near Denau, where vines and cotton grow in the sunlit valley of the Surkhan Darya River, not far from the Afghan border to the south of Uzbekistan.[1]

The Old Man had time on his hands. To fill the time, he wrote letters to the newspapers.

This was a time of great change in the public life of the Soviet Union. Stalin died in March 1953. After a brief struggle, Nikita Khrushchev picked up the reins of power as Soviet leader. Rejecting Stalin and forsaking mass terror, Khrushchev began to pursue a policy of greater openness. Although the new honesty was strictly limited, Soviet citizens began to engage tentatively with the chief problem that Khrushchev raised: the abuse of power to suppress knowledge of the misdeeds of the powerful. One of those citizens was Old Man Nikolayenko.

Letters to the press

Mr. Nikolayenko was a Civil War veteran and pensioner. In the record he is described as having a disability of the "second group"; this official classification implies something serious, possibly a war wound. His pension most likely arose from his disability, because most Soviet rural inhabitants did not have an age-related retirement pension at this time. Despite his disability, the Old Man had reasonable health. Until 1951, he worked as carter and storekeeper of a collective farm where his daughter, Valentina, still worked. In retirement, he kept a private land allotment and went hunting and fishing to supplement his family income.

In the Soviet Union, farms and factories were often named after grand ideas and celebrated people. The local farm was originally called "Communism." In 1951, the year that the Old Man retired, there was a merger and the newly enlarged farm was named after Nikita Khrushchev.

The Old Man held strong opinions. It was his opinion that the "Khrushchev" farm was grossly mismanaged. While his wife and daughter made his home and waited on him, he had time to brood and not much else to think about. In due course, time to brood became time to act. One avenue open to him was to write to the press.

In the conditions of the Thaw, public opinion was being voiced openly again. Newspapers received far more letters than could be published. A flood of letters washed into the mailbox of *Izvestiya*, the government newspaper in Moscow: 130 a day in 1955, rising to nearly 600 a day by 1960.[2]

Old Man Nikolayenko wrote at least three such letters. He wrote twice to the Uzbek Republic paper, *Pravda Vostoka* (Truth of the East).* His opening shot, in March 1954, took aim at a low-level target: abuses by a team leader on the farm.

Nothing happened. Two years passed. The Old Man wrote again in March 1956. His second letter aimed higher, this time, at the top managers on the Khrushchev farm—the farm chairman, Keldyev, and his deputy, Alikulov. He alleged that Keldyev had unfairly dismissed the farm's plant technician and was now running the farm without expert advice. He also complained about abuses committed by Alikulov. The Old Man cast doubt on Alikulov's family origins, claiming he was a child of kulaks, the Bolshevik term for the better-off peasant farmers in the countryside before private landholdings were collectivized. Alikulov, the Old Man implied, was a "usual suspect" (recall the Second Principle: *start from the usual suspects*).

The field of fire of the Old Man's second letter was not limited to the farm bosses. He also took aim at the local party boss. Khaidarov, secretary of the Denau district party committee, had shown an "incorrect attitude to the question of the elimination of defects." It's natural to infer that Nikolayenko had previously contacted Khaidarov to raise the issue of the problems on the farm, which were the "defects" that ought to be eliminated; and that Khaidarov's "incorrect attitude" was to ignore him or tell him to get lost.

Still nothing happened. Two more years passed. In early 1958 the Old Man sent a third letter to the Surkhan-Darya provincial

---

*It may help to recall the Soviet territorial hierarchy. The Soviet Union's basic constituents were *republics*—the Russian, Ukrainian, Uzbek, and other Soviet Socialist Republics. Republics were parcelled up into *provinces*—for example, the Surkhan Darya province. In turn, provinces were made up of *districts*—for example, the Denau district. So, USSR ⟶ Uzbek Republic ⟶ Surkhan Darya province ⟶ Denau district.

paper, "Lenin's Banner." This time, the Old Man complained about the poor postal service ("No, Mr. Nikolayenko, I'm certain we never received your letter"), abuses on the pig farm, unsanitary maintenance of the vegetable plot, and so on.

Three letters in four years does not seem like a lot of action, but more went on behind the scenes. Over this time the Old Man became increasingly angry. He was already angry about things that he could see happening (or not happening), and he was angry with the people who were doing (or not doing) them. He wanted the world to know about it—at least, the little world of the Surkhan Darya valley. He had plenty of persistence, and he needed this because he faced many obstacles, often put in his way by the people he was complaining about or their friends. Every time he hit one of those obstacles it fueled his anger and increased his determination—and it also added another thing for him to complain about. Finally, as a pensioner the Old Man had time and not much else to do. Or maybe his wife or daughter would have liked him to shut up and do something else, like prune his fruit trees, but he didn't care. To him, this came first. So, he kept the letters coming.

In the close-knit community of the Denau district, Old Man Nikolayenko was an outsider. Of all the local people in this story he is the only one to have a Slavic family name. The other characters, starting with Alikulov, Keldyev, and Khaidarov, have Turkic names (Alikul, Keldi, Khaidar) to which some Russian bureaucrat once glued the ending –ov or –ev. As for the Old Man, his family name was Slavic, but not Russian. The ethnic roots of the Nikolayenko family name, which the Old Man shared with the quack scientist Trofim Lysenko and the poet Yevgeny Yevtushenko, lay in Ukraine, two thousand miles to the west. Over two centuries, migration and intermarriage had scattered these names far and wide across the Soviet Union. Even so, a Ukrainian name in the distant valley of the Surkhan Darya was exceptional. In the end it will still be a good question: what exactly was the Ukrainian-sounding Mr. Nikolayenko doing in Uzbekistan? We'll come back to that.

Whistle-blowers and troublemakers

Soviet citizens had limited ways of confronting corruption, injustice, or other abuses of power. In Russia before communism, traditions of public and legal redress were always weak. Instead, the subjects of the empire relied on private petitions to the tsar, the little father of all the Russians, calling on him to correct injustice and punish wrongdoers from his throne in the Kremlin. When this failed, they turned to drink or to insurrection.

The Bolshevik leaders cultivated the tradition of personal appeal to the ruler for several reasons.[3] They shared a preference for the private petition over outlets for discontent that were public and collective. Since they understood the importance of managing the public face of society from behind the scenes, the changing tenor of personal petitions also gave them insight into the real mood of the masses. This also suited the Bolsheviks privately. In their individual capacity, many leaders exploited the personal appeals they received to deal selectively with favored petitioners and to form personal networks of patronage and loyalty. For the citizen of lower rank, the question was then: if you were in trouble, who would you go to? As the poet Osip Mandelstam famously remarked, "Everyone goes to someone; there's no other way." The Mandelstam "went to" Nikolai Bukharin, Stalin's great rival.[4] But in 1938 Bukharin was executed as a traitor, making this a poor choice with hindsight.

The volume of petitions was huge. Over the decade of the 1970s, for example, the party Central Committee alone received more than five million letters from citizens. Citizens also wrote to the press. In 1975, more than 7,000 letters reached the Central Committee and the three biggest daily papers in Moscow on an average working day.[5]

The volume was so large that nearly all letters went unanswered. And still people wrote. This seems to be a feature of human behavior. The expected value of a single ticket in the British national lottery is exactly half what you paid for it. Given a single ticket, you have a 1.75 percent chance of winning the smallest £25 prize. And still people on low incomes buy those tickets in spite of the very poor odds. On the same odds, just 123 of the 7,000 letters received daily would have received a considered reply, as opposed to a brush-off. But probably the number of actual responses was even less than this: think of the effort and organization that would have been required to mount 123 investigations and deliver their outcomes—every day of the year! Yet against the odds, which were probably below the probability of winning the smallest prize in the British national lottery, people of humble circumstances continued to write letters to authority throughout the life of the Soviet Union.

For the not-so-humble people, the managers and officials who had raised themselves above the masses, complaints were a fact of life. No bureaucrat could expect to be loved by everyone. Someone, somewhere, would be complaining about you behind your back. You relied first on the likelihood that their complaint would go unnoticed in the surge of gossip and denunciation. It was bad luck if it got through to your boss, but you could still rely on your personal network to shield you while you ignored it and got on with your life.

It was an entirely different matter when complaints about you were allowed to reach the public through the media. After all, your ultimate boss was the party, and the party controlled the media through censorship. A whistle blown out loud was important not because it alerted the public to your behavior. It was important because it meant that your boss, in other words the party, already knew about your behavior—and had decided not to cover for you but to let the public in on what they knew.

You just couldn't ignore it; in self-defense you had to react at once. But how could you defend yourself? Somehow you had to discredit the evidence against you, so the first person to react against was the swine who was making trouble in the first place. In our story, that swine was Old Man Nikolayenko. His complaints were reaching the media, and this could turn out badly for the people he was making trouble for. Now, they would make trouble for him.

Turning the tables on the troublemaker was the normal response of badly behaved Soviet officials who feared exposure. The historian Nicholas Lampert made a study of cases of whistle-blowing that appeared in the Soviet national press in a later period, between 1979 and 1983.[6] His cases involved sixty-six complainants and eighty persons whose wrongdoing was the subject of a complaint. Lampert was interested not just in what happened to the wrongdoers but also in how the wrongdoers reacted.

Lampert's cases would not be representative of all complaints, because they were the tip of the iceberg: some high official had already made a decision to expose them in the national media. Usually complaints reached this stage precisely because the complainant had tried to find satisfaction locally, and had failed. He then had pressed the complaint in spite of this, and so the complaint had made it into that tiny percentage of cases getting high-level attention.

Given that someone high up had selected all these cases for publicity, it is not surprising that four-fifths of those accused of wrongdoing were eventually penalized in some way. It is more notable that, before they reached this point, three-fifths of the complainants had also been victimized. In fact, there was a clear boomerang effect. The result was that the complaint came whizzing back to hurt the complainant.

The boomerang effect is just another way of saying that complaining about a superior was dangerous. The reason it was dangerous started from the fact that most disputes began in the workplace, and involved employees complaining about the actions of superior managers. The superiors were invariably better connected to power than the complainants, because they were, after all . . . superior. It was easy for them to act against the complainants, so many complainants were dismissed from their jobs before the process came to an end. The complainants could also be victimized in more subtle ways: by ostracism, transfer to a worse job, reprimands, and the denial of bonuses. A few left their jobs voluntarily, which does not look like victimization at first glance but raises the suspicion of resignation forced by bullying.[7]

Lampert explained that, in retaliating against whistle-blowers, bosses would have many allies. To begin, corrupt or illegal practices tended to have many beneficiaries. The factory or farm boss who padded production figures or skimmed off resources would share the gains with the whole management team and workforce; all of these people relied on the boss's wrongdoing to push up bonuses and perks and make life easier for them. The many who gained from wrongdoing were the boss's first line of defense.

In addition, the local party leaders often sided with the wrongdoer for the sake of goodwill and the common good. These people worked together and they partied together. They wanted to uphold the reputation of the district for success in implementing the plan and to avoid washing dirty linen in public. These things made it easy for the bosses under criticism to mobilize both power and opinion against the critics, isolate them socially, and present them as malicious pests.

The desire to suffocate unfriendly criticism had a precedent at the highest level. At this time, the year 1956 was fresh in everyone's memory. When Khrushchev condemned Stalin at that year's party congress he did so in a secret session, not openly. He warned the party "to accept limits, and not feed our enemies, and not lay bare our wounds before them" (see chapter 1). If keeping scandal out of the public eye was good enough for the bigwigs in Moscow, it ought to work for the little people of the Surkhan Darya valley.

The Old Man becomes a victim

By writing his letters, Old Man Nikolayenko annoyed many people. You can imagine them all telling him to shut up. Why did he have to make a fuss? Those he criticized were the pillars of the local community. These men knew each other, worked together, and drank together. They were happy with things as they were, and they were not doing any particular harm to the Old Man, although he was not happy with them. They didn't want to have to change their ways for the sake of this grumpy pensioner with a bee in his bonnet. All they wanted was that he should hold his tongue and let them live peacefully. But he wasn't listening. So, they acted.

The result was a scandal that broke quietly, behind closed doors, in Moscow in the late summer of 1959. It engulfed the farm managers, party leaders, civil police, secret police, and judiciary of the Denau district and ended with the leaders of the Uzbek Communist Party in Tashkent being held to account for their subordinates' crimes and misdemeanors.

The Old Man's first problem was that, no matter what he complained about, nothing was done. He was ignored by those to whom he complained. Nonetheless, those about whom he complained did not ignore him, but began to push back. This was his second problem.

The boomerang came whizzing back to Old Man Nikolayenko in the summer of 1957. His children were assaulted and his property was vandalized. Mr. Nikolayenko complained to the local police, who established the facts, but let off the culprits—the local farm managers—with a warning. In September, a Denau district party official, section chief Badalov, shared the Old Man's complaint with the farm bosses, but then dropped the matter. At some point the Old Man wrote yet another of his letters to *Leninskoe znamya*, because the editors passed it to Denau district prosecutor Alimov the following March. Alimov filed the letter and forgot about it. But let's not forget Alimov or Badalov—we'll meet them again.

At about the same time, the Old Man's targets stepped up their counteraction. On March 28, 1958, farm chairman Keldyev told his deputy Alikulov to send in the tractors. Without warning, farmworkers plowed up the Old Man's private allotment, destroyed his orchard and market garden, and blocked access to his house. This was a dramatic escalation. Since the inception of the collective farms, every Soviet farmer had kept the right to a small private allotment that ensured personal survival when the state had taken everything else. In the countryside, an orchard and a market garden were all that stood between many families and penury.

In justification, Alikulov claimed, the collective farm needed to put more land under cotton, and Old Man Nikolayenko was holding more than his fair share privately. But these were lies. It was later established that the Old Man's share was less than the others' and the land plowed up was not needed; it remained fallow through 1958. Thus the counterattack gave the Old Man new grievances. Again he appealed to the local party for help. But his appeal was channeled to the same Badalov who had ignored him the previous autumn.

At this point the conspiracy widened. Badalov (for the party) and Keldyev (the farm boss) brought in the secret police: the local KGB commissioner Suleimanov. The three called on the Old Man at home and provoked a row. The plan was more sinister than just to inflict physical punishment. It was a provocation. Immediately afterward, they filed a complaint to the effect that Old Man Nikolayenko had threatened to kill Alikulov in retaliation for plowing up his land.

During April 1958, the local KGB gathered "compromising evidence" against Old Man Nikolayenko. For the KGB, Suleimanov sought out farmworkers who had crossed the Old Man's path for any reason over the years and got statements that the target had threatened to murder them or people they knew. One wrote that the Old Man had wanted to kill him "roughly, in August 1955"; another said that the Old Man had "fired a rifle at him and others in the spring of 1951." (Like many men in the Soviet countryside, Old Man Nikolayenko had legal possession of a hunting rifle.)

These statements were evidence for the most serious of charges. Since the Leningrad party leader Sergei Kirov was assassinated in December 1934, the secret police had investigated and prosecuted violence or threats against party and government officials as acts of terrorism. Suleimanov was building a case against the Old Man as a terrorist.

On May 20, 1958, the Denau police confiscated Old Man Nikolayenko's rifle and arrested him. At this point there was a hitch: the police themselves could see no hard evidence of a crime. Still, they understood what was expected of them. They passed the case to the local prosecutor—the same Alimov who had ignored the Old Man's representations just two months earlier. Alimov now indicted Old Man Nikolayenko on the charge of:

> Preparation of the premeditated murder of deputy chairman of the Khrushchev collective farm, party organizer Alikulov; chairman of the collective farm and member of the Supreme Soviet of the Uzbek Soviet Socialist Republic, hero of socialist labor Keldyev; first secretary of the Denau district party committee, hero of socialist labor Khaidarov; director of the Khazarbag state farm, hero of socialist labor Zibrov; and others.

The case now went outside Denau to the court in Termez, the administrative center of the Surkhan Darya province. Twice, the provincial court threw the case out. From Termez, the judge could gain perspective on the case; he saw that the witnesses were all interested parties, and some allegations concerning Old Man Nikolayenko's way of life and means of support were obviously fabricated. The Old Man was not released, however. The case was returned to Alimov for further investigation.

Foiled in the courts, the conspiracy took a new turn. The prosecutor ordered Old Man Nikolayenko to Tashkent, the capital city of Uzbekistan, for psychiatric assessment. Writing letters and attacking people—he must be off his head! As Nick Lampert imagined their thought process: "Some of these people need a medical cure. Isn't it crazy to appeal to Soviet laws all the time and expect them to be observed?"[8] The troublemaker was detained in a psychiatric clinic. At any time this would have been no rest home. Later it became routine for the Soviet regime to silence critics and punish troublemakers by diagnosing "reformist delusions" as a mental illness, so that they could be shut away in psychiatric hospitals.[9] But in the 1950s this was not yet common practice.

In Tashkent, the psychiatrists examined Old Man Nikolayenko. Now they found a flaw in the case: the Old Man wasn't crazy. For sure, he was clearly very annoying: even from the hospital he continued to pester the authorities with dozens of complaints about his unjust detention. But the psychiatrists could not identify a mental disorder. They had not yet learned the script of later years. Now they put professional ethics above the interests of the Denau district clan. On December 22, 1958, the patient was released for lack of grounds on which to detain him.[10]

But there was no triumphant return. During his detention the Nikolayenko family was deprived of the Old Man's pension. His daughter lost her job on the farm. While his wife was away visiting her husband, unknown persons visited their home and burned the storehouse, destroying possessions and grain. Then farm boss Keldyev ordered the house demolished on fabricated excuses: it was built on a site previously occupied by the farm's mill, and it was obstructing the cotton harvest.

Ground down by the remorseless pressure, Mrs. Nikolayenko threw herself on Keldyev's mercy and asked for his protection. He refused her. One night in November an armed gang came to the family. One of them, a farmworker, demanded the daughter in marriage. The threat of abduction, rape, and murder was decisive. The family fled the neighborhood, resettling near Tashkent. The Old Man no longer had a home to return to in the valley of the Surkhan Darya River.

For one guilty pair, retribution was speedy. In March 1959 the prosecutor of the Uzbek Republic fired Denau prosecutor Alimov because of his malicious prosecution of the Old Man, and he also disciplined a local investigator. For the time being, however, the buck stopped there.

Moscow steps in

At this point *everybody* knew what had happened, but there were different circles of knowledge, guilt, and indifference. At the center of the circle was the district of Denau. Everyone there knew everything because they were involved up to their necks. The party organizations, the prosecution service, the local police and KGB were all together in the conspiracy. With Alimov out of the picture, they agreed on the only course of action available to them: pretend nothing had happened. Forced to accept the illegality of the Old Man's arrest, they turned their efforts to protecting each other and avoiding accountability. When the Old Man asked the prosecutors for compensation from the Khrushchev farm, they told him he would have to bring a private claim. He sued the farm for 5,350 rubles—half a year's salary for a wage-earning farmworker. Denying liability, the farm paid him 3,000 rubles out of court. They were that close to getting away with the whole thing.

There was a middle circle of complicity in Termez, the center of the Surkhan Darya province. In Termez, officials knew about the essence of the case but, while they were not really comfortable with it, they did not want to dig deep into the events in Denau. Thus the provincial prosecutor, called Faizylov, asked the Denau district party committee, headed by Khaidarov, to hold deputy farm boss Alikulov to account for his wrongdoing. That was easy; Khaidarov ignored it and filed the letter in the archive. And that was fine, because Faizylov was not really trying in the first place. When the Uzbek Republic prosecutor ordered him to hold a special inspection of the Khrushchev farm, Faizylov refused; he said there was no point, because a routine inspection had just taken place.

The outer circle extended all the way out to Tashkent, the capital of Soviet Uzbekistan. Even there, we will find that people were surprisingly well-informed. Knowing all about it, they were going to do just the minimum to show they cared.

Just from Denau to Tashkent was a four hundred–mile journey through the mountains, and from Tashkent to Moscow was another two thousand miles and more. Who would have expected it? Suddenly, a man from Moscow showed up in the little community of Denau. Moscow's man was Instructor Fedorenko of the Commission of Party Control. Old Man Nikolayenko had written an appeal to the commission—the Soviet leadership's watchdog on party members—and his appeal had been heard.

Immediately, the party committee for the province of the Surkhan Darya took defensive action. The day Instructor Fedorenko arrived, the provincial committee passed a resolution that condemned Old Man Nikolayenko's illegal detention. It was carefully worded to exclude the possibility that any specific person was responsible for the campaign of harassment and intimidation. This was a crime without a perpetrator.

Instructor Fedorenko was not fooled. He reviewed the papers and interviewed the principals. It was like pulling at a loose thread: quickly, the fabric of local power in the Denau district unraveled.

The easy part of his investigation was to establish the facts of the Old Man's persecution. After that, Fedorenko turned back to the Old Man's original complaints. One of these was that the Khrushchev farm was being run without the services of a trained plant technician. The technician had spoken up in criticism of the farm bosses at party meetings. They fired him while he was away at an agricultural show. He protested that he had been unfairly dismissed, and he pressed his case as far as the party Central Committee for the Uzbek Republic in Tashkent. Tashkent ordered the farm to give the technician his job back, and told Moscow that this settled the matter. But the truth was the opposite, Fedorenko found. The technician did not get his job back, and had been forced out of the province.

And again: Instructor Fedorenko found that the farm had allowed its members to take more land and livestock for their private use than the law allowed. A farmworker complained to the Denau party committee that Keldyev was selling off farm livestock to friends and relatives. The farmworker was disciplined for "slander." Without much difficulty, Fedorenko established that the farmworker's accusation was true, not slanderous.

As Fedorenko delved into these things, he found that the abuses that Old Man Nikolayenko had sought to expose led everywhere. As he widened the spotlight from the original allegations to the coverup on the Denau district party committee, Fedorenko found more and more suppressed complaints. Other whistle-blowers had tried to expose faults and abuses on the Khrushchev farm and elsewhere. They were silenced, disciplined, removed from their jobs, or expelled from the farm altogether.

Fedorenko found that Denau party boss Khaidarov had been busy upholding the honor of his district in more ways than one. Recall the list of "heroes of socialist labor" that Old Man Nikolayenko allegedly intended to murder. In 1956 Khaidarov had colluded with other local party officials and farm managers to underreport the district acreage under cotton. In both years they "lost" more than ten thousand acres. By reporting less land under cotton they were able to push up the reported yield of cotton per acre, and so exceed the center's target for the cotton yield. As a reward, in January 1957 Khaidarov and his colleagues received a state decoration: Hero of Socialist Labor.

Many people worked together to pull this off, and knowledge could not have been limited to a few people. Among those who became aware of the fraud were some who wished to discredit the organizers, whether from jealousy or from a sense of honor. Anonymous complaints reached Moscow, which passed them back to the provincial committee for investigation. The provincial committee passed them down to the district committee, and the district committee filed them away.

An Uzbek affair

This was not the last time that games would be played with the cotton harvest in Uzbekistan. In 1959 Sharaf Rashidov became first secretary of the Communist Party of Uzbekistan. Under his regime, accounting fraud became a bigger business than the cotton crop. Everyone boosted results, took the money from Moscow for cotton that had not been grown, shared out the proceeds so that the buyers of the nonexistent crop would keep their mouths shut, and lived quietly.

The country was always short of cotton, but until the last months of his life Rashidov was never short of friends.[11] His best friend was Leonid Brezhnev, who protected him until the end of his life. Among his many decorations, Rashidov was twice a Hero of Socialist Labor. He had his critics but was able to neutralize them or fend them off. When whistle-blowers wrote to the center to complain about abuses and corruption, Moscow returned the letters to Tashkent asking for the local authorities to look into it. Rashidov dutifully wrote back to say the letters were all lies; everything was in order. Thus, with Rashidov's clan rule under Brezhnev's protection, Uzbekistan was shielded from scrutiny.

Brezhnev died in 1982, and former KGB chief Yuri Andropov succeeded him as general secretary of the Soviet Communist Party. For Rashidov, everything changed. At first Andropov could not get through the impenetrable thicket of the Uzbek leader's defenses. You might have thought that having the KGB at his disposal would give Andropov the upper hand. But Rashidov had even bought the Uzbek KGB. According to historian Stephen Kotkin, Andropov finally got his evidence of the Uzbek cotton fraud not from KGB agents on the ground but by means of photographs taken from space by Soviet military satellites.[12]

Andropov made Rashidov an offer: go quietly and stay free. Rashidov turned the offer down and committed suicide. After a lengthy, confrontational, and controversial investigation, two top Uzbek officials were executed. Twenty or so others were imprisoned, among them Yuri Churbanov, the USSR's first deputy minister of the interior and Brezhnev's son-in-law.

Homes for heroes

Not all the energy of the Denau party boss was given to "the good of the cause." Khaidarov's personal life spilled over into his party activities—or was it the other way around? He had an affair with an unmarried party worker and gave her money. This became a problem, for he was already blessed with a large family. Mrs. Khaidarova protested loudly to the district party, where her husband was the boss, and also to the provincial committee in Termez, which stood over him. Evidently she was not afraid of the boomerang effect. Khaidarov assured everyone that the affair was over. The young woman left the province, and no more was said about it (or her).

Khaidarov benefited his own family in other ways. He built himself a large private residence using timber from the Khrushchev farm. Underlying this was a complex exchange of favors. Khaidarov reportedly paid Keldyev, the farm boss, for the timber with cash. The construction was done by workers from another farm, the neighboring "Stalin" cooperative, where Khaidarov's brother was a member. Supposedly, the work done on the house paid off some amount that the Stalin farm owed Khaidarov's brother for work he had done. At the same time, Khaidarov's brother built his own house—and then left the cooperative.

As Fedorenko found, there was a private housing boom in the Denau district. The boom reflected supply and demand. On the demand side, several local farm managers and party functionaries seemed to have money to spend beyond their official means, and were putting the money into building homes. On the supply side, the labor and the timber to build the houses were being provided by local farms.

What did it all mean? It is easy to see what drove demand. The Soviet economy provided few legal instruments for personal saving: cash, savings bank accounts paying low interest, and government bonds that not only paid low interest but were non-transferable and redeemable only after relatively long terms. Neither cash nor bank accounts were secure; in living memory the government had compulsorily converted both on unfavorable terms. Other instruments that were secure, such as foreign currency and precious metals and stones, could not be held legally. How could a family with surplus income spread its risks and diversify its assets? Building a private home in the countryside was one of very few options.

From Moscow's point of view, turning money into private homes undermined the plan for national economic development. In the plan, the top priority was given to public investments in the economic and military infrastructure. These investments depended in part on the food and materials produced by the country's farms, including the Khrushchev farm in the distant valley of the Surkhan Darya. When the cronies of the Denau district saved their money and held it in cash or at the bank, what they saved could be matched with the investments that the government wanted. But if householders invested their surplus income in private homes, and if the building of these homes diverted farm resources from supplying the state with what it needed for public investment, then the state plan for investment and defense would struggle.

Instructor Fedorenko found that the party Central Committee of the Uzbek Republic was well-informed about the private housing boom in the Denau district. In Tashkent, party officials told him that the provincial party in Termez had the matter in hand. They had gone to Denau to tackle the people who were responsible for undermining the national security by building their own homes. The culprits, Fedorenko learned, were being fully cooperative, and were now willing to turn their new homes over to the social housing stock, as long as they were compensated at the state's valuation. To pay for this, the provincial housing authority was currently seeking a "large" additional grant from Moscow's budget. (But this grant, if allowed, would eventually have to be paid for out of higher taxes or cutbacks in public spending in the rest of the country.)

Fedorenko's fact-finding suggests how precious private residences were to the owners, with how much energy they were defended, and how those with connections could defend them. In a related story that Fedorenko uncovered, a gasoline tanker driver accidentally damaged the home of a farm bookkeeper. Instead of pursuing the legal remedies available, the man's boss held the tanker hostage, siphoning off fuel and removing the tires, until the driver had personally compensated the homeowner.

An uncensored expression

Secretary Umarov, one of the big shots on the Surkhan Darya provincial party committee in Termez, was driving on a journey. This journey took him over the railroad tracks near the Denau train station. When he tried to use an unauthorized crossing, he was detained by a railroad worker. A bitter row followed, in the course of which the worker let slip an "uncensored expression." (The Russian language has a rich vein of obscenities that are strictly excluded from public discourse to the present day.) For this breach of the peace, Umarov had the police arrest the worker and keep him in the cells for ten days without pay.

The worker's complaint rose to the Uzbek Republic party Central Committee in Tashkent. There, Umarov gave an assurance that he had apologized to the worker. The reality was different, as Fedorenko established. Far from apologizing, Umarov had sought the worker out, abused him, and demanded a meeting of the other railroad workers to investigate their colleague's misdemeanor. Only the intervention of bystanders held him back from starting the scandal up all over again.

The Old Man is vindicated

Fedorenko's report vindicated our hero in all respects. But how to proceed? This was a party investigation, not a police matter. In the future it might become a police matter, and go to trial, but only if the party allowed it to go there. As a general rule, the party did not like to see its members in court on criminal charges. This did not prevent prosecution, but it meant that party investigation took priority. The party had to reach the decision to remove its protection and expel its members before they could appear in open court. Once the party had turned its back on mass terror, therefore, a party card conferred a degree of protection on wrongdoing by party members.

Fedorenko's main recommendation, therefore, was not to punish the guilty but to convene another meeting. The next step, he said, should be to summon farm boss Keldyev, along with party officials from every level, to meet the Commission of Party Control. So the meeting would also be attended by party secretary Khaidarov from the Denau district, which was the lowest-level party boss; by first secretary Khakimov from the middle level, the Surkhan Darya provincial party committee; and by a bunch of people from Tashkent, representing the central party committee for the whole of Uzbekistan. The Uzbek prosecution service was also invited to send someone; this sounds ominous for Keldyev and Khaidarov, but actually it did not mean anything.

To judge from the record, this meeting took place in the late summer of 1959. As a direct result, the Uzbek Republic party took steps to "correct the indicated faults and punish the guilty."

The only specific measure of punishment that showed up in the record, however, was a reprimand and demotion for provincial committee secretary Umarov, who had tried to cross the railroad in the wrong place.

In the end, therefore, the victory of Old Man Nikolayenko over the party mafia of the Surkhan Darya province was a moral one. His voice was heard in Moscow, and when Moscow finally spoke it was to say that his cause was just.

What enabled this simple pensioner to triumph over the local power elite? Why did Moscow listen to him, when the local authorities were not only deaf to his complaints but conspired to break him? At this time, even after Stalin's death, the Soviet Union remained a harsh, centralized dictatorship with a censored press; the citizen's voice had no right to be heard against the decisions of the party and state. Between 1917 and 1991, millions of Nikolayenkos were silenced and trampled underfoot without a second thought. As long as the vital interests of the Soviet state were not damaged, no one in power was much concerned about an individual miscarriage of justice. What made the Old Man different?

The answer lay partly in timing, which we'll come to. The fundamental thing was this: from Moscow's standpoint, the Old Man's enemies were enemies of the state! If the state was to stand up for itself, it had to stand up for the Old Man.

Cheerleaders of the Revolution

Stalin was a brutal and bloody tyrant but he was not at all stupid. Stalin had clear goals for the country that he led. At least four times in the quarter-century of his rule, Stalin set about mobilizing the resources of the entire country into huge nation-building efforts. At the end of the 1920s, Stalin organized the industrialization of the country and he ordered the peasants into collective farms that would supply the country's new towns and factories with bread, meat, and milk. In the late 1930s, Stalin set about eliminating his enemies at home and arming the country against his enemies abroad. In the early 1940s, he had to marshal the army and the economy to fight off Hitler's devastating surprise attack and conquer Germany. In the late 1940s, Stalin took a country ruined and decimated by invasion and war and launched it into the atomic age.

At every stage, Stalin faced resistance and disloyalty. He understood its sources and he learned to anticipate it. An obvious source was the enemies he could see: the leaders abroad and at home who could turn against him. More challenging was resistance by the enemy he could not see: the ordinary citizens. These were the millions who, as they went about their daily lives, worked to frustrate the dictator's plans. Most of those who did this were not following a conscious intention; when they worked against the plan, they did so unconsciously, just by doing what came instinctively. So, when Moscow spoke, they nodded, then watched and waited to see how things turned out. They were slow to respond and avoided responsibility. At meetings they cheered socialism and saluted the banner of Lenin and Stalin—often sincerely. Afterward, they went home to build their own homes and futures and those of their families and friends. Above all, they helped each other appear to the outside as if they were utterly loyal servants of the proletariat and heroes of socialist labor, and this was not so hard because they did not necessarily *dis*-believe. But at heart they were just doing their best to protect themselves and their families.

The strategy of cheerleading in public and lining pockets in private came naturally to these people. They were still doing it naturally when they became pillars of the community and joined the party, got appointed to the farm management team, and were selected for the district and provincial party committees. For them, politics was just a continuation of everyday life by other means.

This strategy worked better in some places than in others. The places where it worked best of all were a long way from Moscow. Such places tended to have more stable populations—most people would know each other and each other's background, and many would be related by blood or marriage. Most people knew whom they could trust. Even if they didn't entirely rely on each other's goodwill, they often knew about their neighbors' peccadilloes and secrets to the extent that they could still rely on cooperation. Perhaps it worked still better where a dominant non-Russian ethnicity clearly marked insiders from outsiders. In fact, the remote valley of the Surkhan Darya probably had just about the best conditions imaginable for a local clan to work up some protection against the guys from Moscow.

To the extent that they succeeded in quietly going about their everyday business in this way, such little people could win a modest degree of security and private prosperity. This was something to which they had no legal right, so it could easily be taken away. In fact, that was the problem: it gave them something to lose. Anyone who threatened to spoil things could quickly become a problem for the whole community—a troublemaker, for example, like Old Man Nikolayenko.

Most likely Keldyev and Khaidarov could have dealt quite easily with their troublesome neighbor, if only they could have confined the matter within the Denau district, where they were in control. In Denau they knew everyone and could contain the repercussions. For the same reason, Old Man Nikolayenko kept taking his information outside the Denau district to Termez, Tashkent, and beyond. To match his counter-move, Keldyev and Khaidarov needed a few key people on the outside who would collude with them. Some were willing: for example, the provincial party officials and provincial prosecutors. Fatally, some were not. If only the provincial judge had not tossed out the evidence against the Old Man for planning terrorist acts, if only the government psychiatrists had agreed to declare him crazy, we would never have heard of Old Man Nikolayenko.

Ruling without terror

Now think about the same problem from the perspective of Moscow in the mid-1950s. Stalin was dead. But Stalin's problem had not gone away. Stalin's problem was to ensure Moscow's supremacy over local communities and clans the length and breadth of that vast country, a sixth of the world's land surface, five thousand miles from end to end. Nikita Khrushchev now faced the same problem, but he had chosen to throw away Stalin's solution: mass terror.

The Kremlin's new tenants wanted to rule in a new way, with less emphasis on violence and more on loyalty. They had closed down the Gulag and purged the secret police, replacing the old ministry of state security with a new government committee under "party control": the KGB. This new regime was still fragile. What if . . . they must have wondered: what if mass terror had been the *only* thing that was making all those millions of party members in the faraway republics, provinces, and districts fall in line? Would the country hold together without more violence?

For Moscow in transition to new times, Old Man Nikolayenko was a godsend. Unexpectedly, he gave the Kremlin a direct line of microscopic vision into the inner working arrangements of a local power elite. And that vision was frightening! Suddenly, the men in Moscow could see with their own eyes a little mafia at work—the self-protection club of the Surkhan Darya valley. This club had formed because the leaders had neglected the First Principle: *your enemy is hiding*. While they were busy trying to get away from Stalin, they'd forgotten what he told them: "the strength of the present-day wreckers . . . lies in the Party card [which] enables them to be politically trusted and gives them access to all our institutions and organizations."[13]

The scale and multiplicity of local corruption would have set alarm bells ringing in the Kremlin offices. Loudest may have been the bell rung by the collusion of the local KGB. This was a society without free expression or public opinion, in which everyone tried to look loyal, whatever they were actually doing or trying to do. Given that, how was Moscow to uncover disloyalty? The secret police was essential to the stability of the regime. Everywhere, under and after Stalin, before and above all, the secret police was the Kremlin's eyes and ears in the farm and factory, in the village hall and community center, and on the streets. The KBG's loyalty to Moscow was a fundamental tenet.

Under Stalin, loyalty to Moscow meant personal loyalty to the tyrant that Stalin became. Stalin used the secret police any way he liked, and that included policing the "ruling" party. In moving the Soviet political system away from Stalinism, Khrushchev took a calculated risk. He reformed the secret police and brought it under "party control." The party would control the KGB, not the other way around. But who was the party? The party had millions of members and was organized in every establishment and locality of Soviet society. The party in Moscow was not the same as the party in the Denau district. "Party control" created scope to divide the loyalties of the secret policemen. In the Nikolayenko affair a KGB officer went native. He threw in his lot with a local clan, with the Keldyevs and Khaidarovs. If that pattern became widespread, it was the worst news that Moscow could imagine.

There was also good news for Moscow: Old Man Nikolayenko was not alone. Not everyone in this story was a crook or a timeserver. Many Nikolayenkos had been trying to speak the truth to Moscow. These were special people; each and every one of them needed Moscow's attention and support.

Fault lines in the Surkhan Darya valley

Old Man Nikolayenko was a special person. One special characteristic was his tremendous persistence. A lesser person would have quickly swallowed his protests and made his peace with the local mafia. Another special characteristic was surely his preference for Moscow's objectives and Moscow's rules over those of his neighbors. How do we know that? Not directly, but we can work it out.

Old Man Nikolayenko was not, apparently, a party member. If he was, Fedorenko's report would surely have said so. But a party membership card was not everything; in fact, in the faraway Surkhan Darya valley it was the party members who were Moscow's problem. And it was the non-party member, the Old Man, who was behaving like a true believer. And this was not the first conflict in which the Old Man had sided with Moscow. Long ago he had fought in the Russian Civil War—presumably, on the side of the Bolsheviks. And there is more.

Buried in the Old Man's original complaints is a reference to the family origins of Khrushchev farm deputy boss Alikulov. In the 1930s, Alikulov's parents were allegedly kulaks, wealthy farmers who were dispossessed and driven out on Stalin's orders. The process was called "dekulakization"—an ugly word that exactly translates a Russian term invented at the time. Instructor Fedorenko gave substance to the Old Man's story by noting: "Whether Nikolayenko, as he writes, took part in the dekulakization of [Alikulov's] family cannot be established." In short, the Old Man was trying to explain his persecution partly on the basis that Alikulov was resurrecting a vendetta against one of Stalin's loyal agents that originated in the 1930s.

In telling the story of the 1950s we've already stumbled across the ethnic divide in the Denau district. At the center was a community of Uzbeks. On the outside was an old man whose origin lay in far-distant Ukraine. But the conflict between them began not in the 1950s but two decades earlier, in the 1930s, when a Ukrainian immigrant somehow got involved in the dispossession of a family of Uzbeks.

How did that happen? Here's an educated guess: once upon a time, the Old Man was a "twenty-five-thousander." In November 1929, Stalin's Politburo launched a campaign to send twenty-five thousand urban workers to the countryside to force the pace of farm collectivization. This plan, like many others of the time, was "fulfilled and over-fulfilled." The total number of party activists mobilized from the cities for the war against the peasantry eventually reached a hundred thousand. But still they were called the twenty-five-thousanders.

The historian Lynne Viola has told their tale. The twenty-five-thousanders were volunteers, and no one volunteered for this battle unless motivated by an idealistic commitment to Stalin's party line. To the peasants in the countryside, however, the twenty-five-thousanders were outsiders sent by Moscow to impose a violent "revolution from above" that few wanted. In the villages where they were ordered to settle, the twenty-five-thousanders' ideals were tested to the limit. Conditions of dreadful isolation and extreme deprivation were commonplace. Many fell out of the ranks; some lost their health, others their ideals, and more than a few lost their lives. Those left behind when the battle receded were hardened in their convictions, quite unable "to merge with their local surroundings, to cast off their proletarian identity."[14]

A few of the original twenty-five-thousanders settled permanently in the countryside to work, to uphold the new villages, and to raise their families there. It's possible, even probable, that the young Nikolayenko was one of these. He would have arrived in the Surkhan Darya valley around 1930. A quarter century later he was still there. And he was still an outsider who stood apart because of his appearance, his speech, and even his Ukrainian-sounding name.

This would explain for sure why the Old Man never bonded with his Uzbek neighbors. He kept himself aloof from their little local games; he wouldn't endorse their parochial ambitions. As for the neighbors, they wouldn't let him in. By the 1950s the neighbors all looked like loyal citizens, stalwarts of collective farming, and pillars of the party. But only one generation had passed since the expropriations and deportations of Stalin's "great breakthrough." The Old Man remembered the past, and they remembered him.

Perhaps the past wasn't over yet. Mr. Nikolayenko was getting on in years. The children of Stalin's victims were getting on with their own lives. But still they did not feel much need to play fair with him if he was still making trouble for them.

Whose side are you on?

Instructor Fedorenko has left us a historical epic of everyday life in the middle of the twentieth century in a faraway valley of Soviet Uzbekistan. In the background, a far-flung dictatorship and its vast bureaucracy struggle to turn from mass terror to controlled repression. In the foreground a quarrelsome old man carries on a bitter feud with his neighbors. He survives, battered but finally triumphant.

In complicated times the protagonists dressed themselves up in complex identities. The Old Man cast himself to carry the sword of truth and the shield of justice against a self-interested cabal that corrupted the legality of the proletarian state. The network that opposed him was made up of ordinary people, not master criminals. Scarred by their own history, rough and ill-mannered, they had no interest in trust or mutual aid as fundamental moral values, only as means to survive. By cooperation they aimed to hollow out a niche for themselves and their families, to defend their homes, to hold up a roof against brutal, distant outsiders, and to close the curtains against an intrusive, confrontational neighbor.

Surely the Uzbeks of the Surkhan Darya valley would have echoed the words of Nick Lampert's protagonist:

> What principle do the "truth seekers" represent? They represent a world of thorough and cold-blooded state control. The whistle-blowers are the totalitarians of the piece, spying on their colleagues and fellow workers and setting themselves up as agents for the prying eyes of the state.[15]

CHAPTER FIVE

You Have Been Warned

Until the Bolshevik Revolution came to Russia in 1917, Lithuania was a province of the Russian Empire. The governor's court was accommodated in the center of Wilno, the Polish name for Lithuania's capital city. The building was square and solid, in the governmental style of the empire, at the corners of a wide street and an open square lined with trees. Sixty-one years later, Polish Wilno had become Lithuanian Vilnius. The building had become the headquarters of the KGB of Soviet Lithuania, with offices upstairs and cells in the basement.

On a cool, dry day in October 1978, a nervous young man entered the KGB headquarters through the front door.[1] He was there by invitation, but he did not know why. Age thirty-four, Algirdas was a section head in a radio-electronics design bureau. Radio-electronics had military applications, so his work required access to "top secret" government paperwork. The young man, Algirdas, had already been vetted and cleared by the KGB. He was also a candidate for full party membership. His record was clean—until now.

Algirdas was interviewed by three KGB officers. From the moment they opened the conversation, he knew he was in trouble. They told him they needed to talk about "the causes of his inappropriate behavior in the collective, expressed in the dissemination of politically damaging propositions that denigrate our Soviet actuality."

An informer had reported Algirdas to the KGB as "telling anti-Soviet jokes, denigrating Soviet society and party and government leaders, belittling the role of the party and its youth league, and continually praising the American way of life." Through other informers, the KGB confirmed the allegations. To protect the informers' identities, the KGB also secured formal witness statements from Algirdas's past and present colleagues.

We are told that the stages of loss—denial, anger, bargaining, depression, and acceptance—are universal.[2] So too were the stages of a warning conversation with the KGB.

Denial. At first, Algirdas "behaved mistrustfully and insincerely, and tried to show that he is not expressing ideologically incorrect and damaging judgments." (These are the words of the officer who made the record.)

Confession. "But, after he was provided with the concrete facts of his unhealthy propositions, he admitted that among his circle he actually did sometimes repeat jokes, without hostile intentions, and express other incorrect propositions."

Bargaining. At this point Algirdas came up with some excuses. He blamed his own lack of political understanding, and his inexperience and lack of preparation as a section chief. By joking about the party, he claimed, he was just aiming:

> To amuse people so that their work would be worthy of the name. Comparisons with the USA served only as a benchmark for evaluation of work. After the conversation he understood that in making comparisons it is necessary to consider well so that everyone will understand it properly.

Warning. Algirdas "was warned of the unacceptability of similar facts in the future."

Acceptance. In response, Algirdas promised to change his behavior with immediate effect.

Moving on. For a while, Algirdas would be on probation. The KGB would share its information with the party committees at his places of work and residence, so that they knew to keep an eye on him. Based on his promises, the interviewers recommended not to keep him under direct KGB surveillance. But this recommendation was countermanded by their superior officer: "Set up surveillance for a period of one year."

From sword to shield

The secret police was the "sword and shield" of the Bolshevik Revolution. When it acted as the sword, officers took part in arrests, executions, assassinations, and "low intensity" military operations. Accounts of the sword are more sensational and better known than those of the shield. Yet for much of Soviet history KGB officers, especially in the provinces, spent more time acting as the shield of the regime.

The documentary evidence for this chapter comes from Soviet Lithuania. The history of Soviet rule in Lithuania shows both shield and sword at work. In the first years after World War II, Lithuania was under military occupation. KGB records from this time tell of nationalist resistance and Soviet counterinsurgency. The security police took part in military operations, mass arrests, and deportations.[3] The insurgents were suppressed and Lithuania became quiet. As that happened, the sword gave way to the shield.

As the shield of the Soviet state, the Lithuanian KGB still had plenty to do. Although increasingly quiet, political life in Lithuania was never completely "normal." Because of its history of nationalism, strong Catholic congregation, large emigration, open coastline, and land border with conflict-ridden Poland, the

KGB continued to regard Lithuania as a frontline theater of the Cold War.

When the KGB was shielding the Soviet regime, it continued to operate according to the basic principles of the police state. For the sake of the First Principle (*your enemy is hiding*), the Second Principle (*start from the usual suspects*), and the Third Principle (*study the young*), the KGB listened to the citizens in public and private, at home and abroad. It watched the borders and the coming and going of strangers. It covered the business of the state and party in a blanket of secrecy. It reserved its closest scrutiny for anyone who showed undue curiosity about secret business. The information that the KGB gathered was used in many ways. One important use of this information was to support its strategy for the stabilization of Soviet society: the strategy of prevention.

The logic of prevention, in Russian *profilaktika,* was simple: prevention is cheaper than cure. The sword was still available to chop off the heads of the real, inveterate enemies of the state. But the shield was designed to protect the potential enemies from the bad influences that might turn them one day into real enemies and so expose them to the sword.

Prevention was not for highly motivated dissidents or nationalists, those who had already committed "state crimes." In the eyes of the Soviet authorities, these persons were real enemies who deserved retribution and isolation, not dialogue. Prevention was reserved for people who committed nothing more than "politically damaging misdemeanors," which were not yet crimes.[4] Such people needed patience, understanding, and advice; they were suitable cases for treatment. Intervention could save them by forestalling "the emergence of criminal intention and its realization."

This was a clear change from Stalin's time. In the 1920s, Stalin developed the idea that many people were potential enemies who were likely to betray the state under pressure, even if they did not know it themselves. In the 1930s, Stalin's treatment of choice was mass terror, including preventive arrest, imprisonment, and execution.[5] Compared to this, the technique of preventive warnings was humane. It was also absolutely necessary, if Stalin's successors were to manage the consequences of releasing millions of embittered former prisoners back into the community.

Foreign as well as domestic factors were at work. Stalin's successors began to open up Soviet society to the outside world. In that context, the strategy of prevention met the challenges of the outside world. It repaired some of the damage done to the Soviet Union's international reputation by the cruelty of the Stalin years. And it offered a way to inhibit the spread of imported fashions and youth culture from one impressionable young person to another.[6]

The "preventive discussion" was the defining moment in the KGB's strategy of prevention. It was a discussion, not an interrogation; no one was accused of a serious crime. Although the discussion gave both sides the chance to explain themselves, it was never open-ended; it always ended with the subject receiving a clear, unmistakable warning. The person at the focus of the discussion had set out on a path that, if followed to the end, would lead to a collision with the state. If it came to a collision, the state would win. The message of the interview was that this collision was entirely avoidable. All that was required was an immediate change in the subject's behavior.

The discussion ended when a promise was given to do so. But the end of the discussion was not always the end of the process. Sometimes the KGB accepted a promise to mend behavior at its face value; at other times it maintained surveillance for a period.

Surveillance lay at the foundation of the strategy of prevention. Surveillance meant the gathering and collating of data from neighbors and work colleagues, informers, street watchers and followers, and mail and telephone intercepts. The KGB relied on mass surveillance to identify suitable cases for treatment and to signal the moment when the subject's behavior required intervention. After an intervention, the subject's expectation that surveillance would probably continue was one factor that helped ensure compliance. It was not always necessary to target continued surveillance on any particular subject, for there were enough informers that no one could expect to go through life unobserved.

A wide range of interests

The KGB sought preventive interviews across a wide variety of cases, including many that would not seem remotely political at first glance. In Lithuania's seaport of Klaipeda, for example, many cases involved young Lithuanians who were bored, looked for amusement, and found it on the dockside. Foreign sailors were continually in and out of the port, handling Western currency and goods. Even if they started off just looking for a good time, the young people soon found themselves involved in petty currency violations, black-market trading, and casual prostitution. State security did not care about petty crime or prostitution; it did care about contact with foreigners. The KGB picked up these young people and warned them off, sometimes singly, sometimes in groups.[7]

A stream of related cases was provided by Lithuanian sailors who returned from the West with foreign goods and currency. These gave them entry tickets into the same underworld of petty criminality and easy sex. The KGB used its strategy of prevention to impose a cultural and moral quarantine, aimed at stopping the spread of "unhealthy" Western-style values at the border.

For similar reasons, it was the task of the KGB to control the conduct of Soviet citizens abroad. No one was allowed a passport to leave the country without detailed, intrusive checks into his background and reliability. Abroad, Soviet citizens had to conform to a fixed code of conduct (described in chapter 6). Some of those who traveled abroad would inevitably violate the rules by going off on their own, by having unauthorized dealings with foreigners, or by reselling foreign goods or currency. On their return to the Soviet homeland, those involved were reported, called in, and warned.

Some cases, like that of Algirdas, had a clear political dimension. The KGB was particularly interested in anyone who expressed nostalgia for "bourgeois Lithuania" (the KGB's name for the independent state that had existed from 1918 to 1940), denigrated Soviet leaders or the Soviet way of life to colleagues or neighbors, or wrote indiscreetly to relatives abroad.

In KGB eyes, young people were a problem in a way that older people were not (recall the Third Principle: *study the young*). To the KGB, older people were a known quantity. But every new generation threw up its own surprises. The state had many ways to integrate young people into society—for example, through guaranteed employment, the Communist Youth league, and official youth clubs. But the opportunities these provided lacked variety, and any group of young people would include a few rebels who were naturally inclined to push at the limits.

While some young people just wanted more fun, others developed romantic feelings about political freedom and national identity. The KGB was continually treading on the heels of groups that discussed independent Lithuania, read nationalist poetry, or planned escapades involving leaflets and slogans. These were often students. The 1960s and 1970s were a time of student revolution; if in Paris or Prague, why not in Vilnius? Some students were children of the Lithuanian party elite; the party wanted them to aspire to lead Soviet Lithuania, not an independent state. Such young people were too precious to destroy, but sometimes they needed to be taught a lesson, so that they would return to the path of "healthy" behavior.

On losing one's sense of humor

Algirdas was one who came to attention by telling jokes against the regime. He was a joker, in Russian an *anekdotchik*. He was treated leniently, in that he merely received a warning. In the past he might have been dealt with more severely. While writing his wonderful history of communist humor, Ben Lewis interviewed Roy Medvedev, the historian and Soviet-era dissident.[8] According to Medvedev, the first assignment of trainee operatives of the Stalin-era NKVD was often to hang around public places and listen for subversive jokes. This was their homage to the Fourth Principle (*stop the laughing*). By prosecuting the citizens who spread underground humor, the state exercised its zero tolerance for the sharing of dissenting attitudes.

On Stalin's death, according to the well-informed Medvedev, the Soviet labor camps held around 200,000 *anekdotchiki*. When Stalin died and the regime went soft, the jokers were among the first wave of releases from the Gulag.

After that time, Lewis notes, it's hard to find more than a handful of people imprisoned under Soviet rule just for telling jokes. He suggests that official attitudes became so relaxed that disrespectful jokes became a matter for conservative protest. In 1964 one such protest appeared in *Pravda*:

> How should one deal with all these mudslingers? [. . .] We cannot behave as our woodcutter used to do, when he pretended to be a gardener. But we have to fight them.[9]

The "woodcutter" is an oblique reference to Stalin, who used to lop off the mudslingers' heads with a sharp ax.

In reality, things never became as relaxed as this might imply. The state continued to wage war on humor, but it stopped pruning the jokers by snipping them off from society and turning them into compost. Instead, the jokers were disciplined more gently, as the gardener might fasten a rambling wildflower to a trellis. In the struggle with the *anekdotchiki*, the gardener's main tool became the preventive warning. Jokers like Algirdas were summoned to the KGB for a discreet conversation. The outcome was usually to take away their sense of humor, which was better for them than taking away their liberty.

What was the secret of the Soviet anecdote? A typical joke took some official slogan or formula and gave the words a playful twist. A newspaper headline imagined in the time when young volunteers were building a railroad in the Far East declared: "Young Communists: Your Place is in Siberia!" Or, for coal miners: "Communists: Your Place is Underground!"[10] What was the danger in such jokes?

Where was the treason in a moment's amusement? It's important to have in mind that the danger to state security did not lie in the joke itself. It lay in the fact that you were willing not just to think it but to share it. A joke is more than a joke; it's a medium for the exchange of feelings. It's a moment in which two people (or more, which is worse) can share a grain of disbelief, of disloyalty. It's a moment in which the people who share it can learn: I am not alone.

The KGB mistrusted all networks of affinity that did not have official authority: artists, Jews, hippies, and so on. One such network was the network of jokers. Thus the KGB did not find Soviet jokes funny, and for good reason. For the same reason, perhaps, while the KGB was willing to record the fact that jokes had been told, they generally did not record the jokes for themselves. So, with rare exceptions (there will be a rather poor example in our final chapter), the documentation of the KGB does not contain any jokes. To make up for this, however, it reports events from life that are as funny as any joke. Here is one such story from the files of the Klaipeda town KGB in 1972.

Like every Soviet town, Klaipeda had few restaurants open to the public. In fact, to get into any Soviet-era restaurant in any town, you had to do two things. First, you had to go between mealtimes, because this was a workers' state where all the restaurants in every town would close for lunch and dinner so that the staff could take a break. Second, when you got there, you had to wait in line outside the door because, with few restaurants and restricted opening times, there were always many would-be diners looking for a table in the middle of the afternoon and those who knew the doorman would get in first.

In 1972 someone was going around Klaipeda jumping queues and bagging tables by pulling the rank of a major in the KGB. He got a table at the Meridian, telling the doorman that he was on surveillance duty, watching foreigners. After dinner at the Neringa he left his compliments in the visitors' book ("excellent service!"), signing with his supposed KGB rank and an important clue: his real name and address.

A report found its way back to the Klaipeda KGB, where no such officer was listed. So the KGB officers went looking for their man and tracked him down: Tomas, a fitter in the building industry. At work, Tomas was a reliable employee who regularly met his performance indicators. At home, he drank and quarreled with his neighbors.

The KGB pulled Tomas in for a "preventive" discussion. To prevent what, exactly? They said: "In order to prevent the disclosure and discrediting of certain methods of work of the organs of the KGB."

The interview took place on December 4, 1972. Tomas was happy and content, he said, in his work and family life. From 1968 he had been on the police register as a low-level informer. He let his friends find out, and they began to call him "Major." So it all began with a joke, and Tomas went along with it. Then, the joke got out of hand.

In the end, Tomas made four mistakes. He shouldn't have bragged to his friends about his police contacts. He should not have inflated his status to an officer of state security. He definitely should not have tried to exploit that status for enjoyment, for, in the guise of a KGB officer, Tomas found he could demand a table and be served in a restaurant while others stood in line. And it was just insane of him to have left a written record of his enjoyment in the restaurant visitors' book.

Tomas knew he should not have done these things. He promised his interrogators he had never put his little pretense to any more sinister purpose. He swore he would never, ever do it again.

Of course this was not the only society in which citizens had an incentive to impersonate an officer of the security service. In Western societies, too, citizens sometimes impersonate the police. They do this often to get money, sex, or drugs.[11] When they do this they are often taken to court and hit with a fine or jail time. But Tomas lived in a socialist country where the rewards and penalties were different. In the Soviet Union, impersonating a KGB officer enabled you to jump the queue for a decent meal. And the punishment? Tomas was made to acknowledge his guilt, write an explanation, express contrition, and seek forgiveness. And that was it, for this, they considered, was already communism with a "human face." The KGB let Tomas go home, as long as he ate his dinner there from now on.

A life-changing moment

Like the KGB, every police force tries to reduce reoffending. The results do not always impress. In England and Wales, first offenders may be given police cautions for minor violations. Between 2002 and 2013, the police issued more than three million cautions. Proven reoffending in the twelve months after the caution was approximately one in six among adults and one in four among juveniles.[12]

An innovation in the struggle against petty crime in England and Wales was the Anti-Social Behavior Order. ASBOs were introduced in 2000 and replaced in 2014. An ASBO was issued by a court against a person and was designed to inhibit the sort of behavior that would be recognized as antisocial but would not normally warrant prosecution. Once an ASBO was issued, however, to breach it was a criminal offense. Between 2000 and 2014, more than twenty-four thousand ASBOs were issued. Over the same period, more than half of the ASBOs issued were violated. In cases where an ASBO was breached, it was breached five times on average.[13]

The KGB strategy of prevention was astonishingly effective by comparison. In eight years from 1967 through 1974, according to KGB figures for the whole Soviet Union, just over 120,000 people were "treated" by *profilaktika*. Around 70,000 of these were warned for saying or doing things that were "politically damaging," and another 11,000 for "suspicious contacts with foreigners and nurturing inclinations to treason." Only 150 of those who received a warning—just over one per thousand—were subsequently prosecuted or punished administratively for an actual offense.[14] One per thousand is a reoffending rate that Western justice systems can only dream about. At last—an aspect of Soviet society that actually worked!

It is clear that the preventive discussion could be a moment that changed your life. What made it so effective? Fear was the key. The subject of a preventive discussion with the KGB was made to feel fear—not just everyday anxiety, but a deeper fear that the young person issued with an English police caution or ASBO does not feel. There is no other reasonable explanation for the extraordinary effectiveness of *profilaktika*.

The presence of fear leaves few traces in documentary records. Perhaps there were varieties of fear. For some of those interviewed, the KGB would have had a terrifying reputation, rooted in its history. Despite the reform of 1954, KGB leaders themselves emphasized continuity with the secret police of Lenin and Stalin. In living memory the KGB's predecessors had brought about the death of millions and the imprisonment of tens of millions. In the western borderlands, including Lithuania, many young people were likely to know of relatives or family friends of the older generation who had been imprisoned, deported, or caught up in armed conflicts that the KGB's forerunners had waged ruthlessly, with total commitment, and won.

For others there would have been a more immediate fear. In this most centralized society, the KGB spoke not only for the police functions of the state. If necessary, it could give instruction to your employer, teacher, landlord, doctor, and psychiatrist—and those of your parents and children. All of these were agents of the same state and answered to the same government and ruling party as the KGB itself. As a result, because of your behavior, you or your loved ones could be barred from promotion or foreign travel or expelled from the university. If you persisted, as Old Man Nikolayenko found (in chapter 4), you could be put on trial or detained in a psychiatric hospital. There was no aspect of a person's life, however private, that the KGB could not touch if it wished.

In the course of a short conversation, each person experienced a collision with the state. For most such persons, it tilted the axis of their lives forever. The conversation altered their relationship with authority, and it also altered their feelings about friends, colleagues, neighbors, and even loved ones. When the KGB asked you to consider your behavior, you learned two things, perhaps in the same instant. One lesson was: the KGB knows everything about you. The other lesson followed: they know everything about you because among those closest to you are your betrayers. *You are alone.* Devastated and isolated, you nearly always took the only option on offer: the path of compliance. At the end of the psychological demolition, it was not uncommon that you thanked the KGB officers for their helpful advice.

Many preventive interviews were conducted in the privacy of the KGB offices, but another version of the drama was enacted in semi-public meetings in schools and colleges, offices, or neighborhoods. This "social" form of prevention was sometimes applied to groups such as student networks on the edge of nationalist activity or young women who were going together to meet sailors in the ports. The emotional beating was administered, not by KGB officers, but by work colleagues, teachers, fellow students, and community leaders. When young people were living at home, parents would be drawn in so that they could be beaten up too.

A hard case to crack

Preventive discussions rarely deviated from the script. An exception was that of the stationmaster at Leplauke on the Baltic railway between Šiauliai and the coast. The stationmaster, age thirty, was Juozas. From here on you'll need to get used to some Lithuanian given names. In Lithuania, men's given names generally end with the letter S. In this chapter they include Algirdas, Juozas, Jurgis, Ljudas, Romas, and Vytautas. Women's names usually end with an A or E. In this chapter we have only Aldona and Maria. You can say these words pretty much the way they are spelt, except to remember that the letter J always sounds like a Y. Juozas should sound like *Yoh-AH-zahs,* which is not exactly what you'd expect but it's near enough. Anyway, I'm trying to tell a story, not teach you Lithuanian.

The KGB had Juozas in their sights over several years in the 1960s. Eventually, on December 19, 1968, they prompted his bosses to call him into the Šiauliai railway office for a preventive warning. By this time the evidence on Juozas was considerable. He had said to one of his subordinates:

> I'm going to kill you. The communists' time is ending and your time will come too. We'll shoot all the communists and the same with the Jews.

He ordered a second subordinate to avoid contact with the party member:

> He's a communist, a swine through and through . . . We need to isolate him.

Still others confirmed these menaces. Juozas was continually threatening to settle accounts and take revenge; he saw a time coming to deal with the communists as they were handled in 1941 (when they were massacred by the Germans or by Lithuanian nationalists).

Juozas did not stop at personal threats. He was reported as castigating Soviet rule for repressing the church and impoverishing the people:

> They give no freedom to the church or to live freely, they put pressure on [us] until there's not enough air to breathe, even . . . Look at how they live in America, how many cars they have . . . They don't let us make money and they send all the best abroad.

Another dimension of the case against Juozas was his attitude toward classified information. As a railway official he was responsible for the military freights passing through his station, blanketed by darkness and secrecy. Juozas talked openly about explosives and weapons delivered to a missile base in the woods near Šateikiai.

Confronting Juozas with the accusations, his superiors told him there was enough to dismiss him. Juozas took this badly. He flatly denied everything. He said he had no idea that military freights passed through his station. He blamed the accusations on a workplace intrigue against him.

This did not go down too well. His bosses brought additional factors into the conversation: Juozas had a previous conviction for disorderly conduct, including threatening behavior. He had been fined for financial violations. He could not be ignorant about the military freights because it was his job to see them through the station. He was known to have a big mouth. They reminded him that his job was at risk.

Juozas was one of a small minority who remained defiant after a warning. As far as he was concerned, they could take away his station. They could sack him altogether. He could easily get another job. This was not just cheap talk. Soviet factories and building sites were always hungry to recruit more workers. In the Soviet economy, job creation was never a problem; the problem was to motivate the workers and make the jobs productive. As the saying went: "They pretend to pay us and we pretend to work."

After this bruising encounter, things went downhill. While the railway authorities worked on demoting Juozas and moving him to a station away from the lines used for military shipments, the KGB officers discussed bringing criminal charges. Meanwhile, they continued to receive reports. Through the winter of 1968, Juozas drank heavily, lost interest in work, and appeared to look forward to leaving his job. In workplace conversations he was open about the charges against him and did not deny them.

Yet the redeeming power of *profilaktika* was such that there was still a happy ending. The same informers who had brought his bad behavior to the authorities' attention continued to work alongside Juozas. In the spring of 1969, Juozas recovered his spirits and won back his self-control. He drank less, changed his friends, and focused on work. By March, his job was no longer under threat. The KGB was content to maintain surveillance for a short period, before leaving Juozas alone to manage his station.

Setting a trap

In business it's a cliché that a threat is also an opportunity. For the Lithuania KGB, the military shipments that crisscrossed the country were a threat—a continual security headache. But they were also an opportunity. Like the hunter who stakes out a lamb as bait to catch a wolf, the KGB staked out the railways to catch the suspicious characters who showed undue interest.

A KGB counterintelligence plan dated January 28, 1972, shows how this was done. The plan was drawn up to anticipate thirty-two military trains that would enter the country over the next ten days. The plan had many elements, which I'll paraphrase:[15]

- Tighten scrutiny of the usual suspects who were already under surveillance to see whether any of them showed heightened interest in the railways over the period of the military freight movements.
- Mobilize the KGB informers on the railways to watch their colleagues (and anyone else) for suspicious behavior.
- Watch the outgoing mail from the districts affected for letters and packets going abroad.
- Tighten scrutiny of the other usual suspects: those previously convicted of espionage and so on, now living in the territory of the republic after serving out their terms.

- Mount a watch on the stations where military trains would stop for servicing to spot bystanders showing a suspicious interest.
- Keep a check on the timetable for movement and delivery of the military freights.
- Use the KGB informers on the railways to avoid or manage timetable disruptions affecting the military freights.
- Tighten scrutiny of foreigners visiting Vilnius who might have connections with foreign intelligence; this was done separately for diplomats and tourists from capitalist countries and for students.
- Monitor international telephone calls to identify callers who coincide repeatedly with the passage of military freights, and to listen in on any conversations involving people who have called abroad before.
- Monitor the radio frequencies for suspicious transmissions.
- Use the KGB informers on the railways to watch for suspicious contacts with foreigners and possible caches of secret material on trains leaving the country.
- Collate the information acquired.

In the file, the plan is followed by a summary of intercepted correspondence and copies of many of the letters themselves.

The KGB rarely caught any real spies, but real spies were not their only target. Soviet citizens could also show undue interest in secret matters for private reasons. Some were just curious, or liked to show off to neighbors and workmates. A few might have dreamed about turning up at the American embassy in Moscow and using what they knew to buy a ticket out of the country. Whatever their motives, they were not conducting themselves as loyal Soviet citizens should. The KGB liked to find out about them and keep them tabbed in its card catalogs.

From this angle, the positive thing about secrets was that they naturally attracted the very people whom the KGB wanted to observe, like moths to a flame. The KGB understood this perfectly well and even exploited it. In the spring of 1965, for example, under an operation code-named "Neman," the KGB organized two months of unusually intensive military rail traffic. The purpose of this operation was not to move troops and weapons into the right positions but to create a bustle of secretive activity. Lots of people would be charging around in the middle of the night saying loudly: "Hush! It's a secret!" The bustle would draw the attention of enemy agents and disloyal citizens, who could then be identified and exposed.[16]

The first resort for those who disclosed an unhealthy interest in secret matters was, once again, a preventive discussion. Ljudas of Kretinga, Lithuania, liked to brag about his service in the missile troops. Among his drinking companions he would show off his technical knowledge of weaponry and boast about storing photographs and films at home. Unfortunately for him, his audience in the local bar included a KGB resident who reported him. In January 1973, Ljudas was pulled in for a quiet chat. It turned out that his talk was mostly empty; there was no cache of secrets under his floorboards. He promised to hold his tongue from then on.

Another veteran of the missile troops was Vasily, a Russian from Moletai. Vasily bumped into a former comrade and they chatted about old times. Vasily asked his friend to get him a photograph of a rocket in its launcher. Supposedly he wanted a memento of his time in the services. But the old comrade was a KGB informer, so the KGB identified Vasily and invited him in. Since they could not establish any sinister motivation, they decided he was one of those who were too curious for their own good. They warned him, let him go, and kept him under surveillance. According to reports, Vasily immediately changed his ways and took on a new job and new friends. But he also began to drink and became so tiresome that not even his new friends would drink with him. He lost his new job and was soon well on the way to losing another. Eventually the KGB lost interest, and wrote him off as just another hopeless alcoholic. This was not a happy ending for either Vasily or society, but it was no longer the KGB's problem.

Controlling infection

The word *profilaktika* translates directly as "prophylaxis" or "prevention." In medical science, prophylaxis means the prevention of conditions that are spread by human contact, which could include disease or pregnancy. This turns out to be a good metaphor.

Soviet rulers correctly believed that their power depended on maintaining mass conformity. The state endorsed a fixed set of "healthy" ideas and behaviors that loyal citizens should follow. Anything outside this set was a sign of potential disloyalty. Moreover, disloyalty was like an infection because examples could spread like a disease. The Soviet authorities were afraid of infectious disorder that could take hold and propagate rapidly by example, as in the Fifth Principle (*rebellion spreads like wildfire*). They developed the technique of preventive warnings to quickly isolate individual examples of "unhealthy" expressions before they could spread to others.

The KGB did not employ any sociologists, but the idea of disloyalty as a social infection is easily understood in social science.[17] Mixing with others makes us more likely to catch their germs. In much the same way as we catch a germ, we can also "catch" habits and ideas. According to behavioral science, we human beings follow each other from birth, beginning with copying our mothers' expressions, gestures, and words. As we grow up, we imitate those around us in fashion, sexual attitudes, family size, religion, investments, and voting. In deciding whether or not to steal, speed, or drive when drunk, we are influenced by the example of others. There is a lot of imitation in self-harming behavior, from overeating, drinking, and smoking to suicide.

The KGB's job was to keep down Soviet society's vulnerability to infection by examples of disloyalty. They did this by continual surveillance and rapid intervention. A new example is like a new virus. Some people have low resistance. If a new virus is going around, they need only a single exposure to catch it at once. Another group of people has medium resistance and will catch the virus only after ten exposures. Beyond them is a high-resistance group that needs at least a hundred exposures to catch the virus. The result is that the introduction of a virus (or a new idea or new fashion) can have two outcomes. If you intervene quickly and isolate the first sufferers, the spread will stop there. The middle group will fall short of ten exposures and remain unaffected. But suppose you allow the infection to spread into the middle group, and suppose that middle group is large. In that case, enough people will soon catch it that *everyone* will catch it in the end, even those who are highly resistant. If the infectious new idea is "multiparty democracy" or "national independence," the patient may not survive.

The Sixth Principle (*stamp out every spark*) required the KGB to keep a vigilant watch on society and stay alert for the very first signs of the "unhealthy" examples that could raise society's temperature. It might not be able to prevent the first handful of cases, exemplified by people with poor self-control like Juozas, the stationmaster, or by highly motivated enemies or traitors. But by acting quickly and resolutely, it could hope to prevent the example from multiplying.

In the panopticon

The strategy of prevention required the KGB to stand ready to clamp down on each and every example of disloyalty in the moment that it first arose. This was a demanding requirement. The KGB could not operate the strategy of prevention without raw data. The data were the thousands of reports or "signals" from informers and other observers that flowed into KGB offices around the country about petty acts and expressions of disloyalty. To keep up mass surveillance and produce a steady stream of signals was one of the most important duties of the KGB's network of informers.

In Lithuania the KGB achieved this on the basis of a relatively small operation. In 1971, roughly 1,200 officers and civilian staff and 11,500 informers kept watch over 3.1 million citizens.[18] This gives us an idea of how many people the KGB had on hand to do a job at a given moment—and it is not that many. If you added them up, the proportion to the total population was about four per thousand, which does not seem much. (It was well below the ten per thousand in Lithuania during the postwar insurgency and seventeen per thousand in East Germany in 1989.) There was considerable turnover in the ranks of the KGB and its informer network, so if you asked how many people in Lithuania worked for or with the KGB *ever*, you would get a much larger number, perhaps as many as 100,000.[19] This is informative of how many people ended up with some reason to identify their personal safety with upholding the Soviet regime, but it was still only thirty per thousand, and it does not tell us how many people were on hand at a particular time.

The effectiveness of mass surveillance did not lie in numbers alone. It lay partly in priorities: the KGB did not scatter its resources thinly across the whole of society, but focused on particular installations and groups. In line with the Third Principle (*study the young*), it concentrated informers in the places where students and young educated workers would gather: schools, colleges, and science-based facilities.[20]

Mass surveillance was effective partly because of the way it spread fear and suspicion. The eighteenth-century English philosopher Jeremy Bentham wrote about this because he was interested in the management of prisons (and designed a prison providing constant surveillance) and other large-scale institutions where the behavior of residents is of concern:

> The more constantly the persons to be inspected are under the eyes of the persons who should inspect them, the more perfectly will the purpose X of the establishment have been attained. Ideal perfection, if that were the object, would require that each person should actually be in that predicament, during every instant of time. This being impossible, the next thing to be wished for is, that, at every instant, seeing reason to believe as much, and not being able to satisfy himself to the contrary, he should conceive himself to be so.[21]

In short, mass surveillance was not just a support for the strategy of prevention, but was itself an active element in that strategy. Everyone knew it happened, and that knowledge had its own chilling effect on the way that each person acted and expressed his or her views.

In the Soviet setting there was one more twist that Bentham did not consider. Three strangers are gathered round the office teapot: Adomas, Barbara, and you. Into the conversation, Adomas drops a joke about the time of "bourgeois Lithuania" when the country was free and independent. How should you respond? You know you're not an informer, and Adomas is not behaving like one. But what about Barbara? If she is an informer, and if she reports the conversation before you do, what will that mean for you that you listened and said nothing? As for Adomas, clearly he does not fear you—but why not? It's not as if he knows you well. Perhaps he is testing you both. This fear, ever-present in the company of strangers, is recalled by someone who grew up in Odessa after the war:

> If someone would tell jokes, and you didn't report, someone might report you that you were not one who reported . . . [When I heard a joke from someone I didn't know] I would refrain from reacting at all. I just played the role of an idiot. I didn't get it. And it was a signal to them. Take it any way you want, and try and repeat it and expose yourself more without knowing why I didn't react. Or just get that I don't want to hear it.[22]

In short, the Soviet system of mass surveillance was designed to do without the establishment of a vast formal apparatus. It was designed to spread mistrust and to inhibit informal networks that might spread dissenting attitudes—including jokes. In the ideal outcome, each person would watch everyone and all would become informants.[23]

They are ahead of us in Kaunas

From time to time, the strategy of prevention failed. In Lithuania in 1972, some of the KGB's darkest fears were realized. In March of that year, the underground *Chronicle of the Catholic Church in Lithuania* first began to circulate. In April a church petition for greater religious freedom in Lithuania reached the United Nations. Under the nose of the KGB, it gained an astounding total of seventeen thousand signatures.

Suddenly, things got much worse. On Sunday, May 14, a student, Romas Kalanta, set himself on fire in the square before the

Kaunas Musical Theater. This was a symbolic location, the place where the incorporation of Lithuania into the Soviet Union was announced in 1940.[24] He died the next morning in the hospital.

Kalanta's funeral was set for Friday, May 18. In the days beforehand, the authorities did all they could to quiet the mood among young people and to discourage shows of solidarity. The official line was that Kalanta was mentally unbalanced and killed himself in a fit of depression. The subtext was that his tragic end was completely nonpolitical, but others were exploiting it for political ends.[25] In reality, there was certainly a political aspect to Kalanta's final act, for he had left a note, scribbled on a page torn from a calendar: "Blame only the regime for my death." Hardly anyone knew this, however, because the note quickly disappeared into KGB files, where it was found again only in 1988. To the frustration of the authorities, this did not stop ordinary people from putting their own interpretations on what had happened.

When the day of Kalanta's funeral came, the KGB tried to forestall any kind of public manifestation by advancing the ceremony without notice. The result was to provoke exactly what the KGB feared: hundreds of young people gathered, found that the funeral had already taken place, became angry, protested, and marched to the Musical Theater, where their numbers grew to around two thousand. They were dispersed violently and more than four hundred of their number were arrested. The next day, another 1,500 protesters gathered. The police and troops of the interior ministry intervened; this time no one was arrested but hundreds were beaten in and off the streets.

After two days of disorder, Kaunas became quiet again, but it was some time before the country settled down. In the two weeks after the Kaunas events, the KGB recorded many incidents of nationalist or pro-Kalanta graffiti and flier-posting in a dozen towns across Lithuania.[26]

The elements that came together and reacted so violently in Lithuania in 1972 were many.[27] Underlying features of Lithuanian society were strong memories of national independence and a strong church with a degree of independence of the state, both kept alive by a large community in the West and frequent correspondence with family members abroad. There had been recent upheavals in other communist states. Czechoslovakia had seen the Prague Spring of communism with a "human face" in 1968, suppressed by Soviet military intervention. In 1970, the neighboring northern region of Poland had been rocked by riots against food price increases, violently put down. Growing student protests across Europe were an important part of the 1960s. An aspect that is sometimes forgotten is that it was preceded by a ripple of young men burning themselves to death as public protests against communist rule across Ukraine, Hungary, Czechoslovakia, and Poland after 1968.[28] Nationalism, utopianism, romance, self-destruction, and youthful exuberance proved an inherently combustible mixture.

It was bad enough that Kalanta had been able to plan and execute his own death, possibly with the connivance of others, without any signal reaching the KGB. It was still more shocking that this had become an occasion for mass disorder. Such disturbances were exactly what KGB surveillance and prevention were supposed to avoid. There was more bad news in the composition of those detained, who were mostly young, male, and politically and socially aware. Nearly all were either in school or in the first year of employment (so just out of school). One in four belonged to the party's own youth league.[29] Thus, while they were not exactly a cross-section of Lithuanian society at the time, they were a cross-section of Lithuania's future.

But not all the news was bad. While the main demonstration in Kaunas on May 19 was suppressed by force, the KGB did not abandon the logic of its preventive strategy.

The KGB treated a few of its detainees as enemies who merited punishment. Eight of them were brought to court, tried on charges of antisocial behavior or violent disorder, and jailed for one to three years. These were singled out, it seems, because they were among those who demonstrated on the first day and they marched in the front row; or because they already had a police record. Around thirty more received police detention (ten to fifteen days in the cells).

But those who were punished formally made up only one-tenth of the four hundred detainees. The rest—that is, the overwhelming majority—were treated not as enemies, but rather as *potential* enemies who could still be saved. If they had jobs, they were required to attend "cautionary conversations" with the KGB and police; this could involve being named and shamed in workplace meetings. A few, described as "ill-intentioned," were demoted to lower-paid work. Among school and college students there were more cautionary conversations; a number were quietly expelled from their courses.[30]

In other words, in managing a crisis the state did not deviate from its primary reliance on the strategy of prevention, and acted on the belief that most of those caught up in the troubles could be set back on the right path. Later in the year, the KGB concluded that this response had been a success: preventive warnings had succeeded in suppressing bad examples that others could copy:[31]

> Such measures, as a rule, have positively influenced not only *those preventively warned* but also *those around them*, and have helped to uncover the factors giving rise to undesirable manifestations, to eliminate defects, and to improve educational work in the college and workplace collectives of those being warned.

The Kaunas events did not take everyone by surprise. The KGB had its own anonymous prophet. Six weeks earlier, the Lithuania

KGB's chief of information and analysis signed off his divisional plan of work.[32] Item no. 6 was: "Summarize and study evidence of unhealthy manifestations among young people, expressed in imitation of the so-called 'hippie' movement. Present the documents of the investigation to the Central Committee of the communist party of Lithuania." Using a fat, black nib, an unidentified reader marked the paragraph, heavily underlined the words "'hippie' movement," and wrote over the typescript: "They are ahead of us in Kaunas."

As Lithuania returned to "normality," the KGB resumed routine operations. To have suffered an uprising of young people, suddenly and out of the blue, was a serious blow. But the KGB was able to contain the uprising firmly and decisively using a minimum of force, without mass arrests or widespread bloodshed. The most important weapon in its armory continued to be *profilaktika*.

Thereafter the KGB continued to watch Lithuanians warily, especially after the sudden rise of the Solidarity movement in neighboring Poland. The Poles were in the grip of a mass epidemic; how easily would it slip across the border and take hold in Lithuania? This risk assessment was essentially correct, but

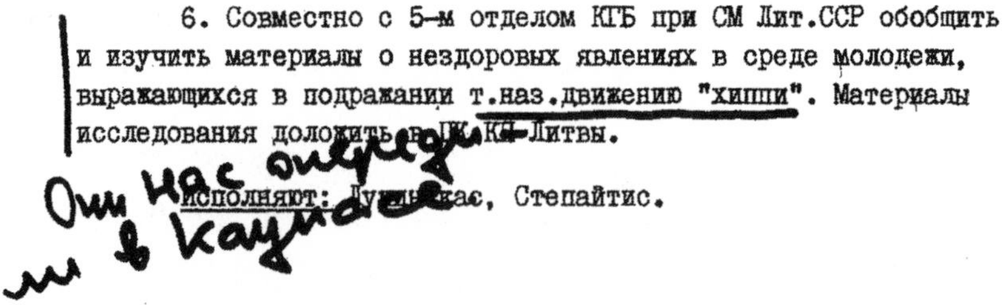

6. Совместно с 5-м отделом КГБ при СМ Лит.ССР обобщить и изучить материалы о нездоровых явлениях в среде молодежи, выражающихся в подражании т.наз.движению "хиппи". Материалы исследования доложить в ЦК КП Литвы.

Исполняют: [illegible]кас, Степайтис.

Figure 3: "They are ahead of us in Kaunas"

Source: Hoover Institution Library & Archives, Lietuvos SSR Valstybes Saugumo Komitetas, Selected Records of the Lithuanian Special Archive (Lietuvos ypatingasis archyvas – LYA), K-1/3/793: 4.

the threat took time to reappear. Mass opposition in Lithuania was resumed suddenly in 1988. This time it spread widely and unstoppably, leading directly to national independence in 1990.

After the Kaunas events

Many people were caught up in the aftermath of the Kaunas events, including some who were nowhere near the events themselves. It was their feelings that betrayed them. In June 1972, the Klaipeda KGB heard that Aldona, a port dispatcher, was talking about Kalanta at work. The official media claimed that Kalanta's death had nothing to do with politics. To the contrary, Aldona said to her workmates, Kalanta had died in protest against the denial of free speech under Soviet rule. She went from this to even more dangerous ground: in her view, an independent Lithuania would freely choose "a state of the type presently existing in Yugoslavia."

You could read the desire for Yugoslav-type independence in two ways. From one angle it illustrates how dissenters often limited their aspirations under Soviet rule. Yugoslavia was marginally more liberal than the Soviet Union, but it was still a Communist Party dictatorship under which several national republics were welded together by force. From another angle it shows why Soviet rulers from Stalin onward regarded the Yugoslav experiment with such intense mistrust: the smallest deviation from orthodoxy abroad could become a banner for malcontents at home.

When the KGB made enquiries about Aldona, it found grounds for both reassurance and anxiety. Or rather, the good news was also bad. Reassurance came from the fact that Aldona was a bright, young, professional woman, a graduate with an unblemished work record, previously secretary of her Communist Youth branch. But herein also lay cause for profound anxiety. She was not a "usual suspect"; she was not some aging, unreconciled nationalist. There was nothing in her background to explain why she should suddenly be spouting such nonsense! She was young, Soviet-educated, and upwardly mobile; people like her were supposed to be Lithuania's future.

The warning was delivered, not directly, but through her party committee secretary, thought to be a person whose influence she respected. Like others when confronted, Aldona at first denied everything, then prevaricated, then reached the stage of acceptance. She now understood, she said, "where an incorrect interpretation of the Kaunas events could lead." She promised to avoid any repetition. And the KGB left it there.

With my own eyes I saw

Others became entangled in the consequences of Kalanta's suicide when they tried to exploit the tragedy for some incidental benefit. Here's the story of Vytautas, a factory worker from Radviliškis in Šiauliai county. On the weekend of the events, Vytautas visited relatives in Kaunas, which meant a bus journey of more than seventy miles. The following Monday Vytautas was absent from work. When he showed up on Tuesday his colleagues asked him where he'd been. He told them a long story. It began on Sunday with a visit to the square before the Musical Theater in Kaunas. With his own eyes, Vytautas related, he had witnessed a young man pour gasoline over himself and set himself on fire. Other youths with long hair had stood around. No one had stopped the young man and no one had intervened as he cried out for someone to put him out of his misery.

Vytautas had more to tell about the aftermath. When the police arrived in the square, he claimed, the long-haired lads had attacked them with knives. The police were reinforced, but more "hippie" types also gathered and began to throw rocks and bricks at them. Order was restored only when troops arrived. A number of young people were arrested and driven away in vehicles. The parents of the dead man were brought to identify him.

This detailed account led up to the reason Vytautas gave for absence from work the next Monday: he had missed the Sunday evening bus to Radviliškis because of the intensive police checks along the way.

Among the listeners that Tuesday morning at the Radviliškis factory were two informers who soon reported what they had heard to their KGB officers. It was decided to invite the loose talker to visit the KGB for a preventive discussion.

Under KGB questioning, Vytautas withdrew his story. A new, simpler narrative emerged. He had not been in the square at the time of Kalanta's suicide, but he had been close by—perhaps 100 yards away. He learned what had transpired there at second hand, from people leaving the square. On Sunday evening he did not miss the bus to Radviliškis; on the contrary, he caught it and returned home, arriving late. On Monday morning he overslept and decided to skip work. On Tuesday he needed an excuse for his Monday absence and at the same time his workmates asked him if he had heard about the events in Kaunas. He made up the rest.

The KGB made Vytautas sign a statement. He admitted making up an excuse for absence from work, apologized for spreading false rumors, promised never to do anything similar again, and asked not to be punished. He had been warned.

What had Vytautas really seen? Most likely, not what he claimed on the Tuesday of his return to work. Then, he had told his co-workers that a crowd of young people was already present in the square at noon on Sunday when Kalanta set himself alight, and that they went on to attack the police. But according to other accounts, the square was relatively empty at midday. Kalanta's parents were not called to identify his body, because he did not die in the square; he was taken to a hospital and died there the next morning. No one attacked the police on Sunday afternoon, and no other witness saw a riot in the square.[33] So it seems that Vytautas just wanted a day off work, and his mistake was to invent an excuse that inevitably drew the attention of the KGB.

The students are on strike

Skaudvile is a pretty village in western Lithuania. From there to Vilnius, the road lies through Kaunas. On May 24, 1972, a telegram was handed in at a post office near Skaudvile. Addressed to the commandant of a hostel for building workers in Vilnius, it read:

> Inform the management that I cannot get from Skaudvile to Vilnius. The roads are jammed. In Kaunas the students are on strike.

At 5 p.m. the telegram reached the district center of Šilale. The Šilale postmaster notified the local KGB.

The KGB officials authorized the cable's transmission—reluctantly. The same evening, they identified the sender and pulled him in for questioning. Jurgis was an employee of the building trust that maintained the Vilnius hostel. From April 25, he was on leave, staying with his girlfriend, a dairymaid on a farm near Skaudvile. (The KGB checked her out: "compromising evidence not found."). He should have been back at work on Tuesday, May 16, but claimed to be unwell—or perhaps he was just reluctant. Having heard about the Kaunas events from villagers nearby, he decided to use them as a reason for further delay.

The ruse was all too transparent. In fact, from May 20 the streets of Kaunas and thereabouts were quiet again.

The KGB did not have the slightest interest in the fact that Jurgis had made up a story in order to take time off work. It was the story he made up that bothered them, combined with his use of the state telegraph system to disseminate it. So the interrogation of Jurgis turned into a preventive warning. He was instructed in "the damaging nature of the content of the telegram and what might be its further consequences." He "acknowledged his incorrect behavior and promised not to engage in similar acts in future."

The matter did not end there. The unfortunate post office clerk who had accepted the telegram in the first place was hauled up before the Šilale postmaster. What was she supposed to have done? He told her: "In similar circumstances she should attempt to persuade the client to alter the content of the text."

In other words, under Soviet rule censorship took many forms. There were the professional censors, whose work was described in chapter 2. But even those whose work was completely unrelated to censorship had a duty to censor the public expressions they encountered at work or in their leisure time. And the ideal citizen censored herself.

Restoring appearances

By warning the people whom they saw as standing on the brink of anti-state criminality, did the KGB hope to change their hearts or just change their behavior? Did they require the psalmist's "broken and contrite heart" of true repentance, or only the simulation of it?

The written record doesn't tell us exactly what happened in the room, let alone what happened in the soul. But fear was the key. It's likely that many encounters were much more threatening and humiliating than appears from the typed summary. No one would leave the room with their sense of the person they were and the person they wanted to be, their integrity, whole and untouched.

Still, it is hard to imagine that many people would change deeply held beliefs and preferences as the result of an hour or so in the hands of the KGB, no matter how difficult and frightening. It is much easier to suppose that most victims quickly understood the script they were supposed to follow and adopted a strategy of obedience and conformity. The KGB could make hostages out of your job, your home, your loved ones, and your children. Wouldn't you prefer to say what had to be said and just get it over with and get out as quickly as possible?

In many cases the confessions of guilt, the realizations of harm done, and the renewed vows of loyalty to Soviet rule were surely insincere. Well, if we can guess that, the KGB officers who witnessed it could probably guess it, too. Yet it seems they were content with lip service.

You could think that this all was part of the decline of the Soviet system: everything now depended on appearances. The KGB demanded the pretence of loyalty and the citizens pretended to supply it. This is true, in a sense, but it also underestimates the importance of appearances.

Forty years before the opening of the Russian archives, when Stalin was barely in his grave, the sociologists Alex Inkeles and Raymond Bauer put their finger on the issue.[34] Soviet leaders, they wrote, did not expect loyalty; on the contrary, they expected their policies to create hostility and assumed that every citizen was at least potentially disloyal. All their efforts went, therefore, into modifying behavior and giving the citizen "no viable alternative except to conform."

Conformist behavior, in turn, had a striking effect. Each person tended to conform, and by conforming mirrored the conformity of those around them. The result was "an exaggerated picture of actual loyalty." Each person concluded that he was the only one to feel alienation from a society in which he had no choice but to live and get along. The Seventh Principle told them: *order is created by appearances*. It was the appearance of order that stabilized the Soviet system of rule; in turn, stability forced everyone into loyalty.

But this was also the weak point in the system. When the first person with enough youthful optimism and irrational courage to stand up and differ did so, all around that person were others who suddenly realized for the first time: "I am not alone." This was the basis of the Fifth Principle: *rebellion spreads like wildfire*. Here is why mass surveillance, unceasing vigilance, and zero tolerance were so important for the KGB. Its answer to the Fifth Principle was the Sixth: *stamp out every spark*. Officials had to be ready to step in at the first sign of some "politically damaging misdemeanor." If they sat back and waited for the second or third sign, it might be too late to prevent a conflagration.

The case is closed

Maria was excited. She heard about the Kalanta affair by listening to foreign radio broadcasts. Married, in her mid-twenties, she was a quality checker at the Sirius factory in Klaipeda. Talking to her workmates, she related what she had heard about the young man's suicide and the disturbances in Kaunas. She went on to raise:

> . . . the lack of freedom in our country, the supposed state of occupation in Lithuania and the Kaunas students' struggle for its independence, and the outrages supposedly perpetrated by the authorities in suppressing the "demonstrations."

The KGB asked about Maria at work. "A frivolous, lazy woman with primitive views and interests, who leads an unrefined way of life." In the official language of the Soviet Union each of these words would carry a particular meaning. "Frivolous": easy-going, possibly in sexual matters. "Lazy": not interested in going the extra mile. "Primitive": not interested in the party line. "Unrefined": not interested in Dostoevsky or Dickens.

Maria was interviewed at work by her bosses. A personal story emerged. She came from a working-class family. Her father drank away his wages. When her elder sister gained a place at the university, Maria had to leave school to bring money into the family.

When challenged to explain the reports, Maria denied them. Then, confronted with more detailed testimony, she crumbled. She blamed her living situation. She and her husband did not have a place of their own; they were living with her parents. Then she blamed her poor understanding of government policies. Finally, she blamed the foreign radio stations for distorting her perceptions of Soviet "actuality."

Then Maria had to listen to a lecture about those government policies that she did not understand, especially about the government policy on nationalities that allowed Soviet Lithuania to exist in the "indissoluble union of free republics" (the opening words of the Soviet Union's national anthem: the union was forever and beyond question, yet the national republics were somehow also free). She also heard about the harm that was done by listening to the voices of Western radio.

As she listens, Maria does not fail to "get" these lessons. A bright light has been switched on inside that supposedly empty head. Now she appreciates how wrong she was, and she says so. More than that, she realizes how bad is the influence on her of those Western radio stations that she listened to. She sees that she herself became part of the infectious spread of bad influences through Soviet society, by passing her harmful thoughts around her workmates. This smart young woman will never in her life do these things again; she will change her ways "fundamentally."

Her bosses have the last word, speaking the lines written for them by the KGB:

> At the end of the preventive-warning discussion, [Maria] was warned that, in the event of a repetition of similar utterances on her side, more severe measures of influence would be applied to her.

There was no need for further surveillance. They closed Maria's case.

CHAPTER SIX

A Grand Tour

In April 1955, the Central Committee of the ruling Soviet Communist Party made a momentous decision: to permit citizens to leave the country as tourists. At first, this permission covered only visits to friendly socialist states, but it was soon extended to the capitalist world. Numbers going abroad were two thousand in 1955, half a million the following year, and a million ten years later.[1]

When Soviet tourists traveled abroad, they did not go alone. Typically, they traveled in groups. A team of watchers accompanied each group at every step. The group typically included a KGB officer under the cover of a tourist, and one or more genuine tourists who were also incidentally—but not accidentally—KGB informers who worked with the officer as a team.

To travel abroad was a privilege, not a right, and only a tiny proportion of Soviet citizens ever qualified. A million outward journeys in 1965 might sound like a lot, and it *was* a lot if you recall that in Stalin's time the borders were entirely closed to tourists. But this was a country of 230 million people, so the rate of foreign travel was still much less than half a percent of the population in a year.[2] In 2014, for comparison, when Russians were more or less free to travel if they had the means to do so, 35 percent of a representative sample reported having traveled abroad at least once, and 8 percent said that they did so at least once a year.[3]

Several barriers had to be overcome before you could go abroad. Most groups were sponsored by a place of work or a cultural organization, so you first had to belong and be well-thought-of in that context. Then, you had to get a passport.

An external passport, that is. The Soviet government issued every citizen what it called a "passport" at age sixteen, but in any other setting this would be recognized as no more than a government ID and residence permit; it did not grant any right to travel abroad. The internal passport was an integral part of the Soviet system of social control because the government used it to store basic information about who you were and where you lived. In fact, whenever the Soviet Union absorbed new territory, one of the first steps was to "passportize" the local population. (The next step was to collate the resulting lists with the findings of political intelligence and mass surveillance and work out who to arrest and imprison or resettle.[4])

The internal passport had no validity at an international border. To cross that border, you needed an external passport. In fact, even an external passport was not enough. To leave the country you needed an external passport with an exit visa, which required you to belong to an approved tourist group with an agreed itinerary and a fixed date of return to the homeland.

To get an external passport with an exit visa was an arduous task with many stages. It began with opportunity. In the "simplest case" described by the Russian biologist Zhores Medvedev, you saw a notice pinned to the board at work: "In the Central Committee of the Trade Union for Medical Workers there are the following tourist places for trips abroad in 1967. To Socialist Countries. . . . To Capitalist Countries: France 10 places, Italy 8 places, Belgium 12 places . . . Cost of the trip 450 rubles. Length of trip: 14 days."[5] It caught your eye. You thought: Paris! Rome! And I can just afford it. And then your troubles began.

A code of conduct

The trouble started with your "exit file." Several months in advance of departure, you began to prepare your documentation. You listed all close relatives with full details of their birth, death, homes, employments, and their war records: how and where did they serve, were they taken prisoner or deported? Then you listed your own details, including everywhere you ever lived and worked. (You're thinking: this is like a foreigner applying for a US visa. But remember: that's for a visa to *enter someone else's* country. This is for a visa to *leave your own*.) Then, you wrote a detailed autobiography. You added a medical report with blood and urine tests, a printout of your heartbeat, X-rays, and the rest. You dropped in a dozen photographs, your marriage certificate, and your children's birth certificates. (You weren't taking your relatives with you. They were to prove that you had good reasons to return.)

To complete your exit file, your boss wrote your character reference, which was confidential. Let's hope the boss thought well of you—your dreams lay in his (or, rarely, her) hands. After that, your file went to the party. First to consider your suitability were the party members in your workplace. Your standing at work and in the community, your political loyalty, marital status, moral fitness, cultural preferences, and personal habits could all be up for discussion. If your case passed this first filter, the file went up to the neighborhood or town party committee, and then to the provincial committee. At the provincial committee the KGB would add what was held in the security files. What you needed at this point was a signal that no "compromising evidence" could be found.

Sometimes the signal was bad, with life-changing consequences. Twice in 1968, for example, a Lithuania KGB informer reported on women who had applied for temporary exit visas to visit relatives in the United States. In both cases he claimed that they intended to defect. And so their applications were rejected.[6]

After making it through all these stages, your case finally reached the officials of the Central Committee in Moscow. There it joined a long queue and waited in line. At this final stage, it had to be scrutinized by the party officials of the "exit commission," who were especially skilled in catching the mistakes made in all the previous stages of consideration. These were the mistakes that allowed unsuitable people through. There was no check for the opposite kind of mistakes, the excessive caution that might have prevented entirely suitable people from traveling.

The final stage would not be complete without a face-to-face interview, so the would-be tourist had to be ready to travel to Moscow. The interview stage gave the party officials the final assurance: Would you give the impression of a worthy representative of Soviet society? Would you stand up for your country against criticism? Would you let it down by getting drunk, into debt, or into bed with a foreigner?

Above all: would you do as you were told? For one purpose of the interview was to provide every tourist with a copy of a 3,000-word secret document, the "Basic Rules of Conduct of Soviet Citizens Visiting Capitalist and Developing Countries." The Basic Rules regulated every aspect of the journey and life abroad: not getting drunk, into debt, or into bed were a small part of it. Above all, the Basic Rules made clear that Soviet travelers should not think of themselves as *going* abroad by their own choice. They were being *sent*, as if on a mission for their country:

> The state, party, and social organizations of the Soviet Union sending Soviet citizens abroad are showing great trust in them. Soviet people are obligated to justify this trust by fulfilling their administrative duties and by irreproachable behavior. Failure to comply with the rules of conduct abroad should be considered as a breach of public duty and of state discipline.[7]

Having passed the interview and signed that you accepted the code of conduct, your *external* passport and visas to travel were almost within reach. Now you had to surrender your *internal* passport; this was to make sure that on return you did not somehow manage to hold onto both documents at once. But after all this, at the last moment even the successful candidate who passed every test might still, suddenly and randomly, be denied permission to leave the country, because this was an economy of shortages and rations. Usually, too many people had applied to travel and been approved, and there was only a fixed number of tickets to go around.

Fellow travelers

In all respects, foreign travel was too important to be left to the individual or to chance. Instead, the KGB had it fully under control. The KGB logged the tourists out and it logged them back in again. More than that, it accompanied them.

To show how it was organized, we'll look into the files of the Lithuania KGB. In January 1972, Lithuania KGB counterintelligence deputy chief Gin'ko listed the anticipated ninety-eight tourist groups leaving the republic month by month between April and December. (As befits a planned economy, it was called "the plan for tourist trips abroad.") Most were visiting other "friendly" socialist countries but a good number were going to Western Europe and a few to North Africa and farther afield. Nearly all groups were sponsored by trade unions, drawing their members from particular industries, trades, and factories. Gin'ko addressed the KGB first ("secret") department chief Kardanovsky:

> We ask you to give instructions to the operational staff to select proven informants that are able to travel abroad and, taking into account the interests of operational expediency, to recommend them to enrol in a tourist visit to capitalist or socialist countries.

Special provisions applied to those visiting capitalist countries and Yugoslavia:

> Decisions about the informants going out to capitalist countries and the Socialist Federative Republic of Yugoslavia are to be sent in advance to the Lithuania KGB second administration, fourth department, for the leadership to determine instructions about to which trade union committees of the republic the informant should present documents in order to take steps to include them in the membership of the tourist group.

Yugoslavia, a communist country, was singled out because its status invited suspicion. Yugoslavia called itself socialist but had gone its own way in foreign and domestic policies. Worse, on the first day of 1967 Yugoslavia had opened its borders to unrestricted foreign travel; this meant that any Soviet citizens who were allowed onto the territory of Yugoslavia could choose to travel onward to any country in the world that would admit them. As a result, visits to Yugoslavia were regarded with as much suspicion as to any NATO member state.

Among more than six hundred citizens allowed to travel abroad from Soviet Lithuania in 1966, one in seven were KGB informers or targets for recruitment as informers. Among the small number permitted to go on private visits, the ratio rose to one in four.[8]

Operationally significant information

The groups went out and came back, and the informants reported. Anne Gorsuch has described Soviet tourism as a kind of theatrical performance.[9] The Communist Party wrote the words. The tourists had to memorize and recite the words for the pleasure of Western audiences. If the tourists were actors, then the KGB watchers mixing with them under cover were the critics. For every tour that went out and came back, the returning watchers wrote a review and evaluated the performance.

They wrote—at length. This was a problem, as we learn from a KGB report (not dated, but 1971 or 1972): "On the unification of reporting documentation on foreign visits." The problem began from the fact that there was no prescribed format for a report. This gave the KGB officers and informers discretion to write freely, and they used this discretion to the fullest. Reports often included page after page of daily schedules, descriptions of activities, character sketches, and other personal impressions. Somewhere in the mass of unnecessary detail were scattered the few "operationally significant" facts, which could be extracted only with great difficulty:

> The information useful for counterintelligence that was contained in the 70-page report of an operative on results of his short-term travel to countries of the Middle and Near East could have been set out in 2 or 3 pages without loss.

Worse, the operationally significant information might be missing altogether; some writers enjoyed reminiscing on paper so much that they forgot the true purpose of the report.

What was the true purpose of such reports? It should have been to "collate facts," "identify persons," to record "the time and place of manifestation of foreigners in the field of view, the objects of their interest, etc." (These are all phrases that the KGB used in the report already mentioned to describe what was required.)

How to ensure that these facts, and only these, were communicated? The answer seemed to lie in information technology. This was the early 1970s, a time when a lot of people thought computers would finally solve all the little glitches and malfunctions of the Soviet Union's centralized command system. The KGB shared this expectation. The idea was to put the intelligence gathered from foreign tourism in a computerized database. The starting point of the database would be the reports of the informants returning from foreign trips. A database is made up of fields, and the way you capture information for each field is on a form. So, the KGB designed a form suitable for gathering this information and entering it on punch cards, which were the last form of physical computer memory before magnetic tape.

When you try to capture information on a standardized form, the most difficult thing is to train people to use it properly. So, the KGB circulated detailed instructions about how to fill in the form. In case that wasn't enough, it also circulated an exemplary record of the operationally useful information arising from a real foreign visit, using the same form. This record tells a story of Soviet citizens on vacation, seen through the eyes of their watchers.

The group assembles

A group of tourists has been sponsored by the trade union council of the province surrounding Kiev, the capital city of Soviet

Ukraine. The group is "non-specialized." This means the members are of varied occupations; they are not all athletes or all doctors, for example. Over three weeks in 1970, from September 30 to October 21, eighteen lucky people will visit New York; Washington, DC; Chicago; Toronto; Ottawa; and Montreal. It won't be all vacation; during their travels they will also pass through a number of North American centers of research on assorted topics.

Among the group are the watchers. Six pairs of eyes belong to tourists who are linked one way or another with the KGB of the Kiev province. In charge is Lieutenant-Colonel Semyonov, traveling as a history teacher from a Kiev secondary school. He can call on the services of five informers, one code-named "White" and four identified by their initials—"BIS," GPI," "KIP," and "USP."

As this list shows, the KGB arranged its informers in two circles, some with code names (such as "White," always in quotation marks) and others known by their initials (such as "BIS"). Code names belonged to informers of the inner circle, who had signed a written undertaking to collaborate with the KGB. The Russian word for the code-named informers was *agent*, but they were mainly civilians, not secret agents in the Western sense. Informers of the outer circle, known by their initials, were known as "trusted persons." The trusties had not signed any agreement to collaborate, and did not have code names, so they were known by their initials (again, always in quotation marks). Lack of formality made it easier to join the second circle, but the political requirements were more demanding. This is because a trusted person could not be untrustworthy—for example, he could not be a usual suspect with "compromising evidence" against him. Informers of the first circle did not have to meet such a high standard, and this might be why they did have to sign a written agreement. While some informers joined the first circle from conviction, the KGB recognized others who were recruited under pressure ("based on compromising evidence")—in other words, because they had got into trouble and could be coerced.[10]

In the group bound for North America, some of the informers have been assigned tasks before departure. "White" is to try to obtain information on a suspect, code-named "Dagger," whom the Moscow city KGB thinks might have a link to foreign intelligence. "USP" is to meet up with a relative to glean some intelligence (he will fail because the relative won't agree to meet). Officer Semyonov will meet secretly with KGB residents in America and another person code-named "Aftermath." And "BIS" will claim to know Semyonov as a teacher and so validate his cover story among the tourists.

The visit will take place in a wider geopolitical context. The KGB warns that Zionists are mounting an anti-Soviet campaign in the West. Another development is a surprise: French-Canadian separatists kidnap the Québecois minister of labor, Pierre Laporte, on October 10, 1970 (while the tourists are in New York), and kill him on October 17 (while they are in Montreal). Soviet diplomats will brief the tourists on how to respond if they encounter Zionist demonstrators, and what to do if one of the tourists disappears.

The KGB's tradecraft will turn out to have surprising gaps. Even before the tourists leave, the report notes, the KGB's own arrangements have damaged Semyonov's cover as an ordinary schoolteacher:

> In agreement with the plan the officer did not disclose his affiliation with the KGB among the tourists. However, because of the established schedule of preparation for the trip and reporting requirements, the officer had to leave Kiev for Moscow earlier than the tourists and after returning from abroad he had to leave Moscow later for Kiev. This circumstance caused some tourists to express opinions about the officer's possible affiliation with the

KGB. For this reason some tourists kept the officer at a distance, which hindered his work to a certain extent.

One of the informers, "GPI," will also be of limited use. The problem is not that his cover is blown, but that it is too good. For no one has instructed him in how to identify officer Semyonov, and Semyonov doesn't know how to identify the informer. And so, no contact takes place between them during the entire trip. In most tourist groups, in other words, most of the tourists will speculate about which of them has been planted by the KGB—the exceptions being the plants, who know. But on this trip, *everyone* wonders who is with the KGB—even the KGB!

Hostile contacts

In the course of a three-week journey there are several incidents of operational interest. The report divides them into some that were forced on the group by hostile strangers, and others that flowed from the unforced errors (or worse) of the tourists themselves. The action begins in the dining room of the Hotel New York at lunch time on Thursday, October 1. Two Americans approach the tourists and sit with them. We'll call them Smith and Jones. Smith is the younger of the two, around forty years old, tall and dark, with a military bearing. Jones, a few years older, is short and fair. Both are Russian speakers. They say they are geologists, but the KGB's New York resident has Jones on file as a CIA member. They fall into conversation with two group members, to whom we must now be introduced.

Alex, a thirty-three-year-old civil engineer, is married. He works in Kiev as a senior manager in industrial construction. His company position is described as "chief of special directorate." In this context, "special" might refer to some technical specialization but it might also signify a security dimension. A party member with a college degree and a working knowledge of English, Alex has been cleared for access to top-secret information (in the Soviet security classification, "top secret" is the second highest level; above it there are only the "special files," restricted to the inner core of Kremlin decision-makers). The record notes "no compromising evidence" in his KGB file.

Paul, who is single at forty-six, is a middle-manager in the petrochemical industry. His plant is described as "secure" (the Russian word is *rezhimnyi*), meaning that the KGB directly regulates its security. The implication is that Paul's work has some kind of defense significance. Like Alex, Paul has been cleared for access to "top-secret" information. Paul went to a specialist secondary school (but not to college) and speaks English.

For a chance encounter the Americans have some surprisingly specific questions, and it turns out that Alex and Paul could potentially provide answers. The Americans want to know about titano-magnetite sand, a mineral that is found in Ukraine and is used for industrial pigments and metallic coatings: where is it extracted and how is it used in industrial construction? They ask about the Kiev chemical plant: what is the chemical make-up of its products? Finally, they enquire after a research chemist employed at the plant; they name him and say they know his published works.

The KGB does not take this lightly. On the contrary, Semyonov writes: "The questions in which Smith and Jones are interested are secret. Information about the utilization of titano-magnetite sand deposits in construction is a state secret, and the chemical products factory is secure." As for the research chemist whom Smith and Jones name, Paul knows exactly who this is and so does the KGB. The object of the Americans' curiosity just happens to be deputy director of the same chemical plant where Paul is a manager.

What should the Ukrainians say? They reply politely but correctly: They are on holiday. They don't want to talk business. The name of the research chemist is a common one, shared by many others at work. It's hard to know which one the Americans would have in mind.

The next instance of hostile activity transpires a few days later in Ottawa. Staying at the Lord Elgin hotel, the tourists daily receive anti-Soviet leaflets sponsored by NTS, the "People's Labor Union," one of the oldest and most persistent emigrant organizations opposed to communist rule in Russia. "Without reading them," we are told:

> The Soviet tourists handed these leaflets over to the group leader who, with the agreement of the [KGB] officer, demonstratively destroyed them before the eyes of the hotel staff. Because this measure did not bring the NTS antics to an end, the group submitted a written protest to the city authorities about the NTS actions. After this, the NTS actions diminished.

Viktor is the object of unwanted attention in the third untoward event, which takes place in Montreal. Married, sixty-one, Viktor is Russian by origin. With a higher degree in engineering science, he is a senior architect at a design institute for industrial construction, which comes under the same ministry as Alex. Although the institute is nominally civilian, it too is classified as a secure facility under KGB supervision. Despite this, Viktor is not cleared for access to classified information. This is his second trip to the States; in 1965 he attended a professional conference in Washington, DC. He speaks English.

On October 15, Viktor enters a bookshop next to the hotel. After half an hour he is accosted by a bespectacled, gray-haired American, who says: "I remember you from the Washington congress in 1965!" This person identifies himself as Lee, an engineer.

Now, a Russian-speaking American engineer of the same name certainly existed, because his reports on Soviet technology can be found in the Library of Congress catalog. And Viktor confirms afterward that he did have a "fleeting encounter" with Lee in 1965, although he doubts it was enough for the American to remember him well. In the bookshop, the American invites Viktor back to his hotel. Politely, the Russian declines: "Our schedule is too full," he says, regretfully.

Rushing back to his hotel room, Viktor finds that his possessions have been disturbed: his notes about the trip, which he usually leaves on top, are now under some books at the bottom of his suitcase. Has his room been searched in his absence?

And a final doubtful circumstance occurs. For the duration of the trip the tourists have a guide and interpreter, a young British woman called Carol who works for the Cosmos travel company. Carol attends to the group exceptionally well—too well, as officer Semyonov and informant "White" agree. The group has a number of North American research centers on its itinerary. The young woman shows too much interest in the more technical aspects of conversation between the visitors and their hosts. The officer particularly recalls a tour of a management research center in Chicago where the questions were more than usually probing, the answers were more than usually detailed, and Carol seemed to be more than usually nervous. Who is she, really?

Breaking the rules

There are no other reports of hostile activity. Everything else that goes wrong is the fault of the tourists. Three of them have blotted their copybooks in ways that will not be forgotten. Alex (the builder) and Viktor (the architect) are caught out badly in Washington, DC, when some Americans become curious about the group. "Who are you? Where are you from?" When it comes out that they are from the Soviet Union, the mood darkens. A woman asks: "Why did your country invade Czechoslovakia?" For it is barely two years since the "Prague Spring" of 1968 was ruthlessly suppressed by the armed forces of its socialist neighbors, including the Soviet Army and the KGB. In the official Soviet version of events, Soviet troops entered Czechoslovakia at the request of the Prague government to help it stabilize the country against a subversive threat. This is the answer the Soviet tourists should have given, but in the pressure of the moment Alex and Viktor forget their lines:

> [They] not only did not explain to the woman the true state of affairs but they also did wrong in this situation by stating that they were not Russians but Ukrainians and so had nothing to say to her about the events in Czechoslovakia.

The officer will have to speak to them afterward to draw their attention to their incorrect behavior, which has clearly violated the Soviet travelers' code of conduct:

> The Soviet citizen abroad must be an active advocate of the foreign policy of the Soviet Union.

Igor takes the stage for the final scene. Married, forty-two, Igor is the only blue-collar worker. A graduate of a specialist secondary school, he works as a senior electrician in a power plant a couple of hours' drive from Kiev. He does not have (or require) security clearance, but he does live in a district that is closed to foreigners. Igor is not a party member and speaks no English.

We might wonder how even a senior electrician could have saved up enough to join these middle-class tourists on a three-week expedition to another continent. But skilled workers employed in important Soviet production facilities were paid well compared with other social groups. Many citizens had substantial savings, not because they were rich but because the economy did not provide them with much to spend their money on. In fact, we'll see that even the cost of his ticket to America did not exhaust the funds at Igor's disposal. He had enough with him to accomplish another purpose, too.

For Igor, this expedition to the metropolises of North America is a once-in-a-lifetime, never-to-be-repeated opportunity, and not for tourism of the usual kind. He has already planned how to exploit it fully. The trusty "BIS" has observed that Igor's suitcases are bulging with goods that he thinks might be novelties for the American shopper: Russian vodka and caviar. Wherever he goes, he sells these to Americans for cash. "BIS" has tried to dissuade him, but without success. Soon, Igor's wallet is bulging with dollars.

As you read the report you start to wonder: what will Igor do with the money? The answer is made clear in Montreal on October 16, when Igor gets stupendously drunk and goes to a brothel. There he runs up a bill of such magnitude that all his accumulated savings cannot cover it. The madam refuses to let him leave and threatens a scandal.

Igor has broken so many of the rules in the book in the Soviet travelers' code of conduct! One rule states: "currency exchange is carried out only in Soviet organizations or with the assistance of Soviet foreign institutions in the banking institutions of the host country." Another warns the traveler: "to hire foreigners for personal services is permitted only in exceptional cases with the approval of the Soviet embassy and consulate." The life of Soviet citizens abroad is required to be "exemplary and modest. You must strictly match your outgoings with your salary, not get into debt, and buy nothing on credit or in installments." It is prohibited "to visit night clubs and cinemas that show anti-Soviet or pornographic films, and other places of questionable entertainment," "to take part in games of chance," and "to abuse alcoholic spirits and to appear intoxicated in public places and on the street." And in all matters the Soviet traveler is obliged "to obey strictly the orders and instructions of the head of delegation, team or group." Igor has left this rule book in shreds and tatters.

What is to be done? The group leader steps in. There is no fuss; Igor's bill is settled. The Soviet embassy staff packs Igor's bags and puts him on a plane home.

So, a failure for Soviet foreign policy. But what about Igor: was it a success or a failure for him? For one day of his life he did exactly as he pleased, regardless of the cost to others. For this he, too, paid a price. Beforehand, he invested his life savings. Afterward, he faced the wrath of the Soviet state and the indignation of his family. Most likely he promised them all that he would never do it again, and on its side the KGB made sure he would never get the chance.

Tourism as a weapon

Tourism as a weapon of foreign policy was an anomaly of the Cold War. It was always a double-edged weapon. When the weapon worked, loyal Soviet tourists went abroad, spoke up for their country's policies, avoided scandal and excess, and returned home with their beliefs unshaken. But the files of the KGB are full of cases where the weapon failed. In those cases, when exposed to the questioning and temptations of a free society and a market economy, men and women like Alex, Viktor, and Igor took a line of least resistance or actively sought the opportunity to misbehave. And many who went abroad and maintained the proper outward appearances during and after their visits must have had their inner beliefs shaken by the visible evidence of the greater freedom and productivity of the Western market economies.

Perhaps Soviet tourism met a domestic need. By sending tourists abroad and watching how they behaved, the KGB found out about their own people. No watcher, however careful and acute, could have learned Igor's innermost dreams by tapping his phone or following him on the streets. No one could have plumbed the shallowness of Alex's and Viktor's convictions by watching them applaud official slogans at scripted party meetings. Let them breathe freely and without fear for a few days, and the watchers might begin to discern their deeper preferences and motivations.

Tourism as a weapon was not confined to Soviet citizens traveling abroad. Just as the Soviet Union tried to use its tourists to gather observations and exert influence, the KGB assumed in turn that every Western visitor to the Soviet Union was a potential spy or enemy agent. Few Westerners visited the Soviet Union before the 1970s. (I was one, making my first visit in a group of English schoolchildren in 1964.) When the tourists began to arrive, the KGB was ready for them, using methods of covert surveillance that it code-named "D" (searching), "F" and "O" (listening and watching), and "U" (photography).

A report of September 1966 from KGB counterintelligence in Moscow, classified "top secret," recounts the experience of applying these methods to foreign visitors—mostly tourists or diplomats.[11] It notes that foreign visitors often carry letters or make notes that they are careful not to leave lying around the hotel room, but keep about their persons, which makes access difficult. For breaking into the target's hotel room, the KGB recommends women dressed as hotel staff or men in the guise of electricians and plumbers. To find out what is being carried, the targets must sometimes be separated from their clothing. This can be done by arranging a visit to a spa, a beach, a medical consultant, or even an underground installation that requires disrobing in order to put on protective clothing.

Covert listening and watching are best carried out by equipment installed in hotel room fixtures, not forgetting bathrooms and vestibules, and in railway and boat cabins, including corridors and gangways. If not all rooms in the hotel are equipped, this has the potential downside that the foreign agencies will try to keep account of which rooms foreigners are placed in, so it is best that static equipment is rotated from room to room periodically.

Finally, remote photography can sometimes achieve what other methods cannot. The example is given of a diplomat who, visiting a town, made notes every evening that he always kept on his person and always shielded from view. The expedient was found of placing a phone call to his room while he was making notes. He went to pick up the phone, placing his notes on the table. This provided sufficient opportunity to take a picture of them.

In fact, the Soviet travelers' code of conduct was written on the assumption that the FBI *would* behave in the way that the KGB actually *did* behave:

> The intelligence agencies of the imperialist states, using modern equipment, apply methods of eavesdropping, covert observation and photography, and also methods of deception, blackmail, fraud, and intimidation. The agents of the capitalist intelligence agencies often operate under the cover of interpreters, doctors and teachers, tailors, vendors, taxi drivers, waiters, hairdressers, and other service providers.

Some of our methods are now known

Did the West have its own code of conduct for citizens visiting the East? There was certainly government advice, which I once received. In 1972 I was a graduate student, interested in Russia's economic history. I applied to visit Moscow University on a scheme that was set up under the British–Soviet cultural treaty of the time. A group of us went out to the Soviet Union together. We were students of history, social science, arts, and math, women as well as men.

All those in the group were asked to attend a briefing at the Foreign Office in London before we left. There, a pleasant chap in his forties told us that we would be objects of interest to the KGB. Among the people we would meet, he said, would be informers who had been instructed to keep tabs on us. We might be watched or followed. For most of us there would be little or no risk and we would never see or hear the KGB around us. However, we should assume we were being observed and we should avoid behaving badly or breaking the law.

In the worst case, our adviser went on, there might be an attempt to compromise us by using alcohol, drugs, or sex. Apparently, a pretty young woman might take her clothes off and climb into my bed late at night. One of us, a female scholar, asked if this might happen to her too. Our adviser had to think about this one before conceding the point. He went on: this might be a prelude to blackmail or intimidation, leading to our recruitment as an informer or spy. If anything like that happened, the best thing was to go straight to the embassy; the staff would do its best to get us safely home. It was fatherly advice, delivered in a manner that was friendly and also a bit patronizing. We listened carefully but skeptically.

Set side by side, the Soviet travelers' code of conduct overlapped considerably with our Foreign Office advice. In addition to being told not to get drunk, into debt, or into bed, we were told that we would be representing our country. The context was very different in other respects. We had foreign passports as a right, not a privilege. We did not have to sign for any government secrets in order to leave the country. Nothing obliged us to follow the advice we were given; we just had to listen. As to whether any of us was reporting back to the security services, I had no idea about that. I believe that one or two of the British students who went out in those years went on to careers in the Foreign Office or MI5, but that was later.

Despite the Foreign Office briefing, the experience of student life in Brezhnev-era Moscow was something for which none of us was fully prepared. In Russia it was easy to make friends. Not everyone wanted to be friends with us for good reasons, so we also had to learn to be careful. We were watchful for would-be friends who might also be informers, and this was a completely unfamiliar way of thinking that I believe each of us found stressful in various ways. Having made friends carefully, we had to learn to be careful in other matters for the sake of our friends. We learned the habits of life in a police state: when to joke and when not to attract attention; when to tell the truth about where we were going and when to pretend; which phones to use and which to avoid; and so on. And we were careful: we probably made a few mistakes, but none of us was sent home in disgrace, as happened from time to time in other years.

But it was all a bit shadowy. There was so much we did not and could not know. We speculated a lot: Was anyone watching us or listening to us? (No idea.) Where exactly were the limits that no one should cross? (We didn't find out because nobody crossed them.) We didn't *feel* like a strategic threat or asset to either side: did they really care about us at all? And the man from the Foreign Office: did he really know what he was talking about, or was he just trying to frighten us with tales of the bogeyman?

So, it was with much more than scholarly interest that I chanced upon a secret memorandum that went around the KGB in the summer of 1969.[12] The subject of the report was the new advice issued by the British security service for "persons visiting communist countries." The British advice is summarized on the following lines: Traveling to communist countries, and especially the Soviet Union, you were likely to meet people who have been commissioned to keep tabs on you. They would be interested in any personal weaknesses that might help to trap you. For most there would be little or no risk but it was a good idea to behave legally and sensibly. In the worst case there might be an attempt to compromise you by means of alcohol, drugs, or sex. This might be a prelude to recruitment as an informer or spy by means of blackmail or intimidation. If that happened, the best thing was to go straight to the embassy; the staff would do its best to extract you safely.

This sounded uncomfortably familiar. As I read on, I was twenty-three once more. I felt an inner tension that was eventually translated into increasing suspense. For I could not anticipate how the report would evaluate the facts that it contained. How would the writer conclude? In what terms would the KGB officer rate the diplomat's advice? What reasons would he give to refute the slanderous implications? How much indignation would he muster? His last words fell on me like the east wind from Siberia:

> When working with emigrants and foreigners, we will need to take into account the fact that they have knowledge . . . of some of the methods of work of Soviet intelligence and counterintelligence.

CHAPTER SEVEN

One Day We Will Live without Fear

The evening of Thursday, November 10, 1966, was cold and clear. At the Vilnius airport, flight 6340 from Odessa was several hours behind schedule. It touched down at 11:20 p.m. Among its passengers was Leila, a young woman.[1] On the airfield, she was greeted by her mother, her older brother, another man, and a teenage boy. Her mother took her to one side; for several minutes they clung to each other and cried. The men gathered her cases. They left in a taxi for the center of town, where they entered an apartment. By this time it was the small hours of the next day.

Leila was wearing an overcoat, brown gloves, and black boots. She was tall, well proportioned, with dark brown hair, an oval face, a straight nose, and mouth and teeth of average size. She looked younger than her age, which was 34.

We know these things because there was a watcher in the shadows, making notes.

"Their ideological banner is Zionism"

Lithuania KGB chairman Colonel Juozas Petkevičius, speaking, "On the tasks of the republic's state security agencies in the struggle with the ideological diversions of the adversary" to a meeting of the Lithuania KGB operative staff, July 19, 1968:

> Jewish nationalists are carrying on malicious propaganda against the USSR. Their ideological banner is Zionism, at the basis of which lies the idea of a "unified Jewish nation," supposedly encompassing Jews of all classes and all countries of the world. A whole range of Zionist organizations is active abroad, among which are counted a grand total of more than 1.5 million people. These organizations, closely bound up with the intelligence agencies of the USA, are directly realizing the tasks of establishing contact with Jews living in the USSR, and are trying to imbue them with the thought that the Soviet state has a hostile attitude to Jews, and incline them to emigrate to Israel.[2]

Lithuania KGB Lieutenant Colonel Kardanovsky, speaking about "The condition of measures to improve counterintelligence work on exposing the agent network of the adversary and verification and investigation of persons suspected of links with them" to a meeting of Lithuania KGB city and district commissioners called to discuss the results of work in 1966, on February 20, 1967:

> As well as seeking sources of military, economic, and political information, the adversary's intelligence looks at the territory of our republic as a trampoline for projection of its agent network into the interior of the Soviet Union.
>
> [. . .] The American and especially West German and Israeli embassies in Moscow are trying to carry out disruptive actions aimed at kindling inclinations toward emigration among persons of Jewish nationality and persons who consider themselves German.[3]

A complicated place to be born

Leila was born into a Jewish family in eastern Poland in 1932, the youngest of three children. She had an older brother and sister, David and Golda.

In this part of Europe, legal discrimination against Jews was centuries old. Until 1917 it was part of the Russian Empire. In 1791, Catherine the Great established the Pale of Settlement and compelled the Jews of the Empire not already living beyond it to convert to Orthodox Christianity or else migrate there. The territory beyond the Pale included much of present-day Lithuania, Poland, Belarus, and Ukraine. Even there, Jews were not permitted to own land or live in the larger cities, so that many small towns developed large Jewish populations. One of these towns was Leila's birthplace, Szarkowszczyzna (Šarkaŭščyzna, pronounced *Shar-KOV-shcheez-nuh*—the stress falls on the second syllable). There and elsewhere, Jews clustered in the professions, the skilled trades, and marketing, making up a significant fraction of the provincial lower middle class.

An independent Poland emerged from World War I and the Russian Empire's collapse. Polish nation-building led to ethnic rivalry and new pressures on Poland's Jews. Their communities suffered economically from adverse discrimination by the government and their non-Jewish neighbors.[4]

In August 1939 Stalin and Hitler agreed secretly to divide Poland between them. In September, Polish territory was torn in half, the western part seized by Germany and the eastern part by the Soviet Union. While most non-Jewish Poles resisted this double betrayal, many Jews were prepared to give the communists the benefit of the doubt. Leila and her family became Soviet citizens. When Germany attacked the Soviet Union in 1941, she was evacuated with her parents and older sister a thousand miles to the east, to Tatarstan. Thus, her family escaped the Holocaust, and the massacre of the Jews in Szarkowszczyzna which took place on July 18, 1942. Her older brother, David, born in 1920, fought in the Red Army and survived. Her father died of some other cause, however, in 1944.

After the war, Leila's birthplace did not revert to Polish jurisdiction because Poland itself was moved several hundred miles to the west. It lost forever the eastern territories that Stalin had seized in 1939, being compensated on the opposite side by the provinces of Pomerania and Silesia, which were taken from Germany. As a result, Leila and her family remained Soviet citizens. Now her brother, David, settled in Vilnius, the capital of Soviet Lithuania, and Leila joined him there with her sister and mother. Leila returned to school.

In 1950, just eighteen, Leila married Adam, then doing military service in the Kaliningrad district. The Kaliningrad district is today a Russian enclave on the Baltic Sea, cut off entirely from the Russian "mainland" by Poland and Lithuania. Leila moved there to be with her husband and to study. In 1952 she had a son.

The aftermath of World War II saw huge forced migrations across Eastern and Central Europe. As frontiers were redrawn, millions of Germans were expelled from their homes in western Poland, previously eastern Germany. Millions of eastern Poles like Leila were stranded on what was now Soviet territory. In the 1950s, agreements between Moscow and Warsaw allowed tens of thousands of former Poles to migrate to the new Poland. This included many of Jewish descent, for whom Poland became a point of transit on the way to a new homeland in Israel.

In 1957 Leila and her husband were able to leave the Soviet Union for Poland with their son. The following year they left Poland for Israel, where they settled outside Tel Aviv. Adam worked as a doctor; Leila trained and found work as a clinical radiologist. They had a second child.

Time passed. Leila's older sister, Golda, who had also gone to Israel, died young. Leila missed her mother and her brother who were still living in Vilnius. Leila's mother was unwell. In the first weeks of 1966, Leila applied to the Soviet embassy to visit her family for two months. The embassy referred her request to the KGB in Vilnius.

In Vilnius the KGB pulled Leila's "exit file" from 1952. They wrote to find out what their colleagues in Kaliningrad had on Leila and her husband. They sniffed around her mother and brother, looked up their files, made floor plans of their apartments, and made enquiries among their neighbors and about their friends. A report on the family's current situation was obtained from an informer, "K," on May 14. On that basis, Major Shneyerov of Lithuania KGB counterintelligence approved Leila's application on July 24.

Since Leila would not arrive until November, this gave both sides four months to make their preparations.

We will be together again

Leila to David in a letter from Israel, early October 1966:

> My dear!
>
> At last I can share my great happiness: I have received permission. I was afraid to write about this to Mama because, although it would make her happy, it would also make her anxious. I imagine that she would immediately lose her peace and quiet (as I have lost mine). So in spite of the fact that I wanted to send a telegram immediately, I have held myself back. Do as you think best, to tell her now or nearer to my visit. . . . Anyway, my darlings, I think we will be together for the November holidays [marking the anniversary of the Bolshevik Revolution on November 7], but I'll say more exactly in the next letter.

Waiting

Thursday, November 10, 8:30 p.m., on the phone at Leila's brother's apartment:

Woman	Yes.
Man	Hello. It's Danny.
Woman	Hello.
Man	How are things? Has she not arrived yet?
Woman	We're waiting. Not so far.
Man	They'll probably arrive tomorrow or the day after.
Woman	Tomorrow, I think.
Man	Is David over there [meaning: not with you]?
Woman	He's there.
Man	Oh well, sorry I disturbed you.
Woman	You're welcome.

Initiating observation

Report from informant "Kharitonov" (called "the source"), taken by officer Chernov, February 14, 1966 (excerpts):

> In conversation with the source, David said his sister Leila would soon [. . .] come to him from Israel [. . .] David invited the source to visit when his sister arrives.
>
> **Assignment:** Suggested to "Kharitonov" that, by corresponding with the brother and in dealing with acquaintances, he should clarify the persons intending to visit the Lithuanian SSR under private visas or as tourists.
>
> **Actions:** Retrieve Leila's file about her departure to the Polish People's Republic from the archive of the Visa and Registration Department and compile a report from it to check against records.

> Collect full verification information on David and implement full checks on him. Copy [this] report to comrade Zakharov.

Report from informant "Kharitonov," taken by officer Chernov, November 2, 1966 (excerpts):

> David promised the source to let him know when the sister arrives so that he can meet with her. The source knows Leila well in so far as she grew up, as they say, in his arms. She herself will visit the source's apartment.
>
> **Assignment:** Suggested to the source that he maintains contact with David and also meets with Leila. In dealing with the latter, to clarify her inclinations, contacts, and conduct.
>
> **Actions:** Copy [this] report to comrade Shneyerov.

Report from informant "Kharitonov," taken by officer Chernov, November 14, 1966 (excerpts):

> On Thursday [November 10] . . . the source went to the station [actually airport] to meet her, because David's wife asked the source to join the reunion. . . . At the reunion, conversation was general, concerning Leila's journey. The source drove them home, that is, to David's apartment. They invited the source to dinner on November 13.
>
> **Assignment:** Maintain contact with David and his sister Leila to elicit her contacts, conduct, and inclinations.
>
> **Actions:** Copy [this] report to comrade Shneyerov.

Leila's movements were watched for three weeks from the night she arrived. But this was not all. Her letters were intercepted. A tap was in place on the phone at her brother's apartment, where she would stay. From within the intimate circle that greeted her on arrival, the KGB would receive several reports from "Kharitonov." Other old friends of the family who would also submit reports on Leila to the KGB during her visit were "Augulis" (November 23), "Tomaz" (December 13), "S" (December 14 and 28 and January 4), "Petrov" (December 17), "Margarita" (December 28), and "Lyova" (January 10). If you're still counting, we should add "K" (May 14) to make eight informers in total.

The resources of the Lithuania KGB were fully mobilized for Leila's visit to Vilnius.

Do you know who I am?

How did Leila spend her first days back in her homeland? It appears that she did not leave her brother's apartment for thirty-six hours. She finally emerged at 1:10 p.m. on Saturday, November 12, with her brother and nephew. They strolled, window-shopped, and made repeated calls from public phone booths. On the first day they met only one old friend, who came out from the shop where she worked to greet them. On another day Leila went out with her nephew. They met with one friend in the street, and surprised another at work:

> At 11:25 they entered Gosbank [the USSR State Bank] on Lenin Prospect, where the nephew asked some question at windows number fourteen, sixteen, and seventeen. When the nephew left window number seventeen ("Income Tax") and went back to the object, he said something to her. After this the object went up to the aforementioned window and said: "Now, citizen, answer my question. Do you know who I am?" The woman bank worker was silent for a minute, and then said loudly: "Leila!" and went round to her, they embraced and talked about something for a minute.

On this occasion, as on others, there was more than one shadow. One followed Leila as she continued around the town, calling on another friend at home (who was out). Another waited at the bank for the employee to leave work and trailed her home.

On every occasion that Leila met with a "new" contact, the same procedure was followed. First, the watcher assigned the contact a new code name. Then, the code name was matched with the real identity of the person, including name, date and city of birth, ethnicity, registered address, the date and police station where the address was registered, and place of work. For completeness the same was then done for everyone else registered at the same address: wives, husbands, grandmothers, children. Finally, all these details were referred to the local records departments of the KGB and the police with a request to search for "compromising evidence" on each person.

In all cases, the form was returned either with the answer "No information" or with a list of names and overseas addresses with whom the subject had corresponded. From such details we know that Leila's circle was generally Jewish and that a number of her contacts had friends and relatives in Israel with whom they were in touch by letter.

To outward appearances, Leila's behavior was ordinary. She went everywhere with her brother, or her nephew, or both. All the time, they talked. But about what? The watcher was rarely within earshot, and all too often could report only "said something," "asked something," "laughed," "said goodbye."

At first, the conduct of Leila and her family could be construed as wary. On Saturday, November 12, their first day "out," they made many calls from public telephones. This might seem odd given that calls from a public kiosk were charged and they had a perfectly good phone at home which gave access to free local calls. (The charge from a public phone was minimal: two kopecks. The problem was to have a sufficient supply of two-kopeck pieces, which were prized for this reason.) But using public telephones was a habit, born of caution. As a visitor to Moscow in the early 1970s, I learned quickly: Don't use the kiosks in the university or the phone in your hotel room to call your friends; these are probably monitored. Use the phones in the street.

The watcher also noted that Leila and her brother were particularly watchful at certain times. On that first day, for example, David talked on a public phone:

> . . . meanwhile attentively watching the street and the passersby, while the object and her nephew stood to one side, talking among themselves, and watching each way.

On Monday, November 21, Leila dined out with her brother and a friend. The watcher notes how they behaved on the way:

> I must remark that, walking on Gor'ky Street and particularly on Geležinkelio Street, David and the foreign woman talked animatedly and more than once stopped one in front of the other so that the citizens walking behind could be seen, and at this time David watched the public and tried to camouflage his actions by a show of affection to the [female] foreigner (he touched her forehead with his finger), giving the appearance of a person intently engaged in conversation.

So, perhaps Leila and her brother were watchful. (They had reason to be, for they were, in fact, being watched.) Or there might be another explanation: they actually were "intently engaged in conversation," so much that they could not do anything else than to stop walking and face and touch each other.

What else happened? One day David came home with two parcels. Another day, Leila went out to dinner with friends, who gave her an envelope. On this occasion, all the couples were followed home. On one outing, Leila and her brother took a taxi. The driver was duly code-named, identified, and checked. There was a day when Leila went to the Vilnius Hotel and dropped a letter into the airmail box. Noting this, the watcher added: "(reported to OTO comrade Burokovaitė)." OTO was the KGB department of technical services, responsible for opening letters and tapping phones. Comrade Burokovaitė arranged for Leila's letter to be intercepted, so that it met with a short delay. The next day, comrade Shneyerov made a note that Leila wrote to ask her husband if he could lay his hands on a white cable for an electric stove, and to ask after a sick friend. Another time, Leila took a letter out of her handbag and read it. But what did it say? The watcher was too far away to read over her shoulder.

It is hard to say that anything else happened. Of course, the watchers might have found out more if they had bothered to work on weekends. The only Saturday they worked was Leila's first in Vilnius, and they did not work on Sundays at all. At weekends, for all they knew, Leila might have been visiting closed military facilities or painting Zionist slogans on the walls of the old Jewish quarter. In any case, after three weeks the street watchers on Leila were withdrawn.

Call me back

Friday, November 11, 9:10 p.m., on the phone at Leila's brother's apartment:

MAN	Yes?
DANNY	Hello, it's Danny.
MAN	Hello, hello, Danny.
DANNY	Well, has Leila arrived?
MAN	She's arrived.

DANNY I'd like to see her.
MAN Well, come over.
DANNY Can she come to the phone?
MAN Do you want to say hello to her on the phone?
DANNY Call her.
LEILA Hello!
DANNY Greetings.
LEILA *Shalom*, greetings, Danny!
DANNY [I congratulate] you on your arrival.
LEILA Thanks. So, are you coming over?
DANNY We're coming over.
LEILA Come over, we'll fix it. How are the children?
DANNY Thanks.
LEILA We'll expect you tomorrow.
DANNY Good, we'll come.
LEILA Thanks.
DANNY Goodbye.
LEILA Goodbye.

In most telephone conversations, the speakers are identified only if their names are used in the conversation. Freda, who is called in the next conversation, is fully identified in advance. Freda lives in Riga, the capital city of Latvia. Most likely she is identified so easily because in the Soviet Union at this time intercity calls could not be dialed directly and had to be placed through an operator in the telephone exchange. The call takes place on Tuesday, November 15, at 9:55 p.m. on the phone at Leila's brother's apartment.

FREDA Yes?
DAVID Freda?
FREDA Yes.

DAVID Greetings.

FREDA Greetings. How come you've remembered me?

DAVID It's not me you'll be interested in, but I called anyway.

FREDA Thanks. How are you?

DAVID Someone wants to say hello to you.

FREDA Who?

DAVID Leila.

FREDA What are you saying?!

DAVID Here she is.

LEILA Greetings, Freda.

FREDA Greetings, dearest.

LEILA How are you?

FREDA Well, so-so.

LEILA I brought you a warm greeting from everyone; they asked me to speak to you if possible and they invite you to come and visit.

FREDA How long will you be here?

LEILA Till the New Year or thereabouts.

FREDA Well, I'll try to come over.

LEILA You must come.

FREDA Well, I'll try and then we can talk about everything.

LEILA Yes, and I'll tell you in detail.

FREDA Thanks. Did you come alone?

LEILA Of course I'm alone. It's a rather expensive treat.

FREDA I understand.

LEILA They miss you terribly; they said you were making arrangements to visit them.

FREDA To visit is a rather elastic idea.

LEILA I understand. Let's meet and talk.

FREDA Yes, I'll try to come.

LEILA You must, if you please. So, keep well.

FREDA Goodbye.

Tapping David's phone was a simple way to track Leila's contacts. These were of two kinds: her old family friends, plus friends and relatives of her new circle in Israel who had asked her to pass on greetings. As time passed she also began to receive requests in connection with her return—for example, for the stove cable that she wrote her husband to find. Another request was for knitting wool. Many invitations were exchanged on the phone and many rendezvous were arranged. And many details of family life were exchanged.

The phone conversations rarely reflected on wider issues or opinions. But here is one conversation that touched a nerve: KGB Major Shneyerov marked it up for particular attention by underlining and sidelining parts of the exchange. It took place on Tuesday, November 22, at 2:10 p.m. on the phone at Leila's brother's apartment:

LEILA	Yes?
SARA	Greetings, Leila dearest.
LEILA	Greetings, Sara dearest.
SARA	How is your Soviet life going?
LEILA	Couldn't be better.
SARA	What are you saying?
LEILA	Yes. What do you think?
SARA	You could agree to stay here?
LEILA	I wouldn't be against.
SARA	Seriously?
LEILA	What do you think? We grew up here, all this has entered into our flesh and blood, so to speak, it's something we are used to.
SARA	Leila, I want to carry you around with me.
LEILA	Me too.

Shneyerov was particularly interested when third parties were mentioned or when strangers called. On one occasion a stranger called and so had to introduce himself at the outset. The next conversation took place on Tuesday, December 6, at 3:20 p.m. on the phone at Leila's brother's apartment:

Kaufman	D. told me you have guests from afar.
Leila	Hello?
Kaufman	This is Kaufman.
Leila	I promised to get in touch with you personally.
Kaufman	Didn't you have the details of my address?
Leila	No. But I found you in the telephone book, but I didn't want to ring and I decided to find you through someone else.
Kaufman	Why didn't you want to ring?
Leila	I don't know.
Kaufman	When can I come to you?
Leila	In an hour. I have visitors now.
Kaufman	You don't know me?
Leila	I might know you. Come and we'll see.
Kaufman	What's your family name?
Leila	My maiden name is Sh–.
Kaufman	Can I come later?
Leila	You can come at 6 or 7, but ring beforehand. I have a headache from visitors and questions, so I'm not sure, but I should be at home all day.
Kaufman	You can call me, my telephone number is 2-90-47.
Leila	It's enough for you to know my number.
Kaufman	Sorry I disturbed you.
Leila	On the contrary, I'm very glad, so I'll be quiet now and speak with you [later].

As with the watchers, Shneyerov is intrigued by Leila's wariness. First she tells Kaufman about her hesitation in contacting him over the phone. Then she struggles to explain her hesitation. On his side, Kaufman has thrown all caution to the wind; he has already had to take the initiative by calling and giving Leila his last name. Although she doesn't ask for it, he gives her his own phone number. Shneyerov pounces on the number with a double underline. On the page itself Shneyerov has handwritten two notes. One is a reminder to check the phone number that Kaufman gave. The second reports his full name, date and place of birth, and place of work. If he wasn't before, Kaufman is now in the KGB files.

Where is Leila's homeland?

To find out what Leila really thought and was telling her friends and family, the KGB relied on informers' reports. In contrast to the phone calls, these disclosed relatively intimate conversations. "Kharitonov," for example, who drove Leila and her family home after meeting them at the airport, was invited to dinner the following Sunday. He told his handler what other visitors were present and what was discussed. Leila, it immediately transpired, was ambivalent about life in Israel. At this first dinner:

> Leila spoke about strong contrasts in the life of the Israeli people, on one side incredible wealth, on the other poverty and unemployment. She spoke about student demonstrations over difficulties with tuition, and about strong religious fanaticism. She said that the Soviet embassy is crowded with people asking to return home. Leila said that, if more attention was given to Jewish culture in the USSR, then the USSR would be the better country. She said she lives well, and her husband has built a radiology facility and an apartment on a twenty-year loan. Her husband is a doctor and radiologist. They subscribe to all kinds of Soviet publications, both specialist and other, including even *Krokodil* [the official Soviet magazine for humor and "satire"]. She said that when Soviet films come to Israel it is very hard to get in to see them;

> they are not dubbed in Hebrew but have subtitles. Leila says that she misses Vilnius a lot and the country generally. When she spoke about this, she cried. Leila is a very intelligent woman, she sees life and existing reality correctly and realistically, both in Israel and with us.
>
> This has a very tough impact on families that arrive in Israel with mixed marriages, especially from the side of religious communities. This is a disgrace for the twentieth century—Leila said.

The underlining of particular phrases is added, most likely by Shneyerov. For context, in 1966 Israel suffered an unusually sharp recession; between 1965 and 1967, unemployment rose from less than 4 percent to more than 10 percent of the workforce.[5] Such difficulties were short-lived. Before this and afterward, the Israeli economy grew strongly. But it was not a happy time. There was a wave of outward migration. On one interpretation, Israel's transitory economic and social dislocation encouraged the neighboring Arab states in plans to attack, which the Israeli leaders then preempted in the Six-Day War of June 1967.

A few days later, Leila was no longer in the first flush of enthusiasm for life in Vilnius. Informant "Augulis" reported on November 23 about a recent gathering at dinner:

> Leila said that [in Israel] she lives better, much better than she lived here. That if you have a profession you can fix yourself up much better, that apartments are better there. She does not openly advocate emigrating there, but on each separate occasion she says roughly the following: "Of course, you could live materially much better there, and you would always find work to match your profession." Or, when my brother was interested in whether a person, say, with a technical college qualification would be of value. She replied to this that he could work as an engineer there as here. To

> a question about whether our papers correctly report on Israeli–Arab relations, she replied in such a way that it became clear that she is a fanatical patriot for Israel.

On occasion, Leila talked about politics. Toward the end of November she was visited by an old friend, the informant "S," who reported in due course:

> Speaking about "democracy" in Israel, Leila said that they have several parties, including a communist one. Many criticize any of these parties on the street or in meetings, and supposedly no one is persecuted for this.

There was a detailed discussion of Israel's kibbutzim, farms organized on lines not unlike Soviet collective farms but without compulsion or political supervision. In the report they are called "communes," always in quotation marks (as with "democracy," just in case the reader might confuse them with the real Soviet thing). The conversation continued:

> The source's husband was interested in the popular mood and why Israel is continually in conflict with the Arabs. Leila answered that the people of Israel do not want war, which is unnecessary, but the Arabs force the Israeli authorities to take measures in response. As an example she referred to the following: the borders are easy to cross, and the Arabs exploit this. At night they attack the "communes" [kibbutzim], beat up young people, abduct some of them, and sabotage tractors and other agriculture machinery in the "communes." In her expressed opinion, the Israeli forces are compelled in such cases to act to defend their citizens.
>
> During discussions in her family circle, Leila talked favorably about the policy of our state, and no anti-Soviet views were

> expressed on her side or on the side of her relatives. In her expressed opinion she did not expect that the people's life would have so improved in Lithuania, that so many good residences have been built, and the city of Vilnius has improved so much since 1957.

As time passed, or perhaps in other company, Leila was more guarded. On December 12, the informant "Petrov" reported on Leila, having called on her twice.

> She said nothing of the details of life in Israel. Because the informant is planning to visit Israel, which the informant told her, she said that you will come and see with your own eyes.
>
> On life in Vilnius, Leila responded positively. She even said she is not against returning to the Soviet Union. Leila's brother, David, behaved normally, and did not allow unnecessary talk with visitors in the presence of the informant.
>
> There was no discussion of war with the Arabs or mutual relations with the Soviet Union and other immediate issues of the present-day international situation.

In the end, Leila did go home. She left Vilnius by air for Moscow, Cyprus, and Tel Aviv on Wednesday, January 4, 1967. Two days before this, "S" met her for the last time. In her presence, however, "there were no conversations among Leila and her visitors presenting operational interest."

Throughout the operation, the KGB officers pressed their informers for more details of Leila's "inclinations, contacts, and behavior." With the saturation of Leila's circle by informers, it is not surprising that by the end of her visit the summary recommendation arising from a report from informant "Tomaz" (on December 13) reads only:

> The report arose on the source's initiative. The persons appearing in the report are known to us. No assignments given to the informant with respect to specific people.

Even so, the prospect of a wider inquiry could not be resisted. When the informant "Lyova" reported (on January 10) mentioning to Leila that his brother was in Israel and he might have an opportunity to visit, the handler noted:

> **Assignment:** to develop further acquaintance with Leila's brother David on the calculation with a view to establishing preconditions, in the event of a visit to Israel on a private visa, for further investigation of Leila there.

The informers

Who were the informers in Leila's circle of friends? In August 1991 the KGB of Soviet Lithuania took its personnel files back to Moscow, so there is no definite proof of their identity in the archives that are now open to scholars or to those with a direct personal interest.

In some cases you can work out who they were. You can be pretty sure about "Kharitonov." This was the friend who met Leila at the airport, drove her home, and went to dinner the next Sunday. It is in the record that the watcher at the airport, who did not know him, gave him a code name, and in turn officer Shneyerov identified him by name and checked his credentials.

The identity of "S" is also betrayed by official indiscretion. Her husband is named in one document, and in another document the wife of the same husband is named as someone with whom the KGB has had "relations of trust for many years."

To work back to "Petrov" takes some guesswork. The documents tell us that "Petrov" is a "fellow countryman" of Leila's, and "Petrov" also reports that in Israel the "fellow countrymen" from Szarkowszczyzna gather annually on July 18, the anniversary of the German massacre of Jews there in 1942. Therefore, "Petrov" is probably from Szarkowszczyzna. On the next page in the file, "Tomaz" names a couple who came to dinner at David's apartment: "They are all fellow countrymen from Szarkowszczyzna, Belarusian SSR." On the balance of probabilities, the husband is "Petrov."

In telling this story, I decided to give equal protection to the identities of the collaborators and victims of the KGB. I have used the real names of the career officers of the KGB and the "real" code names of the informants, but all the other names have been changed to protect their identities.

Why should the collaborators deserve protection? For one reason, collaboration with the KGB was not in the least abnormal in this society, as the sheer number of those reporting on Leila illustrates. For another, without more evidence, we cannot guess at the true reasons why each person made the choice to become an informer.

Did the informers choose freely? Some of them were recruited under duress (as discussed in chapter 6). Others might have collaborated without explicit threats, but still in response to social pressure that did not need to be spelled out. In this story the collaborators, like the victims, were Jews, and all were vulnerable to coercion for this reason. Any person, official or unofficial, could acquire leverage over a Jew without doing much more than pointing to his Jewishness. In the Soviet social and political order, Jews had to prove their loyalty in order to prosper, and sometimes just to survive. Many of our characters had friends and relatives in Israel; this too could be used against them. Not only blackmail, but also a desire to protect other family members, and simple self-preservation in the face of a powerful system that clearly intended to last forever were all compelling reasons to collaborate.

The revolving door that turned victims into perpetrators and back again is a troubled theme in the history of communism. Arseny Roginsky has said: "The memory of Stalinism in Russia is almost always a memory of victims, not of crimes."[6] The victims of Soviet rule were numbered in many millions, but the same system also made perpetrators in very large numbers. Many of the perpetrators of terror became victims of the machine they helped to operate. At the same time, victims were recruited to keep it operating. The revolving door has made it easy to conclude that everyone was to blame and no one was to blame. Partly for this reason, Russia today prefers to remember Stalinism as a crime that had victims but somehow was carried out without perpetrators; no one has been held criminally responsible, and no law has named what they did as a crime.

What should we think about this? I do not mean that everyone was equally innocent. It was clearly one thing to be a victim coerced into collaboration, and a completely different thing to be a perpetrator who for some reason fell afoul of the system and ended up in his own prison or execution cell. There were also those who followed their consciences and lived their lives without much compromise. But I aim to write the history of a society and a system, not to balance one person's guilt against another. It's not important for history that we know each person's degree of guilt in this case, and it's not for me to separate the innocent from the guilty in the absence of proof.

No one is spotless

It is, however, the perfect moment for a joke. The joke comes from Czechoslovakia, and its message is that no one is spotless. First, a history lesson: Once upon a time, Stalin was the general secretary of the Communist Party of the Soviet Union. After Stalin died in 1953, Nikita Khrushchev was appointed "first" secretary—perhaps because no one wanted him to fill Stalin's shoes. The change rippled across the Soviet bloc, and in Czechoslovakia in due course the general secretary became the "first" secretary. But in the Soviet Union in 1966 Leonid Brezhnev restored Stalin's old title, becoming "general" secretary again. After the Soviet-led invasion of 1968 crushed the Prague Spring, Czechoslovakia's new leaders decided to follow Brezhnev's example, and Gustav Husak also became general secretary of the Czechoslovak Communist Party.

Now my story begins.[7] In heaven, the angels were so inspired by the election of comrade Husak as general secretary that they began to feel something was missing in paradise. They had no general secretary! A convocation brought all the angels flying in from all corners of the universe. Nominations were invited for the vacant position of general secretary of the angels. The first nomination was made: Saint Paul. At this, there was jubilation in heaven. Hosannas and hallelujahs rang out, lasting for a hundred years. Eventually they died down. Saint Paul was about to be elected general secretary by acclamation! Suddenly a little angel from the back corner of the universe interrupted the joyous proceedings:

"Comrade angels! No one could be a better candidate for general secretary of the angels than Saint Paul! He is the first evangelist. It's impossible to imagine anyone more suitable. I just have one question. What exactly was Saint Paul doing *before* he saw the light?"

At this, the angels became anxious and began to look at each other. After all, wasn't it true that before he saw the light Saint Paul had been persecuting the first Christians? Wasn't it important to have a general secretary who was without compromising evidence in his file?

Nominations were reopened, and the name of Saint Paul was not mentioned again. A second nomination came in: Saint Peter. At this, there was jubilation in heaven—more than before, because now it was augmented by a sense of relief. Hosannas and hallelujahs rang out, lasting for a thousand years. Eventually they died down. Saint Peter was about to be elected general secretary! Suddenly the same little angel from the back corner of the universe spoke up again:

"Comrade angels! No one could be a better candidate for general secretary of the angels than Saint Peter! He is the rock upon which the church was founded. It's impossible to imagine anyone more suitable. I just have one question. Will Saint Peter confirm that there was a time when he denied Christ?"

This was devastating. Wasn't it true that, when put under pressure by the Roman soldiers, Peter had denied Christ three times? The angels became thoughtful. No more mistakes. Now it was absolutely vital to have a general secretary who was completely clean.

The third nomination came in: Jesus Christ. At this, the jubilation began and exceeded the combined sum of all the previous jubilations. Hosannas and hallelujahs rang out for a million years. Eventually they died down. Jesus Christ was about to be elected general secretary! Suddenly the same little angel from the back corner of the universe spoke up:

"Comrade angels! No one could be a better candidate for general secretary of the angels than Jesus Christ! He is the Son of God, who made us all. It's impossible to imagine anyone more suitable. I just have one question. Is it not true that he spent thirty-three years in emigration in Israel?"

David: a model citizen

In Israel, Leila became homesick. She enjoyed visiting Vilnius, was surprised by the improvements she found on her return, and had mixed feelings about her life in Israel. Her brother, David, had traveled a different trajectory. It is one that you would never guess from the informers' reports on Leila, in which David does and says absolutely nothing that attracts the least attention. But he had previously been under scrutiny under quite different circumstances.

The earliest document in the file goes right back to August 23, 1952. It is a detailed biography of David. The writer, an informer code-named "Pen," claims to have known him "since childhood." Born (as we know) in Szarkowszczyzna in 1920, David left school at fourteen and went to work first for a miller, then as a shop assistant. The family did not have any political affiliations. Once the Red Army showed up in 1939, however, David "took an active part" in nationalizing the larger private landed estates and in "the establishment of Soviet power" in the Szarkowszczyzna district. After that, he found a job in the local government taxation department. This might sound harmless, but it should be taken in the context of the moment: in the early stages of Sovietizing a new country, the main purpose of taxation was to confiscate private wealth and reduce the owners to poverty. In a small way, in other words, David was continuing to build communism.

In 1939 it was not hard for the Jews of eastern Poland to accept Soviet rule. The alternatives were widely seen to be worse. German occupation would finish them off if local anti-Jewish bands did not get them first. "We were saved by the Soviets" was often the immediate reaction, as the historian B. C. Pinchuk recounts.[8]

It is true that under Soviet rule Jewish schools and political, cultural, and Zionist societies were quickly wound up. The social and political order was transformed; this left no place for hundreds of thousands of the Polish elites of every ethnicity, who were arrested and imprisoned or deported, among them tens of thousands of Jews. But for the younger and more secularly minded Jews of small towns like Szarkowszczyzna, anti-Jewish rules and restrictions were lifted and new jobs were created. "A new generation was growing that believed that the new regime opened new horizons for study, improvement, progress," writes one of Pinchuk's witnesses: "The youth literally bloomed." David was one of these.

War came. Evacuated and taken into the Red Army in 1941, David fought and rose to a non-commissioned officer's rank. After demobilization, he lived in Odessa a short while, then Vilnius. He worked once again as a local tax inspector, then in local government finance, and then as head of the finance office of one of the Vilnius city districts. He married Rivka, a Jewish girl from Vilnius. His mother and sisters settled nearby.

By the 1950s, David was a model citizen. "At work," "Pen" reported, David "has recommended himself positively, enjoys authority, and takes a full part in social life. Materially he lives well. In character he is calm, serious, and sets himself high standards. He is working to improve his ideological-political level." David was a full party member. He joined the district party bureau and presided over the district trade union council. He was nominated (and therefore, in this single-party state, "elected") to the neighborhood council where he lived.

David in trouble

What could go wrong? Toward the end of the 1950s, David's life fell apart. While his sisters picked themselves up and left for Israel, David remained in Vilnius. Then, at about the same time, he suffered several blows. He lost his job. He applied to go to Poland, apparently intending to travel onward to join his sisters in Israel, but his application to leave was refused. And his wife, Rivka, suffered ill health and became housebound.

It is clear that David did not lose his job *because* he wanted to go to Israel. Rather, it happened like this—according to informant "Semyonov," reporting on March 23, 1959. Complaints began to come into the district council where David worked. It was alleged that he was taking bribes and living beyond his means. There were rumors that he had altered his family name, implying an attempt to cover up his Jewish ethnicity. There was an investigation. In June 1958 David was dismissed on grounds of financial violations and poor management.

In a case such as David's there could be several plausible interpretations. The fact that he was accused of taking bribes might mean that he was corrupt. Or it might be that David was innocent and victimized. He would not be the first Jew to be accused of stealing from the people. A third possibility encompasses the first two. It is a fact that most Soviet managers could not achieve the results their superiors demanded within the complex limits of the Soviet bureaucracy. Favors and bribes could also serve the plan.[9] By cutting a few corners you could win medals and promotion if the task went well; equally, you could be punished for failure. If David broke the rules it could have been equally for his private enrichment or "for the good of the cause." There was often no way for an outsider to tell the difference.

Notably, David was not expelled from the party. Losing his party membership would have exposed him to prosecution. Thus, whatever David had done wrong was not regarded as a criminal violation. It might be that party investigation had shown his offense to be trivial. But the fact that David lost his job and was not merely demoted or transferred argues against this. Another possibility is that David had friends in the party who protected him. But David's reaction suggests otherwise.

David responded with outraged innocence. From the moment of his dismissal he boycotted the party meetings and refused to pay his dues. He began to talk openly about going to Poland, although "Semyonov" suggests that David was thinking about emigration even before he lost his job. In his apartment, David had said to the source, "This was all I needed"; in other words, his dismissal tipped the balance toward exit. When brought before a party meeting for absences and nonpayment of dues, "Amber" reported, David told them "he would be more valued abroad."

In the course of 1959 no fewer than six informers reported to the Lithuania KGB on David's "inclinations, contacts, and expressions." In addition to "Pen" (again), "Semyonov," and "Amber," there was "Smirnova," evidently a nosy neighbor. "Smirnova" related that David was living amicably with his wife and son, and that he had mysterious visitors from time to time. She reported rumors to the effect that he had female friends in the town, and complained that he wouldn't exchange gossip with his neighbors. "Smirnova" gets the total up to four. To reach six, we have to add informants "Familiar" and "Small."

"Familiar" and "Small" appear together in relation to David's women. On August 1, 1959, "Small" reported to his handler that David "amuses himself with women of easy virtue." "Small" claimed to have been invited by David on a womanizing expedition, but the woman they sought had been out when they called. The handler noted:

> **Report:** [. . .] On the information of informant "Familiar" David maintains intimate relations with object of investigation K. [a Lithuanian family name in the female unmarried form].
>
> **Actions:** Prepare assignment for informant "Small" for a joint visit to object of investigation K.

Thus the KGB showed considerable interest in David's extramarital activities. Whether the curiosity was professional or prurient is hard to say; the KGB appears to have had independent suspicions of Miss K. But informant "Small" disappointed them. On December 16, 1959, that is, four-and-a-half months later, he still had only second-hand information to pass on.

> I have two [women, David told "Small"], one a young Lithuanian girl, who is interesting, and I have another woman for myself, she's not so interesting and she's older. It's not that I'm sorry for her, but she doesn't give herself to everyone.

But it was politics that was David's undoing, not sex. From March 1958, "Small" was reporting his increasingly anti-Soviet expressions. On April 7, for example, David told "Small":

> One has to welcome the situation emerging in the Near East [that is, in the countries around the eastern Mediterranean]. To get such a slap in the face from Nasser after they so cozied up to him, and spent so much money on this United Arab Republic. Whatever Israel is not, a Communist Party does exist there, yet this Hitlerite [Nasser] has jailed all the communists and we have climbed in with him as good friends.

For context, Gamal Abdel Nasser founded the military regime that governed Egypt from 1952 to 2012. The United Arab Republic was his plan, which proved short-lived, to unify Egypt with surrounding Arab states, starting with Syria. In the 1950s the Soviet Union made large investments in Nasser's regime, seeing it as a counterweight to Israel and to American influence in the region, but Nasser's friendship did not extend to the Egyptian Communist Party, which he banned and repeatedly repressed; there were widespread arrests, for example, in March 1959, and this most likely was the trigger for David's outburst. Although a party member himself, David distances himself from his own leaders by referring to them as "they." He contrasts Egypt, the Soviet Union's ally, unfavorably with Israel, where communists had the freedom to associate within the law.

That is what is meant [David concludes his conversation with "Small"] by the wise policy of our party and the Central Committee that we all revere.

Report: On the basis of the source's information David repeatedly appears as a person expressing anti-Soviet fabrications. On the evidence of the source David has been refused departure to Poland.

Assignment: Continue to maintain close relations of trust with David and investigate his political inclination and circle of close contacts.

Action: Open a POP file on David.

David's case is made official

This was a fateful moment. POP stood for "provisional operational verification," an official inquiry into a person "suspected of carrying out activity hostile to the Soviet Union."[10]

Informant "Small" continued to report on David through 1959. Soviet foreign policy was a frequent topic of unfavorable comment. (But you have to wonder how true to life these reports were. On one occasion the informer was able to recall the words of a dialogue exactly as they were spoken a full two years previously.) "Small" also reported David's visitors and their views, for example a woman who commented: "You'll see, America won't begin a war; if anyone begins one it will be us." There were jokes (about Khrushchev), rumors (that Khrushchev would relax restrictions on Jewish emigration), urban myths (a customs officer was driving a confiscated vehicle around Vilnius, not knowing it concealed the fortune of a Jewish emigrant), the experience of an acquaintance who had re-emigrated from Israel back to the Soviet Union, and references to underground literature. The KGB was inquisitive about the latter and commissioned "Small" more than once to get his hands on the copies and find out David's sources, although not with any apparent success.

The joke about Khrushchev was weak. At the riverside, David asked "Small" to write Khrushchev's initials in the sand. Pointing to each letter in turn, going forward and backward, David read out: "The country needs a boss. The boss came up with himself. Nikita Sergeivich Khrushchev." It's barely funny, even in Russian.[11] To make up for that, here's one about the guy who starts to tell a joke in front of a KGB officer. The officer flares up: "May I remind you that I'm with the KGB?" "Don't worry," says the joker. "I'll tell it slowly."[12]

The KGB became particularly focused on David's unemployed status after he lost his job. In fact, on April 14, "Small" reported that David had asked him to help him find a job, and this leads to an unusual outcome. For "Small" spoke to the director of a local consumer society who refused to help *because David was a party member*. The director would hire him only if a superior would provide a guarantee for him. The remark is unexplained. It would seem that, in the post-Stalin climate of forgiveness, it was a particularly bad signal when a party member lost his job altogether. Following this report, the handler gave "Small" a new assignment: "Continue to maintain close relations of trust with David, and do what you can to get him a job with the aim of reinforcing links with him." It was at this time that he raised David's status from POP to DOP. DOP stood for "operational verification file"; there was no longer a first P for "provisional."

David remained without a job through the summer, but by the winter of 1958 he had found work as chief of the supply department of the Vilnius drill factory. A character reference is in his file, written by the factory director, not dated, but countersigned by Major Shneyerov. By the time it was composed, David had evidently returned to the strait and narrow path of Soviet respectability:

> Comrade [David] has been working at the Vilnius drill factory since December 1959 as a department chief. At work he shows himself positively as a proactive, demanding, effective, and literate worker, able to organize work, and takes an active part in social and political activities. He undertakes substantial work on education and agitation within the collective. He is deputy secretary of the party bureau of the factory party organization. He carries out his party tasks well. Since the party-state control group was elected, he has been its chairman and under his leadership much work has been done. He enjoys authority among the factory collective. Comrade [David] works systematically to improve his political and productive knowledge.

A spy story without a plot

To cover Leila's visit to her family, the KGB mobilized its historical records, its shadows, its informers, and the technical systems that allowed it to intercept letters and telephone conversations.

In return for this effort the KGB got what we have seen: an ordinary woman who came and went, who was momentarily reunited with loved ones and friends, who felt the simple hopes and confusions, the love and heartache that one might expect at this extraordinary moment in an ordinary life in an anomalous time and place. On the surface there was a short-lived, bittersweet family reunion. Beneath the spectacle there was nothing, for nothing was going on beneath the surface. It was a spy story, yet there was no plot.

What was it all for—the pitiless invasion of a family's privacy, the tracing of its intimate contacts, and the betrayal of its secrets?

Given that *nothing was going on*, it would be tempting to conclude that the whole operation was a complete waste of time.

This would misunderstand the purposes of the KGB. By the 1960s Lithuania was quiet. The armed insurgency of the first postwar years had been suppressed. Stalinist terror was in the past. But the fact that the country was quiet did not mean that the enemy had gone away. The First Principle remained intact: *the enemy is hiding*.

While the country had gone quiet, the KGB had evolved away from an organization that ruled through mass terror to one that ruled by education and re-education, by watching and warning, and by shepherding the lost sheep. KGB surveillance of the usual suspects (Second Principle) and the young (Third Principle) allowed the authorities to watch for sparks (Fifth Principle) that could set off a rebellion. Through warnings and other KGB interventions, they could stamp out each spark (Sixth Principle) and maintain the appearance of order (Seventh Principle). But to be always ready for every spark of nonconformity and resistance, it was inevitable that they would spend most of their time watching while *nothing was going on*—just in case. And this is exactly what they did in the case of Leila's brief return to her first homeland.

In a society that was quiet on the surface, where outwardly nothing was going on, the sudden reappearance of someone like Leila could be immensely valuable. For Leila had once been a citizen, a sister, and daughter, so that she would arrive in Vilnius with ready-made connections. She had chosen to leave the country and now she was a foreigner; she would carry with her foreign commitments and foreign loyalties, and she would also bring a decade of experiences of life abroad. Naturally, Leila herself was a usual suspect from the moment she arrived. Moreover, everyone whom Leila knew and would communicate with in Vilnius was also a usual suspect. Several things made them into usual suspects. They were mostly Jewish. Every one of them had a friend or relative abroad: Leila herself, and sometimes others too. Among them were some who had a doubtful past—her own brother, David, for example. Finally, all these usual suspects were not isolated individuals. As well as knowing Leila, they knew each other. Together, therefore, they formed an unofficial network based on kinship and ethnic and cultural affinity. No one had given party or government authorization for this network to be formed, and yet there it was beneath the surface, under the nose of the KGB.

From this angle Leila's arrival in Vilnius was not only a potential threat to state security but also a rich potential opportunity. She would fall into the still pool of Lithuanian society like a pebble. Around her would spread ripples of disturbance as the society of her friends and relatives responded to her arrival and the news she would bring. Before she left, the KGB would learn everything it could about those she would leave behind.

That is why the KGB devoted such efforts and resources to the surveillance of an apparently innocent tourist and her apparently reformed brother. Indeed, the attention they gave to Leila was nothing special; they gave the same attention to any foreign tourist at that time.[13]

The KGB's system of surveillance was effective, but still it was imperfect. The ceaseless vigilance required to stamp out every spark implied a standard of perfection. Measured against the requirement of perfection, the KGB was only human. Because of this, Soviet rule was ultimately fragile. Twice in the next twenty years, the KGB would miss something really significant, a hotspot that smoldered and sparked into flame under their noses. One such spark was the Romas Kalanta affair of 1972, described in chapter 5. Lithuanian youth suddenly boiled over, but the KGB managed to douse the flame and quickly restore calm. Years later another spark caught hold and blazed up, leading to the collapse of Soviet authority in Lithuania in 1988, and then national independence in 1990. This was soon followed by the disintegration of the Soviet Union itself.

Our greatest treasure

In September 1959 Nikita Khrushchev made the first visit by a Soviet leader to the United States. As the story goes, US President "Ike" Eisenhower asked him what he'd like to see. Khrushchev replied eagerly: "Ike, will you show me Fort Knox? I want to see all that gold!" Eisenhower frowned. "Nikita Sergeivich," he said, "this is a big ask. I'll give the job to Dick." (Richard Nixon was vice president to Eisenhower.) "He'll have to mobilize the Secret Service, the FBI, the Army, the Air Force, and the Marines. Give him a day or two. We'll see what he can do."

A few days later Nixon called Khrushchev: "It's on for tomorrow." The Secret Service roused Khrushchev at 3 a.m. The presidential helicopter flew him into the Federal Bullion Depository at Fort Knox. In the air there was a fighter escort. As Khrushchev looked down he could see the buildings ringed with tanks and guns; there were sharpshooters on every roof. The helicopter landed. He passed through many checkpoints. At last the steel doors swung open, and he entered the Federal Bullion Depository. He gasped to see the heavy gold bars piled from floor to ceiling, row after row, disappearing into the vast distances of the storeroom. Later he returned to Moscow, deeply impressed by the amount of gold he had seen.

Years went by until 1972, when Richard Nixon became the first US president to visit Moscow. In the Kremlin he met

Leonid Brezhnev. Brezhnev said: "Dick, is there anything you'd like to see while you're here?" At once, Nixon replied: "Leonid Ilyich, do you recall that time when Khrushchev visited Fort Knox? I don't know where you keep your gold, but I'd love to see it for myself." Brezhnev brightened up: "Sure! Be up early tomorrow morning."

At 3 a.m. the next morning a man dressed in a pilot's uniform roused Nixon and drove him to the government airport at Vnukovo. They climbed into a fighter plane and flew east, without escort, at supersonic speeds. They landed at a remote Siberian airfield. A personnel carrier was waiting. They piled in, and jolted over rough tracks for a couple of hours far into the empty Siberian space. They pulled up at a deserted farmhouse. The pilot raised a trapdoor in the floor and indicated for Nixon to go down the steps. In the dark, a few candles burned steadily. Nixon gasped to see a vast underground cave. In every direction were chests and trunks overflowing with every kind of precious metal and jewel. In the candlelight, gold, silver, diamonds, rubies, emeralds, and sapphires glittered and glowed. When he had looked all he wanted, they flew back to Moscow. By nightfall, Nixon was in bed, but he couldn't sleep.

Next day, he met Brezhnev again. "What did you think?" Nixon replied that he was mightily impressed, but he had one question. "Leonid Ilyich, I still remember the huge security arrangements I had to make for Khrushchev to go to Fort Knox. Yesterday you showed me your wonderful national treasures, yet in the entire day I did not see one single security guard. Tell me: How do you keep your treasure safe?"

Brezhnev replied: "Dick, you don't understand. That was not our greatest national treasure. Our greatest national treasure is the Soviet people. They're completely safe and that's because *we watch them all the time.*"

Freely and without fear

Report from informant "Small," March 1, 1958 (excerpts):

During a conversation between the source and David the latter said the following:

"I think there is no point going to Poland. To tell the truth I would not mind going but I am afraid of the outcome. It could turn out that you put your papers in to OVIR [the Visa and Registration Department] and they give them back to you, and then you get a ticket to Siberia, or they can put you in jail."

Further, David advised the source to give up all thought of traveling, we will stay in the USSR, and at this point David added:

"We'll stay in Vilnius and live in the hope that *he* [one of the Soviet leaders, not named] and generally this whole system will smash their heads in, and maybe we will live here freely and without fear."

Report: Information on David received for the first time.

Assignment: The source should establish a relationship of trust with David and clarify his contacts. Investigate his political inclinations and way of life.

Actions: Identify David and verify his records.

Conclusion

From the first to the last chapters of this book, from Stanislav Bronikovsky to Leila and David, we see the changing face of the Soviet police state. Stanislav's story took place in one decade, the 1940s, and was uncovered in another, the 1950s. In that time Soviet life underwent seismic change. In Stanislav's story, we see the indiscriminate violence of Stalin's repressions. Through its exposure, we see how the police state changed, as Stalin's successors distanced themselves from mass terror and worked out new ways of ruling. These changes transformed the ways in which ordinary people could live. We see this in the lives and fates of the Old Man of the Surkhan Darya valley, of Tomas, the restaurant gourmet of Klaipeda, and of Leila's brother, David.

The transformation of everyday Soviet lives was profound, yet also limited. One limit is personal: Stalin's successors could not admit their own part in Stalin's crimes, and for that reason they controlled strictly what could be disclosed and who could be held accountable. Another limit is institutional: the Soviet regime, although no longer that of Stalin, was still a dictatorship. After Stalin, the ruling Communist Party continued to monopolize power and to suppress any public expression of significant political and cultural difference. So the police state also continued.

Three and a half decades passed from the foundation of the Soviet police state in the Russian Revolution to Stalin's death. Stalin's successors forced the police state to adapt and learn new ways. For three and a half more decades it did so successfully. In those seven decades, as a result, an entire generation, born around the time of World War I, middle-aged when Stalin died, passed from the cradle to the grave under communism. Most did not see the day when they could live without fear.

The Soviet police state was durable and flexible. Its durability was based on the working principles introduced in chapter 1 and exemplified in our stories. Your enemy is hiding. Start from the usual suspects. Study the young. Stop the laughing. Rebellion spreads like wildfire. Stamp out every spark. Order is created by appearances. These principles proved to be both fundamental and adaptable.

The principles were adaptable in the sense that a system based on them could have more than one face. One face was bloody and cruel, the face of Communist rule in the time of Stalin's terror. Another was the more "human" face that came later, in the time of Khrushchev and Brezhnev, a face that instilled fear only when necessary and killed only as a last resort. Thus, the application of the principles changed, showing their flexibility. But the principles themselves did not change, and not one of them could be neglected, so they were fundamental to the police state.

Each year since 1973, Freedom House has rated nearly all countries in the world for their citizens' political rights and civil liberties. The data show that in the mid-1970s the proportion of countries rated as "free" stood at less than 30 percent. Thirty years later, in the mid-2000s, the share had reached more than 45 percent.[1] A significant contribution to the rise of political and civil freedoms came from the fall of communism in Europe and the end of Soviet support for guerrilla movements and authoritarian regimes elsewhere.

In the ten years since the mid-2000s, however, there has been no change in the proportion of countries rated "free." Freedom has not just stagnated. Across Europe there is impatience with democracy. One expression is the acquiescence to authoritarian trends that is widespread in some countries that became democracies a few years ago, such as Turkey, Hungary, and Russia. Another expression is widespread admiration for China's authoritarian one-party state, a sentiment that political scientist David Runciman has called "dictator envy."[2]

When we falter in the pursuit of freedom, one factor can be that we have misplaced the memory of what it was like to be afraid: to beware of friends and even loved ones; to live in fear of the betrayal of innermost thoughts; to dread the knock on the door, the car that pulls up beside us, or the polite invitation to visit with the security police. These things happened, and at the time they were so vivid that we thought we could never forget. But they lost their salience, and now we have changed and our world has changed. We think the people these things once happened to are no longer us, and we think the world in which they once happened is not our world.

Somewhere in our world, as you read this, an instructor is summarizing his key points for the trainee officers in the class: "Your enemy is hiding. Start from the usual suspects. Study the young. Stop the laughing . . ."

Afterword: Fact and Fantasy in Soviet Records

The stories in this book arise from investigations by either the Party Control Commission or the KGB (Committee of State Security). They raise the question: can the records of these bodies be trusted? Did party investigators really take the trouble to establish the facts without fear or favor? Did Soviet secret policemen not manufacture fantastic threats and invent fictitious agents in order to impress superiors and win funding, like *Our Man in Havana*? In Graham Greene's novel of 1958, a British businessman in need of funds becomes a spy. To please his new paymaster he develops a fictitious agent network using the names of local people whom he meets accidentally, and reports important military installations using diagrams of vacuum cleaner parts.

Could an NKVD officer do that and get away with it? It is true that many investigative documents of the Soviet era, and especially from Stalin's time, contain claims for which there was no independent evidence. These often concerned attributions of treasonous intention to commit particular acts or allegations of conspiracy to carry them out. Many such allegations were fabricated. The story of Stanislav Bronikovsky (chapter 1) revolves around just such a fabricated claim. The weaving of lies by investigators charged with establishing the truth has led some historians to view Stalin as a "weak dictator." Although Stalin's hand can be found in every major decision of the Soviet state over three decades, perhaps he was not truly in control because he could not control the propensity to lie of those from whom he needed to hear the facts.

The weak-dictator hypothesis merits a short digression. It is concisely stated by James Harris in his review article, "Was Stalin a Weak Dictator?" An earlier version of the same argument, much-cited, is by J. Arch Getty, *Origins of the Great Purges*. Getty returned to the subject in "The Politics of Repression," suggesting that in 1937 Yezhov "pursued initiatives, prepared dossiers, and pushed certain investigations in order to promote his own agenda" which "may not have been identical" with Stalin's.[1]

Much of the case for Stalin's supposed weakness, however, is based on attacking a straw man: the idea that the Great Terror was the culmination of a long-term plan to imprison or murder millions of people that Stalin followed over several years, at least from the murder of Leningrad party chief Sergei Kirov in 1934. There is no evidence that Stalin had such a long-term plan, so advocates of the weak-dictator hypothesis swing from one extreme to another, concluding that Stalin was pushed or manipulated by others into mass murder.

This is a false alternative. For Stalin, terror was an instrument, not a goal. He did not have a long-term plan for mass murder, but he did have stable objectives for national power and his own security and the capacity to pursue them in ways that changed as his information changed.[2] At a certain point, mass murder was the result.

At the same time, the reliability of particular historical records cannot be resolved by debates at such a high level of abstraction. Cautious historians have rightly raised concerns about the private agendas of the investigators. Did the secret police of Stalin's time, for example, not invent underground networks and conspiracies so as to justify their own employment and extract more funding from their political masters? And does this not introduce uncontrollable distortions into the documentary record?

Because this is such an important question, it makes sense to consider the veracity of the documentation underlying this book in some detail. Can the documents be trusted to tell us the truth? No. No document deserves unconditional trust. Can the documents be analyzed to extract a reliable message? Can we identify fact from distortion? Yes. My confidence is based on arguments that I will set out briefly.

First, every record has a message; the problem is to work out what it is. According to the political scientist Robert Jervis, "Most communications convey two messages: what the actor is saying and the fact that he needs to say it."[3] The craft of the historian who works with documents is to triangulate the contents of the document with its authorship, with other sources, and with prior knowledge about the authors, their position in the world as it worked at the time, and their need to say what was said.

Second, we are dealing with records of investigations where the investigator could report the facts selectively, and suppress or invent them at key points, so as to favor one interpretation over another. This creates a dilemma for the reader of any document: where, exactly, did invention take over from the facts?

It is helpful to understand that the investigations carried out by Soviet state and party officials were not liable to *free* invention. Invention was permissible only within strict limits. The limits were handed down from above, and corresponded to the revolutionary insights of the party leaders at the time. These insights could be used to fill in the gaps between the facts as they were known and, if necessary, would take priority over the facts.

This is less strange than it might sound. A close analog to the idea of "revolutionary insight" is Stephen Colbert's invention (on his TV show *The Colbert Report* in 2005): "truthiness." Truthiness, defined in a recent brief to the US Supreme Court, is the quality of something that is "felt to be true"; it is known by instinct and therefore "without regard to evidence or logic."[4] (So truthiness goes deeper than mere plausibility or verisimilitude.) Truthy beliefs tend to persist even when they are contradicted by verified facts. This is because they are felt to be true in general, and such feelings outweigh detailed invalidation.

Truthiness may well be a feature of political discourse in every society, but the Soviet and American ways of politics differed in an important respect. In Soviet life, access to claimed truths was entirely monopolized by the party, and within the party by the leaders. A leader like Stalin had revolutionary insight, and you could not be a Soviet leader without it.[5] Stalin based important decisions on instinct, that is, on claimed insights into the true (or "truthy") state of the world that did not require external validation. He worked assiduously to share these insights with others around him and to ensure that they learned to conform.

Here are Stalin's revolutionary insights that are most relevant to this book. Some of them have already appeared as illustrations of the First Principle (from chapter 1: *your enemy is hiding*).

- We have enemies: "We have internal enemies. We have external enemies. This, comrades, must not be forgotten for a single moment."[6]
- War can come at any time: "We could not know just when the imperialists would attack the USSR . . . but that they might attack us at any moment . . . of that there could be no doubt."[7]
- The internal enemy is hand in glove with the foreign enemy: "a gang of wreckers, diversionists, intelligence

service agents, spies, assassins, a gang of sworn enemies of the working class, working in the pay of the intelligence services of foreign states."[8]

- The most dangerous enemy is the one who is already among us: "Wherein lies the strength of the present-day wreckers, the Trotskyites? Their strength lies in the Party card."[9]
- When something bad happens, look for the link to the foreign enemy: "He [a mutinous officer] is, of course (of course!), not alone. He must be put up against the wall and forced to talk—to tell the whole truth and then severely punished. He must be a Polish-German (or Japanese) agent" (a remark that Stalin made during an investigation in 1934).[10]
- Finally, "truthiness" can be more reliable than the truth, and the reason is that we cannot expect to find independent verification of what we believe: "Experienced conspirators don't leave behind a trail of documents in their work."[11]

Stalin used these messages to guide his own fact-finders. He obligated them to make certain presumptions. You must presume that anyone can be an enemy; that anyone who looks loyal can turn out to be an unconscious enemy; that one explanation for gaps in the evidence can be that enemies cover their tracks; and that among the missing facts may be coordination between domestic and foreign enemies.

The prudent investigator would follow these insights when the facts were missing. There were times such as the Great Terror, but not only then, when Stalin's insights would take precedence even though the facts contradicted them. A result was the widespread fabrication of charges, torture, and false confessions. The story of Stanislav Bronikovsky (chapter 1) takes place at one of those times.

Thus Soviet investigators were authorized to apply "Soviet truthiness" in the course of their investigations, and the documentary records of their investigations became correspondingly distorted. But there was no authorization to invent freely. The authority to invent was limited to those things that would confirm Stalin's revolutionary insights.

Stalin died, and his successors modified his insights. They continued to assert the belief in a homeland encircled and penetrated by enemies that strove ceaselessly for the overthrow of communism. But they dispensed with the infamous notion of the unconscious enemy, and they no longer looked for the most dangerous enemies inside the party. They continued to look for the hand of the enemy in every unplanned event and unauthorized initiative. But they sharply increased the burden of proof that was required to identify the enemy. Suspicion of disloyalty would still lead to investigation but it would not lead to arrest and punishment unless independent facts were found that pointed to specific responsibility, including guilty intention. Thus, there was change as well as continuity in "Soviet truthiness."

Stalin was no weak dictator. He and his successors set firm limits on what could be asserted as "truthy" (as opposed to what was verifiably true). Whatever it was that they believed at the time, they set the same limits in both secret business and public discourse. They were fully alive to the possibility that their own officials might push at these limits, and they used multiple strategies to control them.

How, exactly, did Soviet rulers enforce their beliefs on those around them—and specifically on the fact-finders of the party and the secret police? How did they ensure that investigators would follow the authorized presumptions, and not go an inch beyond them?

The Soviet system was designed with this in mind. It began with keeping the fact-finders apart from those they had to investigate.[12] The secret police, in particular, were an elite group:

"Stalin's praetorians."[13] After that, it was important to keep them few in number and close to hand. Stalin kept his fact-finders modestly staffed and funded. As their numbers grew he also limited their influence at the center by dividing them into smaller, more specialized agencies.[14] He understood what modern democracies forget at their peril: a fact-finding apparatus that is bloated by too much money and too little supervision is dangerous because it can attract empire-builders who acquire their own vested interests and become a political lobby. Stalin wanted conduits of reliable information, not rival centers of power. Stalin's successors took these lessons to heart. We saw in chapter 5 that the KGB, for example, remained a relatively small organization right up to the last days of the Soviet Union.

The Soviet system of rule also limited the fact-finders' scope for straying beyond prescribed limits by denying them the capacity to engage in policy analysis. Stalin never allowed his party investigators or secret policemen to criticize policy, form or frame policy choices, or even just consider broader implications of the facts they found. Analysis was his prerogative, which no one else could assume. The Party Control Commission, responsible for investigating wrongdoing by party members, had no right to analyze the conditions that might lead party members to do wrong. When investigating threats to security, the KGB was restricted to finding facts; it had no right to analyze the factors behind the threats.

Here, perhaps, is an important but neglected difference between intelligence work in a democracy and under a totalitarian dictator. Americans consider that the intelligence officer has a duty to "speak truth to power," even when the truth is painful.[15] The KGB could not speak truth to power. It could speak only facts. This was a surprising discovery for Vadim Bakatin, a provincial party boss whom Gorbachev appointed to bring the KGB under control after the attempted putsch of August 1991. Bakatin did not foresee that as KGB chief he would be expected to handle an avalanche of "almost unprocessed" facts that landed daily on his desk from below. The facts that reached him were undigested because it was nobody's job to make sense of them before they reached his desk. He looked for the cause of this and decided that the party itself had monopolized the role of data analysis, and did not want to share this role with any other body, including the KGB.[16]

This leads me to discount those interpretations of Soviet rule in which a weak ruler was manipulated by his security officials, who fed the paranoia of the regime with fabricated plots of their own devising in order to win funding and job security. The Soviet system was designed to ensure that subordinate officials had neither the freedom of action nor the capacity to manage their superiors in this way.

Where does this leave us? The documents underlying this book are records created by the Soviet rulers' fact-finders. They were written to serve the rulers, and they must be understood in that light. Those who wrote them shared the rulers' mind-set, including their "insights" into what must be true yet cannot be confirmed. Thus our records show characteristic biases that are easily identifiable based on knowledge of the period. These biases arise from the investigators' obligation to conform to the party leaders' insights and to elaborate on them without going beyond them by an inch. The biases do not arise from the investigators' preference for framing the rulers' choices or their desire to manipulate power from below.[17]

In that light I approach the records of party and KGB investigators that form the basis of this book: like any historical documents, they require consideration of the circumstances and motives of the authors, always paying particular attention to the facts that are missing and the facts that were sacrificed to the truthiness of the time and place.

Endnotes

Notes to the Preface

1. Yevtushenko, *Selected Poems*, p. 81.

2. Interview with German television channels ARD and ZDF, May 5, 2005, http://archive.kremlin.ru/eng/speeches/2005/05/05/2355_type82912type82916_87597.shtml.

3. Bruce, *The Firm*, p. 9.

4. Bacon, "Reconsidering Brezhnev," p. 5.

5. "Ideal'nyi pravitel' dlya Rossii—vchera i segodnya" (VTsIOM press release no. 1943, February 2, 2012), http://wciom.ru.

6. "Rol' lichnosti v istorii Rossii," Levada Center press release, January 20, 2014, http://www.levada.ru/20-01-2015/rol-lichnostei-v-istorii-rossii.

7. "Sozhaleete li Vy seichas o raspade Sovetskogo soyuza?" (VTsIOM, December 2, 2012), http://wciom.ru/zh/print_q.php?s_id=879&q_id=61215&date=02.12.2012. Earlier surveys can be found on the VTsIOM web site by searching in both questions and answers on "raspad soyuza" (in Cyrillic characters).

8. Speech to the Federal Assembly, April 25, 2005, http://archive.kremlin.ru/eng/speeches/2005/04/25/2031_type70029type82912_87086.shtml.

9. "Chto, po-Vashemu, kharakterno dlya togo istoricheskogo puti, po kotoromu nasha strana dvigalas' pri Sovetskoi vlasti?" VTsIOM, July 30, 2000, http://wciom.ru/zh/print_q.php?s_id=338

&q_id=27191&date=30.07.2000. Naturally, opinions were not uniform. While 40 percent recalled the Communist Party's political monopoly in the Soviet period, 35 percent remembered queues, shortages, and rationing.

10. "V svyazi s chem Vy prezhde vsego sozhaleete o raspade SSSR?" Levada Center data categories, September 9, 2013, http://www.levada.ru/archive/pamyatnye-daty/v-svyazi-s-chem-vy-prezhde-vsego-sozhaleete-o-raspade-sssr. Loss of the sense of belonging to a great power was named by 51 percent. Significant minorities also mentioned obstacles to travel freely (i.e., to former Soviet republics, now independent states, in Central Asia, the Caucasus, Ukraine, and the Baltic region), to feel at home anywhere, and to maintain ties of friendship and family across national frontiers.

11. Caplan, *The Myth of the Rational Voter*, pp. 43–48.

Notes to Chapter One

1. Today you can visit such an execution cellar in the KGB museum in Vilnius, the capital city of Lithuania, where more than a thousand prisoners were killed between 1944 and the early 1960s. For variations on the Soviet way of execution, see Solzhenitsyn, *The Gulag Archipelago*, vol. 1, pp. 442–455.

2. The story of Stanislav Bronikovsky is told from the records of the Commission of Party Control, a leading committee of the Soviet Union's ruling Communist Party. To understand the documents, therefore, it is necessary to know a little about the Party Control Commission (described by Getty, *Pragmatists and Puritans*, and Markevich, "How Much Control is Enough?"). The commission's remit was to investigate reports of wrongdoing and the negligent handling of party assignments by party members. Such investigations were of decisive importance for the party members themselves. The party did not like its members to appear in the ordinary courts accused of crimes (as Cohn, "Policing the Party," has discussed). Any prosecution of a party member had to be preceded by an investigation of the offense by the party itself, with a finding of guilt, and

a decision to expel the guilty from the party; only this would open the door to prosecution. The 1950s were a period of particular importance in the history of the Party Control Commission because at this time it had to consider a great many "historical" offenses that party members had committed in Stalin's time, including those committed by Stalin himself.

The documents are held by the Hoover Institution Library & Archives, Archives of the Soviet Communist Party and Soviet State Microfilm Collection, 1903–1992: Russian State Archive of Contemporary History (Rossiiskii gosudarstvennyi arkhiv noveishei istorii—RGANI), *fond* 89, *opis* 55, *delo* 27, pages 1 to 9 (below I will abbreviate this and similar references to "Hoover/RGANI 89/55/27: 1–9"). In the order they appear in the file the documents comprise: a "Memorandum of the Commission of Party Control and the department of administrative organs of the Central Committee of the Communist Party of the Soviet Union concerning violations of socialist legality in 1941–1949 in the Khabarovsk province," unsigned, and dated October 12, 1956; a seven-page "Memorandum of the Commission of Party Control and the department of administrative organs of the Central Committee of the CPSU concerning former chief of the second administration of the NKVD Fedotov," signed by I. Boitsov and V. Zolotukhin, addressed to the Central Committee secretariat, dated September 26, 1956; and a one-page, untitled memorandum to the party's Central Committee, signed by officials of the Commission of Party Control and of the Central Committee's department of administrative organs Zolotukhin and Tikunov, dated September 12, 1956.

It is natural to ask whether the records of these investigations may be trusted. In fact, all the documents used in this book arise from investigations by either the Party Control Commission or the KGB (Committee of State Security). My answer to this question is a strictly conditional "Yes." Because it is not straightforward, and concerns all the chapters, I reserve the explanation for an afterword ("Fact and Fantasy in Soviet Records").

Through the story of Stanislav Bronikovsky, both as it happened and later when it was exposed, we begin to see how the Soviet police state evolved from mass terror to something else. In fact, police states around the world come in many varieties. This chapter concludes by introducing the idea that, however much police states may vary in their working arrangements, and however different they may look and feel, they are all designed to manage a common problem. The problem is hidden opposition that can emerge at any time as sudden rebellion. Because all police states are designed to manage the same problem, there are some common principles that they must observe.

To enumerate the working principles of the police state and explain them briefly is the other contribution of this chapter. My template for these seven principles is not that of my "home" discipline, for I was trained as an economist, and the economist would surely prefer a formal model with assumptions and axioms. Instead, partly because I think of senior secret policemen as professional people with strong incentives toward self-improvement, I chose the template of popular professional and self-help writing exemplified by Stephen R. Covey's bestseller, *The 7 Habits of Highly Effective People*. That's how I came to identify seven principles of the police state, none more than five words long.

To identify and set out the seven principles, I drew on much relevant research in history and social science. As noted in this chapter, my principles rest on the shoulders of giants—of anthropology (Alexei Yurchak), economics (Paul Gregory, Avner Greif, Timur Kuran, and Steve Tadelis), history (Peter Holquist and Jan Plamper), political science (Charles E. Schutz and Ronald Wintrobe), and sociology (Raymond Bauer, Mark Granovetter, and Alex Inkeles). Taken singly, none of the seven principles is an original insight. My contribution is limited to assembling them in one place and giving them a concise formulation.

3. On the Japanese side of the war in Asia and the central importance of China, see Paine, *The Wars for Asia*.

4. Goryachev, *Tsentral'nyi komitet KPSS*, and Ivkin, *Gosudarstvennaya vlast' SSSR*, provide brief biographical data for many Soviet officials, including Sergei Goglidze.

5. Zhirnov, "Davno pora byt' v lageryakh."

6. Among many excellent studies of the Great Terror, see Gregory, *Terror by Quota*, pp. 166–218; Holquist, "State Violence as Technique"; Khlevniuk, *Master of the House*, pp. 166–202; and Shearer, *Policing Stalin's Socialism*, pp. 285–370.

7. Kozlov, *Istoriya Stalinskogo Gulaga*, vol. 1, pp. 294–295 (Report from Beria to Stalin, October 30, 1937); and Avalishvili, "The 'Great Terror' of 1937–1938 in Georgia."

8. Gregory, *Terror by Quota*, pp. 238–243.

9. In the movie *Casablanca*, directed by Michael Curtiz (1942), Vichy French police chief Renault orders his men: "Round up the usual suspects."

10. Khlevniuk, "The Objectives of the Great Terror."

11. Fitzpatrick, *Everyday Stalinism*, p. 194, discusses the concept of the unconscious enemy. Stalin first mentioned unconscious enemies writing to his deputy Lazar Kaganovich on August 11, 1932: "Keep in mind, too, that the Ukrainian Communist Party (500,000 members, ha-ha) has quite a lot (yes, quite a lot!) of rotten elements, conscious and unconscious Petliura adherents [nationalists], and, finally, direct agents of [the Polish leader Jozef] Pilsudski." (Davies et al., eds, *The Stalin-Kaganovich Correspondence*, p. 180).

12. Inkeles and Bauer, *The Soviet Citizen*, pp. 265–280. Their study did not address the problem of reverse causation: does arrest experience lead to hostility or does hostility lead to arrest? From the standpoint of the NKVD, this was possibly irrelevant. If you had been arrested before, that provided the needed signal that you were now more likely to be hostile than others.

13. According to Filtzer, *Soviet Workers and Late Stalinism*, p. 235, the average monthly industrial wage in December 1946 was 626 rubles.

14. Shearer, *Policing Stalin's Socialism*, pp. 127–128.

15. Gregory, *Terror by Quota*, pp. 202–218.

16. Kozlov, *Istoriya Stalinskogo Gulaga*, vol. 1, p. 599.

17. Ibid., p. 334.

18. Paine, *The Wars for Asia*, pp. 242–256.

19. Gorlizki and Khlevniuk, *Cold Peace*, p. 154.

20. Rayfield, *Stalin and His Hangmen*, p. 453.

21. Aimermakher, ed., *Doklad N. S. Khrushcheva*, pp. 116–117.

22. These are words that Khrushchev actually spoke, according to Aimermakher, *Doklad N. S. Khrushcheva*, p. 66. The rest of the dialogue is fictional.

23. Wintrobe, *Political Economy of Dictatorship*, pp. 20–39.

24. Stalin, *Works*, vol. 14, p. 256 ("Defects in Party Work and Measures for Liquidating Trotskyite and Other Double-Dealers," March 3–5, 1937); "Wolves in sheep's clothing," p. 242; "Masked enemies," p. 321.

25. Stalin's psychopathology is discussed by Bullock, *Hitler and Stalin*, p. 494; Conquest, *Great Terror*, p. 114; Kotkin, *Stalin*, vol. 1, pp. 462–471; Medvedev, *Let History Judge*, p. 306; Tucker, *Stalin as Revolutionary* and *Stalin in Power*; and Service, *Stalin*, pp. 343–344. Stalin had few scruples, few friends, and a limited capacity for empathy. He also had exceptional talents for organized, logical reasoning. He based his conclusions on complex, consistent models of cause and effect. He was self-controlled and could wait; he was patient in formulating long-term objectives and he was persistent in pursuing them. He was often self-pitying but seldom if ever doubting, depressed, or desperate. Even if he lacked empathy, he had insight and could manipulate others.

26. Discussing how such beliefs take hold and become widespread, Kuran and Sunstein, in "Availability Cascades," p. 696, quote the environmental activist Lois Marie Gibbs when she recalled the Love Canal campaign in the 1970s—a turning point for US landfill regulation that turned out later to be based on false science and panic: "Love Canal taught us that government will protect you from such poisoning only when you force it to. If you think you're safe, think again! And if you're ever in doubt what a company is doing, or what the government is telling you, talk with your neighbors, seek out the truth beyond the bland assurances of the authorities, and don't be afraid to dig in your heels to protect your community. We are more organized now than ever before, and there *is* help available—just a phone call away."

27. On Bolshevik beliefs generally, and Stalin's in particular, see, for example, Davies and Harris, *Stalin's World*, pp. 59–130; Getty and Naumov, *The Road to Terror*, pp. 15–29; Gregory, *Terror by Quota*, pp. 106–139; and Rittersporn, "The Omnipresent Conspiracy."

28. Quoted by Davies and Harris, *Stalin's World*, p. 90. Stalin used these words in conversation with the German writer Lion Feuchtwanger.

29. Holquist, "State Violence as Technique," p. 154.

30. Gregory, *Terror by Quota*, pp. 106–131.

31. For the Chinese maxim advising a ratio of a thousand innocents to one guilty, see Hiroaki Kuromiya, "Stalin's Great Terror and the Asian Nexus," p. 786. For twenty to one (Stalin's "5 percent rule") see Gregory, *Terror by Quota*, p. 196. For ten to one (Yezhov), see Sebag Montefiore, *Stalin*, p. 194.

32. Greif and Tadelis, "A Theory of Moral Persistence."

33. A respondent cited by Oring, "Risky Business," p. 212. On dissimulation see also Havel, *Living in Truth*, pp. 49–51, and Kharkhordin, *The Collective and the Individual*, p. 357.

34. "The exploitation of man by man": this one is so familiar that I have no idea when I first heard it. But it is quoted independently by Lewis, *Hammer and Tickle*, p. 60; Yurchak, *Everything Was Forever*, p. 280; and Mel'nichenko, *Sovetskii anekdot*, p. 153 (no. 410).

35. Mel'nichenko, *Sovetskii anekdot*, p. 170 (no. 522).

36. Orwell, *Complete Works*, vol. 16, p. 483.

37. The phrase of Peter Sloterdijk, quoted by Yurchak, *Everything Was Forever*, p. 277.

38. See Lewis, *Hammer and Tickle*, pp. 18–21; and Davies, *Mirth of Nations*, pp. 224–225. Oring, "Risky Business," presents an insightful survey of a wider range of interpretations.

39. As argued by both Orwell, *Complete Works*, vol. 16, p. 483, and Schutz, "Cryptic Humor," pp. 52–53.

40. Kuran, "Sparks and Prairie Fires."

41. Here I draw not only on "Sparks and Prairie Fires" but also on Kuran and Sunstein, "Availability Cascades," especially pp. 714 and 729.

42. Feinberg, "Die Durchsetzung einer neuen Welt." I thank Melissa Feinberg for access to her original English text, from which I quote.

43. Granovetter, "Threshold Models of Collective Behavior." For more intuitive discussion and applications, see Kuran, "Now Out of Never."

44. Inkeles and Bauer, *The Soviet Citizen*, pp. 282–283, 290–291.

45. This is also the argument of Kuran, *Private Truths, Public Lies*, pp. 261–276.

46. This paradox is the subject of Yurchak, *Everything Was Forever Until It Was No More*, but the first and best explanation of the paradox is by Kuran, "Now Out of Never."

Notes to Chapter Two

1. This chapter reveals the working arrangements of Soviet censorship in more detail than I believe is available in other accounts. The result is a tale of pressure, frailty, and disaster. Perhaps nothing shows up the working of a system better than the moment when it fails and everyone has to sit around scratching their heads and trying to work out what should have happened that didn't. And there is a bonus: the story turns out to revolve around the police state's intolerance of ambiguity, and this serves to clarify some of the working principles of the police state.

Like chapter 1, this chapter is based on records left by the Commission of Party Control of the ruling Communist Party, held on microfilm at the Hoover Archives (Hoover/RGANI, 6/1/74: 147–160). They comprise a memorandum "On the results of verification of comments in *Pravda*, May 8, of this year, 'A subversive photomontage'," signed "in favor" by KPK members Yaroslavsky E., Kaganovich L., and Rubenov R., noting that Kuibyshev V. and Shkiryatov M. are away on business and Akulov I. is on vacation, dated June 9, 1937; a memorandum to Yakovlev, signed by Rubenov R. and dated May 29, 1937; a report "On the results of verification of comments in *Pravda*, May 8 of this year, 'A subversive montage'," by Party Control Commission press group leader Pospelov, to Party Control Commission deputy chairman Yakovlev Ya. A., dated May 16, 1937; and a reproduction of Presscliché no. 431, "Truth stings the eyes," drawn by artist Ilinsky.

I have called our heroine "Katya" Novikova but I admit that this is my guess; her first name is a missing fact. We know her initials, which were "Ye. M." Here the Ye could stand equally for Yekaterina (Katya), Yelena (Lena), or Yevgenia (Zhenya), to name three of the most popular. I chose Katya because it would be more familiar to English-speaking readers. If that was her real name, I am fortunate. If I guessed wrong, I can only apologize to her memory.

2. "Vreditel'skii montazh," *Pravda*, May 8, 1937.

3. TsSU, *Trud v SSSR*, p. 75.

4. As illustrated, for example, by the office typist of Lydia Chukovskaya's novel *Sofia Petrovna*.

5. "1934, 1 aprelya. Struktura, shtatnoe raspisanie, personal'nyi sostav i stavki Glavlita," Otkrytyi tekst, http://www.opentextnn.ru/censorship/russia/sov/org/glavlit/struktura/?id=130.

6. Dianov, "Sotsialisticheskoe sorevnovanie v organakh sovetskoi tsenzury."

7. "1935, 7 marta. Prikaz Nachal'nika Glavlita No. 51 (O poryadke publikatsii rabot Lenina i Stalina)," http://www.opentextnn.ru/censorship/russia/sov/org/glavlit/norm/1935/.

8. Mel'nichenko, *Sovetskii anekdot*, p. 653 (no. 3310).

9. Ibid., p. 653 (no. 3308).

10. "Defects in Party Work and Measures for Liquidating Trotskyite and Other Double Dealers: Report to the Plenum of the Central Committee of the RKP(b), March 3, 1937," in Stalin, *Works*, vol. 14, p. 241. Stalin's speech was published in *Pravda*, but not until March 29.

11. Plamper, "Abolishing Ambiguity."

12. Schutz, in "Cryptic Humor," traces this idea back to Hungarian author Arthur Koestler.

13. Hitler, "Hitlers Rede zur Eröffnung der Großen Deutschen Kunstausstellung."

14. These details are from Goryachev, ed., *Tsentral'nyi komitet KPSS*, p. 338.

15. The events are recounted by Zhirkov, *Istoriya tsenzury v Rossii*, and Nevezhin, *Esli zavtra v pokhod*.

16. Goryaeva, *Politicheskaya tsenzura v SSSR*, p. 210.

Notes to Chapter Three

1. This chapter contributes to our understanding of Stalin's last years. Soviet politics and economics were at their most secretive after the war, but the opening of Russian archives has begun to yield up the secrets of that time (see, for example, Gorlizki and Khlevniuk, *Cold Peace*). The stories in this chapter illustrate how times were changing even before the dictator died: just as before the war, every suspicion of disloyalty was still taken very seriously, but suspicion alone would no longer lead to arrest and imprisonment or worse.

Now, with the war over and Stalin an old man, every allegation would be investigated and the evidence would be weighed to the last scruple before judgment was reached.

The stories in this chapter are drawn from records of the Party Control Commission, held on microfilm by the Hoover Archives: Hoover/RGANI 6/6/1574: 11–19 (the Rybnikov case); 6/6/1543, 20–23 (Demidenko); and 26–28 (Frumkin).

2. Konstantin Rybnikov's biographical data are taken from several sources: the Party Control Commission files on which this chapter is based; the web site of the Moscow State University faculty of mechanics and mathematics at http://www.math.msu.ru/history; and Rybnikov's author page at the electronic library http://www.koob.ru/ribnikov/.

3. Goryachev, *Tsentral'nyi komitet KPSS*, pp. 336–337.

4. Gorlizki and Khlevniuk, *Cold Peace*, pp. 89–92.

5. Fedin, *Filin na razvalinakh*, p. 97. The physicist Erlen Fedin was Lednev's student from 1947 until his arrest in 1949.

6. For these figures and discussion of their approximate nature, see Barber and Harrison, "Patriotic War," pp. 225–227.

7. Ellman, "The 1947 Soviet Famine."

8. Filtzer, *The Hazards of Urban Life In Late Stalinist Russia*, p. 206.

9. Harrison, "Forging Success."

10. Medvedev and Medvedev, *The Unknown Stalin*, pp. 77–78, 136–139; and Holloway, *Stalin*, pp. 138–144.

11. Holloway, *Stalin and the Bomb*, pp. 210–211.

12. Gorelik, "Fizika universitetskaya i akademicheskaya."

13. Andrew and Mitrokhin, *The Mitrokhin Archive*, p. 152.

14. Gorlizki and Khlevniuk, *Cold Peace*, p. 76; and Service, *Stalin*, pp. 523, 568.

15. Zaleski, *Stalinist Planning for Economic Growth*, pp. 689, 694.

16. Filtzer, *Soviet Workers and Late Stalinism*, p. 235.

17. Potatoes keep for well over one hundred days at 5 degrees Centigrade (41 degrees Fahrenheit) with controlled air circulation (but much less otherwise). New potatoes provide around 65 calories per 100 grams, so 650 kilos of new potatoes would have made around 425,000 kilocalories of food. Assume an adult requirement of 2,900 kilocalories per day, of which half is from potatoes. If Rybnikov's family included a woman and two children of varying ages,

their food requirement might be the equivalent of three adult males. Three adult men would eat the potatoes in 98 days (425,000 divided by the product of 2,900 × three × one-half).

18. Ledeneva, *Russia's Economy of Favours*.

19. In the summer of 1970, Lysenko's supporters were possibly implicated in an attempt to incarcerate Zhores Medvedev in a psychiatric hospital. Medvedev was an expert in the science of aging and an established proponent of modern genetics. See Medvedev and Medvedev, *A Question of Madness*, pp. 48–50.

20. This joke is slightly adapted from Lewis, *Hammer and Tickle*, p. 227.

21. This was in a letter, "On the Final Victory of Socialism in the USSR," published in *Pravda* on February 14, 1938.

22. The average life expectancy of a Russian urban male age fifty-five in 1958/59 (as Frumkin would have been) was a further 18.3 years (from Goskomstat Rossii, *Naselenie Rossii*, p. 168). In 1958/59, the collapse of the Soviet Union was still more than thirty years in the future. Whether Frumkin would beat the average depends a lot on whether he smoked or drank, and whether he kept himself fit. He seems to have lived through some stressful times, so quite possibly not.

23. I wrote about this transition in more detail in Harrison, "The Soviet Union After 1945."

Notes to Chapter Four

1. Stories of whistle-blowing and retribution can be found in every time and place, but Old Man Nikolayenko's fight for justice against the party mafia of Surkhan Darya deserves a special place. For one thing, as a story of Soviet life it is uncensored. The story is remarkable for the variety of people and agencies that became involved. There is a twist: the ethics that the whistle-blower seeks to uphold belong to an oppressive, intrusive dictatorship. And there is timing: we catch Soviet society in a historic moment of transition from mass terror to selective repression, just as relationships between Moscow and the provinces are adjusting to the new realities.

The story of the Old Man provides a drama in the best tradition of socialist realism, with high political stakes and a wide cast of characters from many walks of life. To set it in context I have relied particularly on Nicholas Lampert's pathbreaking study of *Whistleblowing in the Soviet Union,* published in 1985. Lampert did his research during the Cold War when Soviet archives were almost entirely closed. His book exemplifies the best social research of the Sovietological era.

Old Man Nikolayenko's story is taken from the Party Control Commission files at Hoover/RGANI 6/6/1765: 6–16 (Instructor Fedorenko of the Commission of Party Control of the Central Committee of the Communist Party of the Soviet Union, "On the results of verification of the complaint of Nikolayenko M. A. about the facts of incorrect attitude to criticism of faults in the Surkhan Darya district of Uzbekistan," August 19, 1959) and 17 (Commission of Party Control member Dzhurabayev, memorandum to the Commission of Party Control, October 22, 1959).

2. Lampert, *Whistleblowing in the Soviet Union*, p. 64.

3. Livshin and Orlov, *Pis'ma vo vlast'* (1917–1927); Livshin, Orlov, and Khlevniuk, *Pis'ma vo vlast'* (1928–1939); and Sokolov, *Golos naroda*.

4. Mandelstam, *Hope Against Hope*, p. 133.

5. Lampert, *Whistleblowing in the Soviet Union*, pp. 63–64.

6. Ibid., pp. 141, 155.

7. The qualitative evidence suggests that this was a common counteraction against critics. See Lampert, *Whistleblowing in the Soviet Union*, pp. 156–157.

8. Ibid., p. 183.

9. Medvedev and Medvedev, *A Question of Madness;* and Bloch and Reddaway, *Russia's Political Hospitals.*

10. It was psychiatrists in Tashkent, again, who examined the dissident Major-General Peter Grigorenko in the summer of 1969 and bravely found him to be of sound mind. The episode is discussed by Medvedev and Medvedev, *A Question of Madness*, p. 94. This was not the diagnosis that Moscow wanted, and it was reversed as soon as Grigorenko was transferred to Moscow.

11. Mlechin, *Yurii Andropov* ("Podarki tovarishcha Rashidova"); and Goryachev, *Tsentral'nyi komitet*, p. 348.

12. Kotkin, *Armageddon Averted*, p. 67.

13. Stalin, *Works*, vol. 14, p. 256 ("Defects in Party Work and Measures for Liquidating Trotskyite and Other Double-Dealers," March 3–5, 1937).

14. Viola, *Best Sons of the Fatherland*, pp. 185, 192.

15. Lampert, *Whistleblowing in the Soviet Union*, p. 183.

Notes to Chapter Five

1. The stories in this chapter describe the KGB practice of *profilaktika* (prevention). The idea of *profilaktika* has been described in histories of Soviet policing and secret policing by Julie Fedor, Paul Holquist, Robert Hornsby, David Shearer, and others, but these appear to be the first detailed descriptions of *profilaktika* from primary records of its practice in the 1960s and 1970s.

The stories are drawn from among hundreds of similar records in the files of the KGB of Soviet Lithuania, now held on paper at the Lithuanian Special Archive (LYA) in Vilnius and on microfilm at the Hoover Institution where I consulted them. The KGB, like the Party Control Commission (the records of which formed the basis of previous chapters), was one of the Soviet Union's fact-gathering agencies. Its documentation requires interpretation, taking into account its mission and the incentives that its operatives faced to report or distort the facts as they saw them. The interested reader may consult the full discussion of these issues in the Afterword.

For the primary documents underlying this chapter, specific references are to the Hoover Institution Library & Archives, Lietuvos SSR Valstybes Saugumo Komitetas, Selected Records of the Lithuanian Special Archive (Lietuvos ypatingasis archyvas—LYA), *fondas* K-1, *aprašas* 3, *saug. vien.* 667, pages 125 to 129 (hereafter Hoover/LYA, K-1/3/667: 125–129) (the story of Juozas); K-1/3/696, 80–81 (Jurgis); K-1/3/697, 44–46 (Vytautas); 67–68 (Aldona); 76–78 (Maria); 83–84 (Tomas); K-1/3/710, 1–2 (Ljudas); K-1/3/713, 4–6 (Vasily); K-1/3/753, 74–76 (Algirdas). I have suppressed all the family names of the subjects of these reports because any of these people could still be alive, and their personal details were collected without their consent.

Additionally, the chapter contributes to the wider historical literature on mass unrest under Soviet rule (for example, Baron, *Bloody Saturday in the Soviet Union*; Central Intelligence Agency, *Dimensions of Civil Unrest*; Kozlov, *Massovye besporyadki v SSSR*). The particular episode that is featured in this chapter is the "Kaunas events" of 1972, which began with a young man's suicide in a public square, followed by several days of demonstrations and other illegal manifestations of discontent and nonconformity. At this point I must also thank Amanda Swain for allowing me to read her fascinating doctoral dissertation, "A Death Transformed," and other writing on these events.

The wider literature understandably highlights the Soviet authorities' resort to violence in order to suppress public disorder, and Amanda's research also shows that in Kaunas in 1972 police violence was certainly a factor in the rapid overpowering of the demonstrators. Nonetheless, the stories in this chapter also suggest another interpretation: in the Kaunas events the use of force was kept to a minimum, extreme violence and mass reprisals were avoided, and for most of the people involved and their sympathizers, KGB *profilaktika* turned out to be an effective response.

This pattern of response to the Kaunas disturbances has significant implications. The fact that the Kaunas events took place was a failure of the KGB's preventive policies. The subsequent victory over the Kaunas demonstrators was one battle in a protracted war that the Soviet police state would eventually lose. We know from the wider literature that in waging this war the KGB was sometimes thuggish and incompetent. Not always, however. The KGB response to the Kaunas events provides a case study of how, in this one particular instance, secret policemen could respond to an emergency and overcome resistance by means of flexible and efficient repression.

2. Kübler-Ross, *On Death and Dying*.

3. Reklaitis, "Cold War Lithuania"; Statiev, *Soviet Counterinsurgency in the Western Borderlands*.

4. Chebrikov, *Istoriya sovetskikh organov gosudarstvennoi bezopastnosti*, p. 503; Nikitchenko et al., eds, *Kontrrazvedyvatel'nyi slovar'*, pp. 237–238.

5. Khlevniuk, "Objectives of the Great Terror."

6. On the origins of profilaktika see Fedor, *Russia and the Cult of State Security*, p. 52, and Hornsby, *Protest, Reform, and Repression*, pp. 211-212. The full story of its emergence as a practical technique has yet to be told.

7. Hoover/LYA, K-1/3/697: 15–20 (Senior commissioner of Klaipeda KGB second division captain Epishov and others, "Report on implementation of preventive work in relation to a group of persons among the associates of foreign sailors," to Lithuania KGB chairman Juozas Petkevičius, March 27, 1972).

8. Lewis, *Hammer and Tickle*, pp. 69–75.

9. Ibid., p. 177.

10. Mel'nichenko, *Sovetskii anekdot*, p. 658 (nos. 3350 and 3353).

11. Pretending to be an agent of the US federal government is now a popular ruse employed by Internet scammers, according to Carol Kando-Pineda of the Federal Trade Commission's Division of Consumer and Business Education, "The Grate Pretenders," March 2, 2015, https://www.consumer.ftc.gov/blog/grate-pretenders.

12. "Proven reoffending tables: July 2012 to June 2013," UK National Statistics and Ministry of Justice, April 30, 2015, https://www.gov.uk/government/statistics/proven-reoffending-statistics-july-2012-to-june-2013.

13. "Anti-social behaviour order statistics: England and Wales 2013 key findings," UK Home Office and Ministry of Justice, September 18, 2014, https://www.gov.uk/government/publications/anti-social-behaviour-order-statistics-england-and-wales-2013/anti-social-behaviour-order-statistics-england-and-wales-2013-key-findings.

14. Hoover Institution Library & Archives, Dmitrii Antonovich Volkogonov papers, container 28 (reel 18) (USSR KGB chairman Yuri Andropov, memo, "Concerning some results of the warning and preventive work of the organs of state security," October 31, 1975).

15. Hoover/LYA, K-1/3/694: 3–7 (Colonels Naras and Ščensnovičius, "Plan of agent-operative measures to ensure secrecy and security of military freights," January 28, 1972); 8–62 (list of mail intercepts and copies of letters).

16. Hoover/LYA, K-1/3/644: 70–75 (Lithuania KGB second administration, first department chief, Lieutenant-Colonel Naras,

report on counterintelligence work around military facilities of special importance, February 4, 1966).

17. On copying, see Banerjee, "Simple Model of Herd Behavior"; on thresholds, see Granovetter, "Threshold Models of Collective Behavior."

18. These and the figures below are from Harrison and Zaksauskienė, "Counterintelligence in a Command Economy," and Weiner and Rahi-Tamm, "Getting to Know You," p. 33.

19. Burinskaitė and Okuličiūtė, *KGB in Lithuania*, p. 15.

20. Harrison and Zaksauskienė, "Counterintelligence in a Command Economy."

21. Bentham, *Panopticon*, p. 3. For more general discussion, see Foucault, *Discipline and Punish.*

22. Reported by Oring, "Risky Business," p. 218. Omissions and insertions are as in the original.

23. For more in this vein, see Kharkhordin, *The Collective and the Individual*, pp. 101–117.

24. The events of May 1972 have been carefully documented and described by Swain, *A Death Transformed*, pp. 62–67; also Swain, "Negotiating Narratives of Kaunas 1972," and "From the Big Screen to the Streets of Kaunas." Earlier accounts include Remeikis, "Self-Immolation and National Protest," and "Eyewitness Report of Demonstrations." For the KGB report of the incident itself, see Hoover/LYA, K-1/3/793: 142–149 (Lithuania KGB chairman Juozas Petkevičius, report, not dated but May 1972).

25. Hoover/LYA, K-1/3/793: 142–149 (Lithuania KGB chairman Juozas Petkevičius, report, not dated but May 1972).

26. Swain, *A Death Transformed*, pp. 121–122.

27. Swain, *A Death Transformed*, provides a fuller analysis.

28. For background, see Weiner, "Déjà Vu All Over Again."

29. Hoover/LYA, K-1/3/793: 146–7.

30. Hoover/LYA, K-1/3/703: 170–174 (Lithuania KGB Kaunas city chief Bagdonas and third division chief Trukhachev, "Report on measures for implementation of the decree of the Lithuanian communist party central committee of May 30, 1972," August 17, 1973).

31. Hoover/LYA, K-1/3/717: 123–130 (Lithuania KGB fifth department deputy chief Stalauskas, second administration third department deputy chief Grishechkin, and senior inspector under

the Lithuania KGB chairman Malakhov, "Report on the condition of prophylactic work in the Lithuania KGB and measures to improve it," October 17, 1974). The emphasis is mine.

32. Hoover/LYA, K-1/3/793: 1–4 (Lithuania KGB information and analysis division chief Major E. Andriatis, plan of work for 1972, dated March 27, 1972).

33. See, for example, Daškevičiūte, "Remembering Romas Kalanta." According to Lithuania KGB chairman Juozas Petkevičius, Kalanta arrived in the square alone. After setting fire to himself he did indeed cry out for help to save him or end his life. At this stage, however, the KGB was already building its own narrative of this terrible event. Hoover/LYA, K-1/3/793: 150–159 (Lithuania KGB chairman Juozas Petkevičius, "Report of evidence of the investigation of the mass anti-social manifestation in the city of Kaunas, May 18–19,1972," not dated but May 1972).

34. Inkeles and Bauer, *Soviet Citizen*, pp. 282–283, 290–291.

Notes to Chapter Six

1. Gorsuch, *All This is Your World*, pp. 10, 18. For Soviet citizens the opportunity to travel to other countries was a rare, often unforgettable experience. This chapter contributes an original account—possibly the first such account, at least in English—of a Soviet tourist group's visit to the United States, seen through the eyes of the KGB officer accompanying them under cover. It also, therefore, adds something new to the wider but still limited literature on Soviet foreign travel and tourism, which for me began with the account of the obstacles facing the Soviet traveler written many years ago by Zhores Medvedev for his collection on *National Frontiers and International Scientific Cooperation*.

The main evidence underlying this chapter is found in Hoover/LYA, K-1/3/698: 1–8 (Lithuania KGB counterintelligence deputy chief Gin'ko and Captain Čejda, memo on the "plan of tourist trips abroad in quarters 2 to 4 of 1972," not dated but January 1972); 10–13 (Lithuania KGB chairman Juozas Petkevičius, memorandum dated April 22, 1972); 14–18 ("On unification of reporting documentation on trips abroad by operative workers, agents, and trusted persons," not signed or dated); and 19–32 ("Example"). I have changed the names of the subjects of these reports because some of them may still be alive, even if elderly by now, and their personal details were gathered without their consent.

2. To compare with one million outward journeys in 1966, the Soviet population in the same year is given as 232.2 million by TsSU SSSR, *Narodnoe khoziaistvo SSSR (1922–1972)*, p. 9.

3. "Rossiyane o poezdkakh v drugie strany," Levada Center press release, April 9, 2014, http://www.levada.ru/09-04-2014/rossiyane-o-poezdkakh-v-drugie-st rany. It is true that Russia is a somewhat smaller country today than the Soviet Union in 1966, so that Russians must now hold passports and cross international borders to make some journeys, such as to the Baltic countries or Ukraine, that would previously have been classified as domestic.

4. As described by Holquist, "State Violence"; and Shearer, *Policing Stalin's Socialism*, pp. 427–431.

5. This quotation is from "How a trip abroad from the USSR is arranged," by Zhores Medvedev, *National Frontiers and International Scientific Cooperation*, pp. 195–215.

6. Hoover/LYA, K-1/3/668: 49 (Šiauliai KGB chief Žilinskas, "Report on results of work for 1968 and measures adopted by the industrial group," March 27, 1969).

7. The code of conduct as amended in 1979 is published by Bredikhin, *Lubyanka*, pp. 162–173. Getting into debt was covered under Rule 13 ("You must strictly match your outgoings with your salary, not get into debt, and buy nothing on credit or in installments") and getting drunk and into bed under various sub-clauses of Rule 14 ("It is categorically prohibited . . . To establish and maintain contact with foreigners directly or through other persons, if this is not called for by business requirements . . . To abuse alcoholic spirits and to appear intoxicated in public places and on the street"). A shorter code (Bredikhin, *Lubyanka*, pp. 155–161) governed visits to friendly socialist countries.

8. Hoover/LYA, K-1/3/656: 11 ("The status of and measures to improve counterintelligence work on exposure of the adversary's intelligence agent networks and verification and investigation of persons suspected of contacts with them," speech by Lt. Col. Kardan-

ovsky A. Ya. to meetings of KGB operational workers in cities and districts of Soviet Lithuania about results of work for 1966, February 20, 1967).

9. Gorsuch, *All This Is Your World*, p. 113.

10. Nikitchenko et al., *Kontrrazvedyvatel'nyi slovar'*, pp. 9–10, 93–94; and Chebrikov, *Istoriya*, pp. 558–559.

11. Hoover/LYA, K-1/3/652: 13–19ob (USSR KGB counterintelligence special division chief Gavrilenko, "On the experience of using operational-technical measures D, O, F, and U in implementing the plan 'Operation-100' in 1965," May 18, 1966).

12. Hoover/LYA, K-1/3/673: 33–38 (Lithuania KGB "secret" department chief, colonel Zenyakin A., memo to Lithuania KGB counterintelligence chief, colonel Naras A. I., dated June 24, 1969).

Notes to Chapter Seven

1. This chapter relates the details of a KGB surveillance operation on a foreign tourist in Soviet Lithuania in 1966. The details of surveillance are the stuff of a thousand spy novels and memoirs. The best of these came out of East Germany: for example, Timothy Garton Ash's autobiographical story *The File* (published in 1997); Anna Funder's *Stasiland: Stories from Behind the Berlin Wall* (2003); and Florian Henckel von Donnersmarck's feature film *Das Leben der Anderen* (2006), based on a fictional Stasi intrigue, released in English as *The Lives of Others*.

What is gained by adding to them? One contribution of this chapter arises because modern Russia has not broken with its KGB past, so that the documentary evidence available to scholars on KGB surveillance is much thinner by comparison with that from East Germany. Another contribution is to illustrate the completeness with which the privacy of the subjects was penetrated and the details of their private lives were exposed *in a case such as this*. Of course I do not wish to imply that any surveillance operation can uncover the inner truth of anyone's personal existence, but nonetheless it is striking to find so many layers of observation and such detail recorded as of "operational significance."

In a case such as this? A further aspect of interest, to me the most compelling of all, is the nature of the case itself: on one side the subjects were completely ordinary people without the slightest political pretensions; on the other side the watchers behaved with complete professionalism. In *The File*, we can understand that the subject, Timothy Garton Ash, is under surveillance because he is a well-connected Western writer. There is surveillance in *The Lives of Others* because a well-known playwright becomes disillusioned and smuggles out a dissenting statement, and among the KGB watchers are a libertine and a voyeur. Leila, in contrast, is completely ordinary. No one in her circle is a dissident. The KGB officers who are interested in her family have only professional goals. Leila's is a story without a plot, in both meanings of the word. There is no conspiracy. There is no narrative that unfolds a mystery. The subjects have nothing to hide beyond the private business on which we would all choose to close the curtains as night falls.

At the same time, as discussed at the end of the chapter, I do not conclude that the KGB was wasting time by watching Leila and her family. On the contrary, watching Leila was essential to the mission of Soviet counterintelligence.

Leila's file can be found at Hoover/LYA, K-1/3/648: 1–134. The file holds many items of official correspondence, intercepted letters and telephone conversations, photographs, identifications, and agent reports, covering a fifteen-year period from 1952 to 1967. Because of the relative completeness of the personal information and the risk of exposure of the innocent, I have disguised the names of everyone but the KGB employees. Informers' code names are as originally reported.

2. Hoover/LYA, K-1/3/663: 49.

3. Hoover/LYA, K-1/3/656: 11.

4. Pinchuk, "Sovietization," pp. 391–392.

5. Barkai and Liviatan, *Bank of Israel*, vol. 1, p. 71.

6. Roginsky, "Pamyat'," p. 22.

7. I was told this joke by the late Jan Šling. Jan and his mother, Marian, were my friends in the late 1970s. Jan's father, Otto Šling, was among the former Czechoslovak Communist leaders executed in 1952 following a major show trial in Prague.

8. Pinchuk, "Sovietization," p. 392.

9. Belova, "Economic Crime," pp. 139–142.

10. Nikitchenko et al., eds, *Kontrrazvedyvatel'nyi slovar'*, pp. 232–233.

11. "**N**uzhen **S**trane **Kh**ozyain. **Kh**ozyain **S**am **N**ashelsya. **N**ikita **S**ergeivich **Kh**rushchev."

12. This isn't one of mine; I owe it to the excellent Lewis, *Hammer*, p. 167.

13. I thank Arvydas Anušauskas for advice on this point (e-mail letter dated December 10, 2012).

Notes to the Conclusion

1. Freedom House, "Freedom in the World 2015," interactive map, https://freedomhouse.org/report/freedom-world/freedom-world-2015#.Vb12H_lViko.

2. David Runciman, "The Trouble with Democracy," *The Guardian*, November 8, 2013.

Notes to the Afterword

1. The quoted words are by Getty "The Politics of Repression," pp. 59–60. See also Getty, *Origins of the Great Purges*, and Harris, "Was Stalin a Weak Dictator?"

2. This case is made in more detail by Gregory and Harrison, "Allocation Under Dictatorship," pp. 732–733; Gregory, Schröder, and Sonin, "Rational Dictators"; and Harrison, "The Dictator and Defense."

3. Jervis, "Signaling and Perception," p. 298.

4. Shapiro et al., "Truthiness and the First Amendment."

5. On Stalin and revolutionary insight, see Davies and Harris, *Stalin's World*, pp. 60–61, 79–80.

6. Stalin, *Works*, vol. 11, p. 67.

7. Stalin, *Works*, vol. 13, p. 186.

8. Stalin, *Works*, vol. 14, p. 252.

9. Ibid., p. 256.

10. For the full story of the so-called Nakhayev affair, see Davies et al., eds., *The Stalin-Kaganovich Correspondence*, pp. 240–242, 246–264.

11. Quoted by Davies and Harris, *Stalin's World*, p. 90.

12. Discussed by Gregory, *Restructuring the Soviet Bureaucracy*, pp. 18–23.

13. These words are used by Gregory, *Terror by Quota*, pp. 33–59.

14. Described by Gregory, *Terror by Quota*, pp. 98–103; Gregory and Belova, "Dictator, Loyal and Opportunistic Agents"; and Markevich, "How Much Control is Enough?"

15. Peterson, "What I Learned in 40 Years."

16. Bakatin, *Izbavlenie ot KGB*, pp. 44–45.

17. For a level-headed discussion that reaches similar conclusions on the reliability of Soviet secret-police records concerning the popular mood, see Davies, *Popular Opinion*, pp. 9–17.

References

Aimermakher (Eimermacher), K., V. Yu. Afiani, D. Bairau (Beirau), B. Bonvech (Bonwetsch), V. P. Kozlov, and N. G. Tomalina, eds. *Doklad N. S. Khrushcheva o kul'te lichnosti Stalina na XX s'esde KPSS. Dokumenty.* Moscow: ROSSPEN, 2002.

Andrew, Christopher, and Vasili Mitrokhin. *The Mitrokhin Archive: The KGB in Europe and the West.* London: Penguin, 2000.

Anušauskas, Arvydas. *KGB Lietuvoje. Slaptosios veiklos bruožai.* Vilnius: Asociacija "Atvažiavo Meška," 2008.

Avalishvili, Levan. "The 'Great Terror' of 1937–1938 in Georgia: Between the Two Reports of Lavrentiy Beria." *Caucasus Analytical Digest* 22 (December 1, 2010): 2–6.

Bacon, Edwin. "Reconsidering Brezhnev." In *Brezhnev Reconsidered,* edited by Edwin Bacon and Mark Sandle, 1–21. Basingstoke, UK: Palgrave Macmillan, 2002.

Bakatin, Vadim. *Izbavlenie ot KGB.* Moscow: Novosti, 1992.

Banerjee, Abhijit V. "A Simple Model of Herd Behavior." *Quarterly Journal of Economics* 107, no. 3 (1992): 797–817.

Barber, John, and Mark Harrison. "Patriotic War, 1941–1945." In *The Cambridge History of Russia,* vol. 3, *The Twentieth Century,* edited by Ronald Grigor Suny, 217–242. Cambridge: Cambridge University Press, 2006.

Barkai, Haim, and Nissan Liviatan. *The Bank of Israel,* vol. 1. Oxford: Oxford University Press, 2007.

Baron, Samuel H. *Bloody Saturday in the Soviet Union: Novocherkassk, 1962*. Stanford: Stanford University Press, 2001.

Belova, Eugenia. "Economic Crime and Punishment." In *Behind the Façade of Stalin's Command Economy: Evidence from the Soviet State and Party Archives*, edited by Paul R. Gregory, 131–158. Stanford: Hoover Institution Press, 2001.

Belova, Eugenia, and Paul Gregory. "Dictator, Loyal, and Opportunistic Agents: The Soviet Archives on Creating the Soviet Economic System." *Public Choice* 113 (2002): 265–86.

Bentham, Jeremy. *The Panopticon; or, The Inspection House.* Dublin: T. Payne, 1791, http://books.google.co.uk/books?id=NM4TAAAAQAAJ.

Bloch, Sidney, and Peter Reddaway. 1977. *Russia's Political Hospitals: The Abuse of Psychiatry in the Soviet Union.* London: Victor Gollancz, 1977.

Bredikhin, V. N., ed. *Lubyanka-Staraya ploshchad': Sekretnye dokumenty TsK KPSS i KGB o repressiyakh 1937–1990 gg. v SSSR*. Moscow: Posev, 2005, http://www.sps.ru/?id=213821.

Bruce, Gary. *The Firm: The Inside Story of the Stasi.* Oxford: Oxford University Press, 2012.

Bullock, Alan. *Hitler and Stalin: Parallel Lives*, 2nd ed. London: Fontana, 1993.

Burinskaitė, Kristina, and Lina Okuličiūtė. *KGB in Lithuania in 1954–1991*, edited by Teresė Birutė Burauskaitė. Vilnius: Genocide and Resistance Research Centre of Lithuania, 2010.

Caplan, Bryan. *The Myth of the Rational Voter: Why Democracies Choose Bad Policies.* Princeton: Princeton University Press, 2007.

Central Intelligence Agency. "Dimensions of Civil Unrest in the Soviet Union." National Intelligence Council Memorandum 83–10006, 1983.

Chebrikov, V. M., G. F. Grigorenko, N.A. Dushin, and F. D. Bobkov, eds. *Istoriya sovetskikh organov gosudarstvennoi bezopastnosti. Uchebnik.* Moscow: Vysshaya Krasnoznamennaya shkola KGB pri SM SSSR imeni F. E. Dzerzhinskogo, 1977, http://www.fas.harvard.edu/~hpcws/documents.htm.

Chukovskaya, Lydia. *Sofia Petrovna.* Evanston, IL: Northwestern University Press, 1967.

Cohn, Edward D. "Policing the Party: Conflicts between Local Prosecutors and Party Leaders under Late Stalinism." *Europe-Asia Studies* 65, no. 10 (2013): 1912–1930.

Conquest, Robert. *The Great Terror: A Reassessment*. New York: Oxford University Press, 1990.

Covey, Stephen R. *The 7 Habits of Highly Effective People: Powerful Lessons in Personal Change*. New York: Simon & Schuster, 1989.

Daškevičiūtė, Dalia. "Remembering Romas Kalanta, the Flaming Herald of Freedom." *The Lithuania Tribune*, May 14, 2012, http://www.lithuaniatribune.com/2012/05/14/remembering-romas-kalanta-the-flaming-herald-of-freedom/.

Davies, Christie. *The Mirth of Nations*. Piscataway, NJ: Transaction Publishers, 2002.

Davies, R. W., Oleg Khlevniuk, E. A. Rees, Liudmila P. Kosheleva, and Larisa A. Rogovaia, eds. *The Stalin-Kaganovich Correspondence, 1931–36*. New Haven: Yale University Press, 2003.

Davies, Sarah. *Popular Opinion in Stalin's Russia: Terror, Propaganda and Dissent, 1934–1941*. Cambridge: Cambridge University Press, 1997.

Davies, Sarah, and James Harris. *Stalin's World: Dictating the Soviet Order*. New Haven: Yale University Press, 2014.

Dianov, S. A., "Sotsialisticheskoe sorevnovanie v organakh sovetskoi tsenzury v epoku 'Stalinisma' (po materialam Urala)," *Nauchnyi dialog* 13, no. 1 (2013), http://cyberleninka.ru/article/n/sotsialisticheskoe-sorevnovanie-v-organah-sovetskoy-tsenzury-v-epohu-stalinizma-po-materialam-urala.

Ehrenburg, Ilya. *The Thaw*. Translated by Manya Harari. London: Harvill Press, 1955.

Ellman, Michael. "The 1947 Soviet Famine and the Entitlement Approach to Famines." *Cambridge Journal of Economics* 24, no. 5 (2000): 603–630.

Fedin, E. I. *Filin na razvalinakh*. St. Petersburg: Nauchno-issledovatel'skii institute khimii Sankt-Peterburgskogo gosudarstennogo universiteta, 2000, http://www.sakharov-center.ru.

Fedor, Julie. *Russia and the Cult of State Security: The Chekist Tradition, from Lenin to Putin*. London: Routledge, 2011.

Feinberg, Melissa. "Die Durchsetzung einer neuen Welt. Politische Prozesse in Osteuropa, 1948–1954." In *Angst im Kalten Krieg*, edited by Bernd Greiner, Christian Th. Müller, and Dierk Walter, 190–219. Hamburg: Hamburger Edition, 2009.

Filtzer, Donald. *Soviet Workers and Late Stalinism: Labour and the Restoration of the Stalinist System after World War II.* Cambridge: Cambridge University Press, 2002.

Filtzer, Donald. *The Hazards of Urban Life in Late Stalinist Russia: Health, Hygiene, and Living Standards, 1943–1953.* Cambridge: Cambridge University Press, 2010.

Fitzpatrick, Sheila. *Everyday Stalinism. Ordinary Life in Extraordinary Times: Soviet Russia in the 1930s.* Oxford: Oxford University Press, 1999.

Foucault, Michel. *Discipline and Punish: The Birth of the Prison.* Translated by Alan Sheridan. London: Allen Lane, 1977.

Garton Ash, Timothy. *The File: A Personal History.* London: HarperCollins, 1997.

Getty, J. Arch. *Origins of the Great Purges: The Soviet Communist Party Reconsidered, 1933–1938.* Cambridge: Cambridge University Press, 1987.

Getty, J. Arch. "The Politics of Repression Revisited." In *Stalinist Terror: New Perspectives,* edited by J. Arch Getty and Roberta T. Manning, 40–62. Cambridge: Cambridge University Press, 1993.

Getty, J. Arch. "Pragmatists and Puritans: The Rise and Fall of the Party Control Commission." *The Carl Beck Papers in Russian and East European Studies* 1208. University of Pittsburgh, Center for Russian and East European Studies, 1997.

Getty, J. Arch, and Oleg V. Naumov. *The Road to Terror: Stalin and the Self-Destruction of the Bolsheviks, 1932–1939.* New Haven: Yale University Press, 1999.

Gorelik, G. Ye. "Fizika universitetskaya i akademicheskaya, ili Nauka v sil'nom sotsial'nom pole." *Voprosy istorii estestvoznaniya i tekhniki* 1991, no. 1: 15–32, http://ggorelik.narod.ru/ZS_etc/Fizika_universitetskaya.html.

Gorlizki, Yoram, and Oleg Khlevniuk. *Cold Peace: Stalin and the Soviet Ruling Circle, 1945–1953.* Oxford: Oxford University Press, 2004.

Gorsuch, Anne E., ed. *All This is Your World: Soviet Tourism at Home and Abroad after Stalin.* Oxford: Oxford University Press, 2011.

Goryachev, Yu. V. *Tsentral'nyi komitet KPSS-VKP(b)-RKP(b)-RSDRP(b). 1917–1991. Istoriko-biograficheskii spravochnik.* Moscow: Parad, 2005.

Goryaeva, T. M. *Politicheskaya tsenzura v SSSR. 1917–1991 gg.* Moscow: ROSSPEN, 2009.

Goskomstat Rossii. *Naselenie Rossii za 100 let (1897–1997). Statisticheskii sbornik.* Moscow: Gosudarstvennyi komitet Rossiiskoi Federatsii po statistike, 1998.

Granovetter, Mark. "Threshold Models of Collective Behavior." *American Journal of Sociology* 83, no. 6 (1978): 1420–1443.

Gregory, Paul R. *Restructuring the Soviet Economic Bureaucracy.* Cambridge: Cambridge University Press, 1990.

Gregory, Paul R. *Terror by Quota: State Security from Lenin to Stalin (An Archival Study).* New Haven: Yale University Press, 2009.

Gregory, Paul R., and Mark Harrison. "Allocation under Dictatorship: Research in Stalin's Archives." *Journal of Economic Literature* 43, no. 3 (2005): 721–61.

Gregory, Paul R., Philipp J. H. Schröder, and Konstantin Sonin. "Rational Dictators and the Killing of Innocents: Data from Stalin's Archives." *Journal of Comparative Economics* 39, no. 1 (2011): 34–42.

Greif, Avner, and Steven Tadelis. "A Theory of Moral Persistence: Crypto-Morality and Political Legitimacy." *Journal of Comparative Economics* 38, no. 3 (2010): 229–244.

Harris, James. "Was Stalin a Weak Dictator?" *Journal of Modern History* 75, no. 2 (2003): 375–386.

Harrison, Mark. "The Dictator and Defense." In *Guns and Rubles: The Defense Industry in the Stalinist State,* edited by Mark Harrison, 1–30. New Haven: Yale University Press, 2008.

Harrison, Mark. "Forging Success: Soviet Managers and Accounting Fraud, 1943 to 1962." *Journal of Comparative Economics* 39, no. 1 (2011): 43–64.

Harrison, Mark. "The Soviet Union after 1945: Economic Recovery and Political Repression." Supplement 6, *Past & Present* 210 (2011): 103–120.

Harrison, Mark, and Inga Zaksauskienė. "Counterintelligence in a Command Economy." *Economic History Review,* forthcoming.

Havel, Václav. *Living in Truth: 22 Essays Published on the Occasion of the Award of the Erasmus Prize to Vaclav Havel.* London: Faber, 1986.

Hitler, Adolf. "Hitlers Rede zur Eröffnung der Großen Deutschen Kunstausstellung im Haus der Kunst, München," 1937, http://www.kunstzitate.de/bildendekunst/manifeste/nationalsozialismus/hitler_haus_der_kunst_37.htm.

Holloway, David. *Stalin and the Bomb: The Soviet Union and Atomic Energy, 1939–1956.* New Haven: Yale University Press, 1994.

Holquist, Peter. "State Violence as Technique: The Logic of Violence in Soviet Totalitarianism." In *Landscaping the Human Garden: Twentieth Century Population Management in a Comparative Framework*, edited by Amir Weiner, 19–45. Stanford: Stanford University Press, 2003.

Hornsby, Robert. *Protest, Reform, and Repression in Khrushchev's Soviet Union.* Cambridge: Cambridge University Press, 2013.

Inkeles, Alex, and Raymond A. Bauer. *The Soviet Citizen: Daily Life in a Totalitarian Society.* Cambridge, MA: Harvard University Press, 1959.

Ivkin, V. I., ed. *Gosudarstvennaya vlast' SSSR. Vysshye organy vlasti I upravleniya i ikh rukovoditeli. 1923–1991 gg. Istoriko-biograficheskii spravochnik.* Moscow: ROSSPEN, 1999.

Jervis, Robert. "Signaling and Perception: Drawing Inferences and Projecting Images." In *Political Psychology*, edited by Kristen Renwick Monroe, 293–312. Mahwah, NJ: Lawrence Erlbaum Associates, 2001.

Kharkhordin, Oleg. *The Collective and the Individual in Russia: A Study of Practices.* Berkeley: University of California Press, 1999.

Khlevniuk, Oleg. "The Objectives of the Great Terror, 1937–38." In *Soviet History, 1917–1953: Essays in Honour of R.W. Davies*, edited by J.M. Cooper, Maureen Perrie, and E.A. Rees, 158–176. New York: St. Martin's Press, 1995.

Khlevniuk, Oleg. *Master of the House: Stalin and His Inner Circle.* New Haven: Yale University Press, 2009.

Kotkin, Stephen. *Armageddon Averted: The Soviet Collapse, 1970–2000.* Oxford: Oxford University Press, 2008.

Kotkin, Stephen. *Stalin*, vol. 1, *Paradoxes of Power, 1878–1928.* London: Penguin, 2014.

Kozlov V. A. *Massovye besporyadki v SSSR pri Khrushcheve i Brezhneve.* Novosibirsk: Sibirskii Khronograf, 1999.

Kozlov, V. P., and thirteen others. *Istoriya Stalinskogo Gulaga. Konets 1920-kh—pervaya polovina 1950-kh godov,* vol. 1, *Massovye repressii v SSSR*. Moscow: ROSSPEN, 2004.

Kübler-Ross, Elisabeth. *On Death and Dying: What the Dying Have to Teach Doctors, Nurses, Clergy & Their Own Families.* London: Routledge, 1969.

Kuran, Timur, and Cass R. Sunstein. "Availability Cascades and Risk Regulation." *Stanford Law Review* 51, no. 4 (1999): 683–768.

Kuran, Timur. "Sparks and Prairie Fires: A Theory of Unanticipated Political Revolution." *Public Choice* 61, no. 1 (1989): 41–74.

Kuran, Timur. "Now Out of Never: The Element of Surprise in the East European Revolution of 1989." *World Politics* 44, no. 1 (1991): 7–48.

Kuran, Timur. *Private Truths, Public Lies. The Social Consequences of Preference Falsification.* Cambridge, MA: Harvard University Press, 1995.

Kuromiya, Hiroaki. "Stalin's Great Terror and the Asian Nexus." *Europe-Asia Studies* 66, no. 5 (2014): 775–793.

Lampert, Nicholas. *Whistleblowing in the Soviet Union: Complaints and Abuses under State Socialism.* London and Basingstoke: Macmillan, 1985.

Ledeneva, Alena V. *Russia's Economy of Favours: Blat, Networking and Informal Exchange.* Cambridge: Cambridge University Press, 1998.

Lewis, Ben. *Hammer and Tickle: The History of Communism Told Through Communist Jokes.* London: Weidenfeld and Nicolson, 2008.

Livshin, A. Ya., and I. B. Orlov, eds. *Pis'ma vo vlast'. 1917–1927. Zayavleniya, zhaloby, donosy, pis'ma v gosudarstvennye struktury i bol'shevistkim vozhdyam.* Moscow: ROSSPEN, 1998.

Livshin, A. Ya., I. B. Orlov, and O. V. Khlevniuk, eds. *Pis'ma vo vlast'. 1928–1939. Zayavleniya, zhaloby, donosy, pis'ma v gosudarstvennye struktury i sovetskim vozhdyam.* Moscow: ROSSPEN, 2002.

Mandelstam, Nadezhda. *Hope Against Hope: A Memoir.* London: Penguin, 1975.

Markevich, Andrei. "How Much Control is Enough? Monitoring and Enforcement under Stalin." *Europe-Asia Studies* 63, no. 8 (2011): 1449–1468.

Medvedev, Roy. *Let History Judge: The Origins and Consequences of Stalinism*. London: Macmillan, 1971.

Medvedev, Zhores. *National Frontiers and International Scientific Cooperation*. Nottingham: Spokesman Books, 1975.

Medvedev, Zhores, and Roy Medvedev. *A Question of Madness*. London: Penguin, 1974.

Medvedev, Zhores, and Roy Medvedev. *The Unknown Stalin*. London: I. B. Tauris, 2003.

Mel'nichenko, M. *Sovetskii anekdot (Ukazatel' syuzhetov)*. Moscow: Novoe literaturnoe obozrenie, 2014.

Michel, Jean-Baptiste, Yuan Kui Shen, Aviva Presser Aiden, Adrian Veres, Matthew K. Gray, The Google Books Team, Joseph P. Pickett, Dale Hoiberg, Dan Clancy, Peter Norvig, Jon Orwant, Steven Pinker, Martin A. Nowak, and Erez Lieberman Aiden. "Quantitative Analysis of Culture Using Millions of Digitized Books." *Science* 331, no. 6014 (January 14, 2011): 176–182.

Mlechin, Leonid. *Yurii Andropov: Poslednyaya nadezhda rezhima*. Moscow: Tsentrpoligraf, 2008, http://www.telenir.net/istorija/yurii_andropov_poslednjaja_nadezhda_rezhima/.

Nevezhin, V. A. *Esli zavtra v pokhod. Podgotovka k voine i ideologicheskaya propaganda v 30-kh–40-kh godakh*. Moscow: Yauza, Eksmo, 2007.

Nikitchenko, V. F. and 16 others, eds. *Kontrrazvedyvatel'nyi slovar'*. Vysshaya kranoznamennaya shkola Komiteta gosudarstvennoi bezopasnosti pri Sovete Ministrov SSSR imeni F. E. Dzerzhinksogo, Nauchno-izdatel'skii otdel, 1972, http://www.genocid.lt/KGB/ci_dictionary.pdf.

Oring, Elliott. "Risky Business: Political Jokes under Repressive Regimes." *Western Folklore* 63, no. 3 (2004): 209–236.

Orwell, George. *The Complete Works of George Orwell*, vol. 16, edited by Peter Davison. London: Secker and Warburg, 1998.

Paine, S. C. M. *The Wars for Asia, 1911–1949*. Cambridge: Cambridge University Press, 2012.

Petersen, Martin. "What I Learned in 40 Years of Doing Intelligence Analysis for US Foreign Policy Makers." *Studies in Intelligence* 55, no. 1 (2011): 13–20.

Pinchuk, B. C. "The Sovietization of the Jewish Community of Eastern Poland, 1939–1941." *Slavonic and East European Review* 56, no. 3 (1978): 387–410.

Plamper, Jan. "Abolishing Ambiguity: Soviet Censorship Practices in the 1930s." *Russian Review* 60, no. 4 (2001): 526–544.

Rayfield, Donald. *Stalin and His Hangmen: An Authoritative Portrait of a Tyrant and Those Who Served Him.* London: Penguin, 2005.

Reklaitis, George. "Cold War Lithuania: National Armed Resistance and Soviet Counterinsurgency." *The Carl Beck Papers in Russian & East European Studies* 1806. University of Pittsburgh: Center for Russian and East European Studies, 2007.

Remeikis, Thomas. "Self-Immolation and National Protest in Lithuania" and "Eyewitness Report of Demonstrations in Kaunas, Lithuania, Following the Self-Immolation of Romas Kalanta, May 18–19, 1972." *Lituanus: Lithuanian Quarterly Journal of Arts and Sciences* 18, no. 4 (1972): 58–69.

Rittersporn, Gábor Tamás. "The Omnipresent Conspiracy: On Soviet Imagery of Politics and Social Relations in the 1930s." In *Stalinist Terror: New Perspectives*, edited by J. Arch Getty and Roberta T. Manning, 99–115. Cambridge: Cambridge University Press, 1993.

Roginsky, N. A. "Pamyat' o stalinizme." In *Istoriya stalinizma: Itogi i problemy izycheniya*, edited by E. Yu. Kandrashina, N. P. Zimarina, M. I. Leiko, L. Yu. Pantina, G. M. Sokolova, E. V. Chagulova, and E. D. Shchepalova, 21–27. Moscow: ROSSPEN, 2011.

Schutz, Charles E. "Cryptic Humor: The Subversive Message of Political Jokes." *Humor: International Journal of Humor Research* 8, no. 1 (1995): 51–64.

Sebag Montefiore, Simon. *Stalin: The Court of the Red Tsar.* London: Weidenfeld & Nicolson, 2003.

Service, Robert. *Stalin: A Biography.* Basingstoke: Macmillan, 2004.

Shapiro, Ilya, Trevor Burrus, and Gabriel Latner. "Truthiness and the First Amendment." *University of Pennsylvania Journal of Constitutional Law Online* 14 (2014): 51–62, https://www.law.upenn.edu/live/files/3381-shapiro16upajconstlheightscrutiny512014pubpdf.

Shearer, David R. *Policing Stalin's Socialism: Repression and Social Order in the Soviet Union, 1924–1953.* New Haven: Yale University Press, 2009.

Sokolov, A. K., ed. *Golos naroda. Pis'ma i otkliki ryadovykh sovetskikh grazhdan o sobytiyakh 1918–1932 gg.* Moscow: ROSSPEN, 1998.

Solzhenitsyn, Aleksandr. *The Gulag Archipelago*, vol. 1. New York: Harper & Row, 1973.

Stalin, J. V. *Works*, vol. 11, *1928–1929*. Moscow: Foreign Languages Publishing House, 1949.

Stalin, J. V. *Works*, vol. 13, *1930–1934*. Moscow: Foreign Languages Publishing House, 1954.

Stalin, J. V. *Works*, vol. 14, *1934–1940*. London: Red Star Press, 1978.

Statiev, Alexander. *The Soviet Counterinsurgency in the Western Borderlands*. Cambridge: Cambridge University Press, 2010.

Swain, Amanda Jeanne. "Negotiating Narratives of Kaunas 1972 from Archives to Oral Interviews." *REECAS (Russian, East European, and Central Asian Studies) Newsletter*, April 5, 2012, http://ellisoncenter.washington.edu/alumni-spotlight/negotiating-narratives-of-kaunas-1972-from-archives-to-oral-interviews/.

Swain, Amanda Jeanne. "From the Big Screen to the Streets of Kaunas: Youth Cultural Practices and Communist Party Discourse in Soviet Lithuania." *Cahiers du monde Russe* 54, no. 3–4 (2013): 467–490.

Swain, Amanda Jeanne. "A Death Transformed: The Political and Social Consequences of Romas Kalanta's Self-Immolation, Soviet Lithuania, 1972." PhD diss., University of Washington, 2013.

TsSU SSSR. *Trud v SSSR. Statisticheskii sbornik*. Moscow: Tsentral'noe statisticheskoe upravlenie pri Sovete Ministrov SSSR, 1968.

TsSU SSSR. *Narodnoe khoziaistvo SSSR. 1922–1972. Yubileinyi statisticheskii sbornik*. Moscow: Statistika, 1972.

Tucker, R. C. *Stalin as Revolutionary, 1879–1929*. New York: Norton, 1974.

Tucker, R. C. *Stalin in Power: The Revolution from Above, 1928–1941*. New York: Norton, 1992.

Viola, Lynne. *The Best Sons of the Fatherland: Workers in the Vanguard of Soviet Collectivization*. New York: Oxford University Press, 1987.

Weiner, Amir, and Aigi Rahi-Tamm. "Getting to Know You: The Soviet Surveillance System, 1939–1957." *Kritika: Explorations in Russian and Eurasian History* 13, no. 1 (2012): 5–45.

Weiner, Amir. "Déjà Vu All Over Again: Prague Spring, Romanian Summer and Soviet Autumn on the Soviet Western Frontier." *Contemporary European History* 15, no. 2 (2006): 159–194.

Wintrobe, Ronald. *The Political Economy of Dictatorship*. Cambridge: Cambridge University Press, 2000.

Yevtushenko, Yevgeny. *Yevtushenko: Selected Poems*. Translated with an introduction by Robin Milner-Gulland and Peter Levi. London: Penguin Books, 1962.

Yurchak, Alexei. 2005. *Everything Was Forever, Until It Was No More: The Last Soviet Generation*. Princeton: Princeton University Press, 2005.

Zaleski, Eugène. *Stalinist Planning for Economic Growth, 1933–1952*. London: Macmillan, 1980.

Zhirkov, G. V. *Istoriya tsenzury v Rossii XIX–XX vv. Uchebnoe posobie*. Moscow: Aspekt-Press, 2001.

Zhirnov, Yevgenii. "Davno pora byt' v lageryakh eshche pobol'she." *Kommersant' vlast'* 38, no. 641 (September 26, 2005), http://kommersant.ru/doc/611989.

Index